Jean-Luc Nancy
and the Future of Philosophy

Jean-Luc Nancy and the Future of Philosophy

B. C. Hutchens

McGill-Queen's University Press
Montreal & Kingston • Ithaca

© B. C. Hutchens 2005

ISBN 0-7735-2982-9   (hardcover)
ISBN 0-7735-2983-7   (paperback)

Legal deposit third quarter 2005
Bibliothèque nationale du Québec

Published simultaneously outside North America
by Acumen Publishing Limited

McGill-Queen's University Press acknowledges the financial support of the
Government of Canada through the Book Publishing Development Program
(BPIDP) for its activities.

Library and Archives Canada Cataloguing in Publication

Hutchens, B. C. (Benjamin C.)
    Jean-Luc Nancy and the future of philosophy / B.C.
Hutchens.

Includes bibliographical references and index.
ISBN 0-7735-2982-9 (bound).—ISBN 0-7735-2983-7 (pbk.)

    1. Nancy, Jean-Luc. I. Title.

B2430.N364H87 2005   194   C2005-900995-0

Designed and typeset by Kate Williams, Swansea.
Printed and bound by Cromwell Press, Trowbridge

Contents

Abbreviations

BC "Of Being in Common" (1991).

BP *The Birth to Presence* (1993).

BSP *Being Singular Plural* (2000).

C "*La Comparution/*The Compearance" (1992).

CMM *La création du monde ou la mondialisation* (2002).

DC "La Déconstruction du christianisme" (1998).

EF *The Experience of Freedom* (1993).

FT *A Finite Thinking* (2003).

GT *The Gravity of Thought* (1997).

HRN *Hegel: The Restlessness of the Negative* (2002).

IC *The Inoperative Community* (1991).

L "*L'Intrus*" (2002).

LA *The Literary Absolute: The Theory of Literature in German Romanticism* (1988).

M *The Muses* (1996).

MMT "An Interview with Jean-Luc Nancy", M. Gaillot (ed.) (1998).

NM "The Nazi Myth" (1990).

OP *L'oubli de la philosophie* (1986).

P "Is Everything Political? (A Brief Remark)" (2002).

R "Responding for Existence" (1999).

RP *Retreating the Political* (1997).

SDC "The Self-Deconstruction of Christianity: A Discussion with Jean-Luc Nancy" (2000).

SR *The Speculative Remark (One of Hegel's Bon Mots)* (2001).

SV "Sharing Voices" (1990).

SW *The Sense of the World* (1997).

TL *The Title of the Letter: A Reading of Lacan* (1992).

Preface

... parallel lines meet at infinity, an infinity that must be truly vast to accommodate so many things, dimensions, lines straight and curved and intersecting, the trams that go up these tracks and the passengers inside the trams, the light in the eyes of every passenger, the echo of words, *the inaudible friction of thoughts* ...

José Saramago[1]

Jean-Luc Nancy is Professor of Philosophy at the University of Strasbourg, co-founder of the former "Centre for Philosophical Research on the Political" and author of numerous influential books about meaning, freedom, community, art and politics. However, he is not merely another academic celebrity seduced by the allures of pedantry. His ideas not only bear on social realities; they also stem from them. For approximately a decade, he has endured the suffering of both a heart transplant and cancer, and written profoundly about both in such works as "The Heart of Things" and "*L'Intrus*". It is from Nancy that we learn that, if each part of a body could take over or spread over the body itself, then there is no such thing as body at all, only a sharing out of bodies and their relations (BP: 207). His misfortunes have inspired a relentless enquiry into the meaning of the body's fragility and fragmentation, the tenuous connections of a community of such bodies, and the plurality of voices that express their sense. The single heart of all things, their sense, he writes, "never stops coming into presence, and putting us in its presence, the presence of this concretion of being, always unique and always 'whatever'" (BP: 188). Clearly, not even the grievance against human finitude that he could so naturally possess has forced him to lose his spirited fascination with the incertitude and undecidability of discourses that incessantly fail to acquiesce in comprehension. One can only admire the fortitude of a thinker whose thoughts are not swayed by misfortune, but encouraged, deepened and even vindicated by it. Perhaps not since Pascal has a thinker's pained musing been more stirringly apt to the human condition.

Jean-Luc Nancy and the Future of Philosophy is a book addressing what this philosopher has written about the future of philosophy and the concept of "the future". It surveys Nancy's timely insights about the unstable conditions under which existence is always endured and fleetingly understood. Philosophical thoughts are master only of those domains they imagine for themselves; they are as vulnerable to the exigencies of a coming future as all human bodies are. It is with that in mind that Nancy writes of the "corpus" of philosophy, the catalogue of the ways that bodies have sense only because sense itself is bound to corporeal states and activities open to their own improvidence. Just as philosophy is troubled by the coming of sense, so are bodies in contiguity with and invaded by strangenesses that never "cease being a disturbance and a perturbation of intimacy" (L: 2). There is something foreign in us all, and in this respect we are each equally exposed to our shared strangeness. When the invader exposes bodies' strangeness to themselves, then the philosopher is exposed to what José Saramago calls the "inaudible friction of thoughts" (see epigraph). But if there are only bodies, then every reader of this corpus should recognize the sharing in the community of bodies this necessarily brings to presence. Despite the cacophony of voices in which we philosophers share, we are nonetheless answerable to this "inaudible friction" between "our" thoughts of what is to come for "our" bodies and what "we" represent "our" bodies to be.

It is appropriate, then, to dedicate this book in gratitude to Jean-Luc Nancy himself. It is as much about the man as it is the stimulations his ideas have undoubtedly provided to appreciative readers.

In this book, it has been my objective to survey the relevance of Nancy's expansive vision to many contemporary philosophical concerns, all of which relate to the question of the future of our time and the status of the concept of the "future" today. I have chosen to present Nancy's critiques of various prevailing contemporary presuppositions: in particular, the substantialist, transcendentalist and immanentist metaphysics are discernible in the context of libertarianism, post-secular theology, communitarianism, contractarianism and specific, timely questions about technology and globalization. There are gaping holes in coverage, some of which are scandalous: literature, the visual arts, love, joy, and justice are some of the concepts that figure only glimmeringly in this book, if they figure at all. Nancy's voluminous work on the visual arts alone would require an independent study I must confess would be beyond my abilities. Nevertheless, I hope that the reader will find what follows to be at least a suitable primer for the study of this fascinating contemporary thinker.

It is hoped that the reader will find this book more accessible than Nancy's own daunting composition. I advise the reader to examine the introduction, interview and conclusion of the book, as well as to consult the glossary for clarification of the meanings of terms as I have used them. Bulleted conclusions are to be found at the end of each chapter.

Special thanks are owed to Tristan Palmer of Acumen, who has guided and encouraged this production from its troubled origins. I am grateful for his faith in the pertinence of the project when many editors would have been incapable of suspending their "ecotechnical" incredulity. Professor William Hawk of James Madison University and Professor Duncan Richter of the Virginia Military Institute deserve thanks for providing ample and desirable teaching opportunities. Above all, warmest thanks to Karen Hutchens, whose inquisitive mind and capacity for wonder have been not only an inheritance, but an inspiration.

CHAPTER ONE
Introduction

What will become of our world is something we cannot know, and we can no longer believe in being able to predict or command it. But we can act in such a way that this world is a world able to open itself up to its own uncertainty as such. (RP: 158)

All that we transmit to ourselves ... has begun to transmit itself in front of us, toward or coming from a "we" that we have not yet appropriated, and which has not yet received its name, if ever it should have one. (C: 384)

Our time is the time that, as it were, exposes exposure itself: the time for which all identifiable figures have become inconsistent (the gods, the *logoi*, the wise, knowledge), and which therefore works toward (or which gives itself over to) the coming of a figure of the unidentifiable, the figures of opacity and of resistant consistency as such. "Man" thus becomes opaque to himself, he grows thick and heavy with the weight of an excessive thought of his humanity: eight billions bodies in an ecotechnical whirlwind that no longer has any other end than the infinity of an inappropriable meaning. (GT: 83–4)

Jean-Luc Nancy is a contemporary philosopher fixated by the parlous future of community and its spontaneous freedoms in a globalizing West. His core commitment is to an alternative view of community dissimilar to those normally offered today. In particular, he regards social relations as an insubstantial sharing in an "impalpable reticulation of contiguous and tangential contacts", not as a substantial cluster of "individuals" determined by common social means and focused on common political ends that produce a controllable future. In addressing this possibility, he proposes a

1

"community of being" (the irreducible plurality of singular "ones") that replaces the intractably traditional question of the "being of community" (the "being" that brings predetermined "individuals" into communion) (SW: 61; BC: 1). With undeniable sincerity, he addresses the possibility of the West's future being determined by the feral interplay between, on the one hand, a democracy of individualism rendered impotent by its "cynical" liberal values and, on the other, an "ecotechnics" of capital (expansively formative of community and sovereignty). He insists vehemently that, despite the political and technological progress of our contemporary "market democracy", we remain unwittingly improvident, closed to an uncertain future and the undecidability of the consequences of agency. Nevertheless, for Nancy, whatever form modern life may assume, each of "us" is a finite being whose radical singularity has been neither eradicated by the demands of political and social reality nor entirely deracinated from community life. It is in our freedom and community that we are open to a future that is always a surprise or shock to our traditional sensibilities. To realize this, however, we must think differently of what freedom and community have conventionally come to mean.

In the main, he is intrigued by the thought that the Westernization of the globe has redounded to become the globalization of the West, leading to a suspended "end" torn between the incompatible options of a reductive Enlightenment and a lyric Romanticism (MMT: 94; BSP: 63). Singularly devoid of the bromides and vatic pronouncements so common in "Continental" philosophy, his work soberly attests a fascination with the West's panoply of immanence: its suspended history and the resulting "crisis of sense"; its exclusionary and appropriative politics (in which "everything is political"); its yearning fascination with exteriority (God, Law, Value); its debilitating nostalgia for lost community, myth and rituals of spiritual sacrifice (already a minatory totalitarianism); the precariousness of its rational and libertarian efforts to establish the self-evidence of "freedom"; its self-deceiving presumption of evil's essential negativity; the intrusion of its ecotechnical values into health and life; its determination of the market value of "being-human" reflected in the media's opinion polling, market research, and human interest stories; and above all, perhaps, its *horror vacui*.

This is certainly not to imply that Nancy is a "revolutionary" philosopher in any traditional sense of the term. Although he calls for a "revolutionary politics", he understands this to mean resistance to the political establishment of formal freedom and community, or alternatively, a spacing within which freedom disrupts the market democratic effort to bestow it with a meaning and put it to a political task. What liberal, libertarian and communitarian philosophies of democracy cannot grasp, he enjoins us to realize, is freedom as the inaugural act itself, the surprising burst of freedom exercised in the social effort to take freedom back from any political cause that has allegedly granted "liberty" as a "right" and then attempted to recover it for political reasons. In other words, he is interested in the revolutionary politics of the "an-archy" of freedom itself, the irreducible and inappropriable surprise that opens singular beings to their own future (a future, it must be said, that political views of freedom and community cannot anticipate) (EF: 76–8).

Ultimately, the focus of his attacks on contemporary views of freedom, community and politics is their implication of "substantialist" and "immanentist" metaphysics, which neglects the futural spacings of modern social relations. (By "substantialist" I mean any commitment to the predetermined existence of beings and the self-evidence of their essence; by "immanentist" I mean the activity of determining such beings' identities through the reflection and playing back of ideals conceived for this purpose.) In this respect, he is not merely another thinker of the "end" of the West's intellectual projects and political missions, but a Nietzschean *Versucher* who wonders at futural possibilities of precisely the intense debilities of that "end". The West is not mistaken in its view of the end of the meaning of community, yet the openness to the uncertainty of its destiny provides the very conditions of that meaning (C: 374). His writings explore the sense of the world, in particular its circulations, relations, singularities, inoperable implications, and certainly the polymorphy and polyphony of the banalities of common life. Aversion to the singular things of such life and inordinate passion for mediation, he proposes, place Western subjectivity at once "in" the world transcendentally but not immanent to it as a finite existent amongst singularities. Celebrating the capricious behaviour of concepts, he shares with many post-structuralist philosophers a determination to discover untapped "an-archic" conceptual possibilities of experience, especially those involving intense disruptions, interruptions and fragmentations of existence and its discourses. Perhaps Nancy's work is a response to the intensities of finitude, the ecstasy of freedom (better: the ecstasy that freedom is), and the rapture of sharing in loving, giving, dying and writing – in other words, the perturbations of philosophical thought. And it must be said that, despite the enriching presence of many influences on his thinking, Nancy is inexorably original in his pursuit of the conditions of another, *futural* philosophical scene of openness to uncertainty, the undecidability of philosophical discourse (that is, its openness to a futural resolution that always "is coming" but never arrives).

From the outset, what is meant by the statement that Nancy is a philosopher of "the future" should be clarified. Of course, Nancy's argumentation has not yet been thoroughly raked through and continues to yield many fecund ideas. However, it might be said with some temerity that Nancy's "future" is not merely the post-Enlightenment's field of opportunity for the deployment of rationality into a progressive scheme; nor is it the fashionable post-secular eschatological "not-yet" or "to-come" in Heidegger, Bloch and Levinas; nor is it even the ecotechnical reticulations of the indefinite power of capital so dominant in the shopping malls and entertainment circles of the market democratic world. Rather, following the thought of "the end" to its end, Nancy is interested in the intrinsic limits transgressed in this culmination of thought, the interstitial boundaries leaped on the way to the end. His self-engendered discourse straddles such internal divisions and strives to nullify each of the terms of their dichotomies. Existential conditions are espoused in the "extensive/intensive dynamic" of singularities exposed to one another, at once "in" and "not in" existence but exposed to it and having a share in it nonetheless. In this way, he is, as Christopher Fynsk has remarked, a "laborer of thought"[1] (BC: 4–8) undaunted by the thinking of the uncertain future of a plurality of singular "ones" and the undecidability of the vectoral relations among them.

Despite being subjected to a modest but respectable degree of commentary, Nancy's work has not yet yielded its primary focus. After all, his erudition encompasses Romanticism and techno music, phenomenology and communitarianism, Hegelian logic and contemporary cinema. Commentators have proposed a number of significant nodal concepts that might provide insights into this focus. For Howard Caygill (who contrasts Nancy with the political scientist Hannah Arendt), Fred Dallmayr (who intersects his work with that of historians Samuel Huntington and Immanuel Wallerstein), Christopher Fynsk (who reads him in conjunction with Rorty) and Simon Critchley,[2] among others, it is the concept of an open community of sharing that is irreducible to political appropriation. Wilhelm Wurzer and Krzysztof Ziarek explore the provocative notions of ecotechnics and globalization in the context of a more general discussion of technology.[3] Alternatively, for Gary Shapiro and Anne O'Byrne,[4] it is the horizons of the body's elliptical contact with others addressed at the very edge of philosophical discourse. Michael Naas hears in Nancy "perhaps the greatest thinker of worklessness and the interruption of the practical on the contemporary scene", that is, one who daringly explores the resistances of meaning to sheer production and appropriation.[5] John T. Lysaker emphasizes that Nancy is the composer of "literary communism", the counter *praxis* posed against the totalizing practices of theory itself.[6] Finally, Peter Fenves[7] proposes that Nancy's primary intent is an empirical exploration of the burst of freedom exhibited most poignantly in the positivity of wickedness. This diversity of perspectives attests to the rich conceptual possibilities Nancy's work advertently offers.

4

However, all commentators agree that, despite the many possible gleanings of Nancy's profoundly endowed texts, the task of his philosophy is to enquire into *the sense of the world*. (By "sense" one might understand preliminarily the condition of truth and meaning that precedes their partial disclosure and that is incommensurate with, yet enabling of, conventional views of both.) Indeed, there is nothing but the world, he avers, and any appeal to a transcendental reserve of meaning from which the sense of the world could be drawn is strictly unjustifiable. Refreshingly, Nancy will not temporize any "alterity" that would be "exterior" and "irreducible" to immanence, a transcendentality that, in contemporary post-secular theories, invariably provides an "opening" anticipating religious discourse. Strictly speaking, Nancy is not another philosopher of "the Other". Christianity, he reiterates adroitly throughout his work, deserves deconstruction even if it is Christianity itself that enables deconstructive possibilities, although the danger remains that spiritual "alterities" will serve as foils for a self-fulfilling interpretative scheme that would preclude or "exscribe" the thought of the insubstantial "community of being". Christianity, he remarks, is not a religion but the "self-deconstruction of religion"; it is an "exit from all religion" in so far as it is necessary "from the inside" to ask: "What does this mean?" (SDC: 3). Along with another stellar contemporary thinker who will have no truck with the theological excrescence of "alterities", Alain Badiou, he insists that the world attests to itself and requires no external foundations. He demands that contemporary critical philosophy rid itself of the foundational "ontology of the Other and the Same" and emphasize enquiry into the ontology of a world of unmediated multiplicities of singular "ones", of a community of others co-appearing in irreducible plurality (BSP: 53, 67).[8] That is to say, there is no closed immanential "inside" of the world, because there could be no "outside" of any diversity of singular "ones". This world is not merely a collection of entities whose meanings could be substantiated through exterior factors (such as God, creation, etc.). The sense of the world, he avers relentlessly against Hegel, should not be sublated into any greater synthesis of the significations of such entities. On the contrary, in order to "think" such sense at all, one would need to examine the question of relations among singularities, especially their trajectories and intersections. In his desire to "let oneself be led to concrete thinking" (BSP: 19, 45, 77, 199; BP: 188), Nancy is fascinated by the behaviours of such "corpuscular" vectors and relations, not merely with the substances and entities they relate (although he regards "sense" to be the material totality, not merely some truant ideality that divagates through tangible reality) (R: 8). And, in a phrase that recurs less frequently than its sentiment, "nothing more can be said". The world is what it is – sense. The task of philosophy is to offer a "finite thinking" (the singular thought of

5

singular beings, double genitive) through the variegations of the disclosure of sense.

Despite the stress on the singularity of sense, it is most obviously discernible on the surfaces or contours of entities, where such relations have an empirical presence, or in particular, where the world can be seen to "come to presence". If one were to imagine erasing the entities of such immanential relations, then the result would be a denuded reality, a nothingness that would still have sense despite the nullification of its entities. In spite of our *horror vacui*, such a world does not "have" a sense (which would imply a transcendental reserve from which it receives it). Rather it "is" sense on the grounds that there could be nothing else. Sense and world are coextensive, perfectly commensurate, with no superfluous meanings overhanging this coextensivity. Of course, relations are a plurality of singular events, at once fissile and feral, which circulate through human experience and are grasped in figments of meaning. In order to "think" the sense of the world, it would be necessary to be sensitive to the nuances of such circulations.

Nevertheless, there are many aspects of Nancy's thought that defy binary reasoning and its constraining dichotomies. For example, we shall hear Nancy say that the sense of the world is that the world "is" sense, that "we" are sense, and that evil is a positive presence or "constitutive decay" in the ground of freedom. Often, as if echoing Samuel Butler, he suggests that something is simply what it is, nothing more, and there is nothing else available to the requisite finite thinking. What Nancy appears to have in mind is that all questions about sense lead it to *collapse* into an infinity of relational moments, each with its own self-attesting and absolutely singular density. Nancy refers to a pure space, an "areality" (area, surface) of points or movements that simultaneously define the exteriority and its common division, which results from a commonality of sense "despoiled" of transcendence and immanence alike (C: 373). Even the process of interpretation is either interrupted or "contracts to a certain point", a prepositional point in which there is "nothing but" sense – we "are" sense, the world "is" sense. It is in this way that he can speak in the same breath of a singular sense and a multiplicity of circulating forms of it. Again, this collapse of existential relations into a singular, "open" immanence defies the imperative (or even the possibility) of a transcendental ground or foundation on which theories of causal necessity are established and from which theories of signification may spring effulgently. To say that there is nothing more to the world than sense, and that nothing more can be said, is to attempt to draw our attention to this collapse of the immanence–transcendence dichotomy into sense.

Although Nancy does not present his thought in this way, one might think of it heuristically. The point of Nancy's enquiry is always to pay close attention to the behaviour of concepts and figures in philosophical discourse. The collapse of existential conditions into sense figures on the axiology of plethora and lacuna, origin and end. Of course, other axes, such as *technē* and *physis*, can intersect these coordinates, but ultimately they merely add detail. To insist that we live in an age lacking sense, for example, is to say that the incessant origin of the question of sense is the end of enquiry. And the absence of sense is itself indicative of an abundance of significations of sense. Nevertheless, regardless of the form of the enquiry, the result is an internal folding of all axes into a singular moment of sense. That is indicative of the tessellating behaviour of the concept of sense, never in isolation and always intersecting with the behaviours of other nodal concepts. Although this is not easy to grasp, it serves as the conceptual possibility reiterated on many registers of Nancy's expansive vision.

With this discourse of the behaviour of concepts in mind, one might say that Nancy's work exhibits a *conceptual delirium*. Dismissive of simulated nostalgias and vengeful calls for cultural renewal, and offering a worthy departure from both the climate of despair and the ignorance of this despair, his thoughts are often conveyed with a contagious passion crackling with an energy often lacking in the feigned, world-weary ennui of so much contemporary theory. Ultimately his gaze focuses unblinkingly on an existence consisting of a multiplicity of singular events of infinite multilinear contact between material entities. Undistracted by theoretical constraints and paradigmatic imperatives, he admires the impenetrable density, granulated surfaces and collective frictions of such relations, as well as the absolute facticity of empirical experiences divorced from philosophical discourse. And for this reason, as many commentators have remarked, he takes philosophy to the limit of its integrity, to the edge of its tolerance, by flirting with the singularities of non-philosophical life.

One might think of this in a more truncated manner. His philosophical fixation is with theory frozen at the absolute moment of contact with (or between) singularities. At this moment, theory is not enabled to move on to conceptual schematization of a universal or essential nature. The result is almost casuistic in form: when elaborating on community or politics, for example, Nancy endeavours to "think" their universal values in terms of singular events, processes and entities. What Nancy finds hermeneutically objectionable is that, in the composition of theories, there is always enthusiasm for generalities that slide past the fascinating richness of singular relations (SV: 211–18). Nancy's textual discipline creates an intensity of focus upon the singularity at hand that refuses the arrogation of reason whereby thought endows itself with protocols of entitlement. He will not relinquish an existent until he has subjected its ineradicable singularity to a rigorous finite thinking, and thereby divested it of conceptual or theoretical accretions that facilitate lazy universalizations. In this sense, there is the suggestion of a radically empirical bias in Nancy's work (that is to say, he is obsessed by the density and tactility of the singular, but does not merely take it as either a "brute given" or a unified construction of sentient being). Finite thinking, singular thoughts about singular relations, must pause patiently over the singular "given" that purportedly takes us beyond the limit of philosophical discourse (which might suggest a certain anti-philosophical, or at least anti-canonical, tendentiousness on Nancy's part).

Hence, regarding Nancy as an empiricist enables us to understand why he often appears to caper nimbly away from analysis: he has assumed the daunting task of clearing a free space around the singularity of contact between singularities in order to think its "groundless" or "an-archical" moment. Indeed, Nancy's concepts are often *nodal* points within descriptions, that is, not concepts applied to a description in order to render it intelligible, but concepts that cannot be divorced from descriptions of singularity and relation. In a sense, Nancy gives us nothing that can be applied elsewhere, only the precious gift of an alternative perspective. It would be pointless to impose logical standards upon his work, for his deconstructive commitments are such that this logic would be imbued with precisely the values incommensurate with the project of finite thinking. Hence, in order to fathom the discourse of the collapse of sense, he resists logical blandishments and instead utilizes *paradox* to isolate and compare the textures and densities of singularities. For example, Nancy mulls the paradox of singularity as such: to think ontologically is not merely to think of the conditions of singularity, but to determine singularity itself as the necessary condition of grounds themselves. Generally speaking, he delights in an almost casuistic inversion of priorities and subsumptions.

Paradoxically (and thus reflective of his fascination with the paradoxical), Nancy thinks of the singular in terms of fragmented corporeal experiences of singular relations, whose profuse nuances require the thinker's passion and patience alike. For Nancy, the "subject" and the "ego" being theological anachronisms, reality is a kaleidoscope of multiplicity whirling deliriously, composing the very limit conditions of experience and resisting appropriation by a meaning-bestowing mind. He is captivated by the *intensity* of intimate sensations and refulgent experiences, that is, of existence as such. The circulation of sense (grasped as mere meanings and significations) and its incessantly different re-creations, "sensing-oneself-sensing", "being-at-the-edge", "coming-to presence", "being-given-over-to-itself", the vertiginous and prodigal "burst of freedom", the "hatred of existence as such", the "haunting" of thinking by an obligation, and even the "enthusiasms" of the rave party are all poignant manifestations of this conceptual delirium. Each is a singular intensity, approachable solely by means of conceptually dense paradoxes suggesting the collapse into sense. Perhaps the ultimate paradox of Nancy's thought is that logic cannot dissolve the paradoxes necessary for thinking of intense relations of singularities. An essential aspect of this paralogic is the notion that the discourse of philosophy is a discourse of fragmentation, of the ruination of systems.

The textual strategy Nancy deploys to consider the multiple forms of sense is worthy of attention. It is analogous to a multi-stranded knot (perhaps similar to those knots beloved of Lacan) whose ends are enclosed by the strands in such a way that to pull on any strand is merely to tighten the knot itself. Alexander's sword, whether as force or as reason, might cut this Gordian knot, which would sever the hidden ends, yet that severance would remove the possibility of learning the knot's valuable meaning. Nevertheless, if meaning is to be gained at all, the knot must be untied meticulously, without impatience or preconception. The Gordian knot is a perplexity: on the one hand, the strand of meaning is meaningful only once the knot is unravelled; yet, on the other, the meaning of the knot itself (tied, untied or cut) is determined by the role the notion of meaning plays in the process of untying itself. Nancy himself has deftly bound these strands together so that the very meaning of the knot remains hidden inside regardless of one's success in struggling with it. Nancy's intellectual acuity is evident in the fact that the meaning is not found when the knot is untied, but in the peculiarly variegated ways the knot itself may be studied. There is nothing pointless in the attempt to study and practise the process of untying, nothing vertiginous or esoteric that might repel the positivistic reader looking for a "point". Once the knot has been tied, Nancy guards against its unravelment, not by disguising it beneath a farrago of recondite metaphysical imaginings, but rather by forcing the diligent reader to enact the very fragmented tableaux of meaning elliptically revealed in the texts themselves. And there can be no doubt that, despite the fragmentations of his texts and the occasionally tortured prose that strives to flit away from traditional conceptualizations, Nancy possesses the requisite finesse to pull off such an endeavour. His books are imbued with commitments to rigour and redolent with proposals for its application. They deftly maintain the fine equilibrium necessary to enquire into the single sense of the world and to explore the reticulations of sense in the openness of human existence.

Textual ruins: the rigours of philosophical fragmentation

In many respects, Nancy's task is not only to write of the sense of freedom and community, but to write freely and to share in community as he does so. This requires a certain rebellion against the protocols of academic philosophical "work". Writing freely of the free play of the plurality of singularities, Nancy shares with Pascal, Schlegel, Nietzsche, Wittgenstein and Blanchot an acute penchant for fragmented philosophical composition. At first glance, his later works in particular are interlarded by fragments in such a fashion that each "chapter" actually identifies merely part of a conceptual domain, the rest of which is to be found in other "chapters". Moreover, each "chapter" might begin with a fragment that reads as if it were an introduction, although in many cases it merely provides clues about which part of the domain will be elucidated in that "chapter".

This is an exercise of superb assiduity, not hermeneutical sleight-of-hand. In a fascinating way, Nancy's fragmented texts enact the very fragments of singularity that compose pluralities. It would be bizarre, after all, if Nancy were to celebrate singularity in multiplicity, only to offer a streamlined text flowing from concept to concept as if there were actually ordered unity on the surveyed tableau of singularities. The primary danger, and it is a severe one, is that this text–theme enactment could be mistaken for a unity. In order to reduce the risk that a certain style of philosophical composition would impose order precisely where there was none, Nancy attempts to maintain minimal integrity within and among fragments by capturing the sense of the theme's proclivity to glimmer spectrally without being taken as a brute given.

He is also insistent that fragmentation of philosophical discourse cannot be disavowed with any resentful or vengeful call for renewal of coherent sense. Indeed, in the contemporary age, fragmentation of discourse is an event possessing its own truth, although this truth offers no possibility of a reconstitution of "original" non-fragmented states. To illustrate this point, Nancy gives special attention to a fragment of Schlegel's that appears to celebrate the vitality of fragmented discourse (LA: 51). It is significant for him that Schlegel conceives of philosophy as a "grotesque", a "tissue of moral discourse from which one can learn disorganization, or in which confusion is properly constructed and symmetrical". Elsewhere, Schlegel anticipates Nancy with the claim that "many modern works are fragments as soon as they are written", perhaps in the sense that mere composition is already fragmented prior to the effort to fragment it.[9] Finally, in *The Birth to Presence*, Nancy exhorts us to acknowledge that, in reference to the work of Blanchot, fragmentation is not something that one does, since writing is already implicitly fragmented (BP: 267). Hence, the implicit task of the fragmentation of discourse is to distort textuality in service to the truth of fragmentation itself, thereby reducing the risk that the disorder of textuality will be buried beneath superficial orders. If he were ever to explain in non-fragmented form why he writes in fragmented form, then that would imply that there is a unifying *logos* facilitating intelligibility. Implying such a *logos* would betray the very strategy of enacting the singularities that could not be presented without fragmentation.

He notes in fragments in *The Experience of Freedom* that, by the standards of philosophical discourse, the textual fragment is ambiguous to the point of near discreditability. In referring to Blanchot's notion of the fragment as a tightening "point of rupture" in discourse, he remarks that philosophy itself has always been surprised by the incessant fragmentation of its own discourses, especially those of freedom, the absence of divinity, the multiplicity of arts, and the impossibility of community. Given the fragmentation of discourse and the imperative of fragmented composition, philosophy has no end, obeys no rules, satisfies no criteria, and never liberates itself from the ruptures of discourse it cannot heal. It is always in "agony" because of its own incompetence before singularity and the fragmentation necessary for enacting it. It is "cheating" to pretend not to discern the fragmentation of philosophical discourse, to strive philosophically for the "end" of a particular discourse that was never surprised (and thus never attentive to itself). After all, he notes in *The Sense of the World*, that which has been fragmented "has not simply disappeared in the process of being broken up", as if, for example, there were nothing of the beautiful in fragments about the beautiful (SW: 124). Being what it is precisely because of this fragmentation, philosophy must acknowledge the surprises, the strangeness, the disconcerting truths that would arise along the path of any philosophical itinerary and that intercalate its discourse.

> But without this risk, despite everything, no matter what I did I would be betraying yet more certainly the experience of freedom. I would claim to offer it as a concept (even if as a concept of the limit of the concept) or to draw it as a conclusion from an analysis, or to identify it with the movements of a discourse, and even with its tightening, its continual fragmentation. But the experience of freedom is already taking place, and it is only a question of this, along with our formidable insufficiency to "know" it, "think" it, or "say" it. So then, fragments, as vague, uncertain marks of this insufficiency. (EF: 150)

In other words, if Nancy were to offer reductive concepts and draw conclusions about the experience of freedom, then the surprising burst of freedom that just is the writing of freedom would be betrayed. One might propose that fragments are at least textual traces of the insufficiency of philosophical discourse in its pursuit of the *logos* of the thinking of freedom. Freedom itself, especially the freedom of the writing of this thinking of freedom, constantly surprises this discourse with unrecognized and often unpalatable truths. One might speak of this "free" rigour as such only if one acknowledges the limits and insufficiencies of the unsurprised thought of freedom.

Such a procedure offers yet other challenges to the commentator. If the task of commentary is not to sustain coherence and continuity among fragments, but instead to disclose the incessant process of fragmentation even within the fragment, then the boundaries of discourse are less vivid than commentary may require. How could a commentator fail to impose cohesion and unity when surveying such fragments? On the one hand, the commentator would need to contextualize each occasion of fragmented discussion, isolating it from all others. That would entail, then, that the presentation of the concept in one "book" could not be aligned in any way with a presentation of the concept from another "book". Doing so would impose cohesion and presuppose unity, as if there were a basic text one were recomposing from the fragments of disparate texts. However, on the other hand, if texts were merely physical media necessary for the presentations of fragments (and thus the commentator might simply reconstruct the basic text that Nancy himself was at pains to disavow), then one would be betraying the very text one imposed. Either way, there would be no surprise in the commentator's (and, needless to say, the readers') thinking of Nancy's free thinking of the *logos* of freedom.

Nancy's fascination with the fragment is extant in some of his earliest work, especially *The Literary Absolute* (co-authored with Philippe Lacoue-Labarthe). This work maintains that a fragment's density and textual insularity enable it to be figuratively self-positing. A work of composition is a singularly determinate statement consisting of "accidental and involuntary aspects of fragmentations", which appears to suggest that fragmentary composition is ecstatic and exploratory in nature. Nevertheless, fragmented composition does not exclude the possibility of systematic fragmentation preceding and proleptically interrupting the process of systematically healing the ruptures of philosophical discourse. "If the fragment is indeed a fraction, it emphasizes neither first nor foremost the fracture that produces it. At the very least, it designates the borders of the fracture as an autonomous form as much as the formlessness or deformity of the tearing." In other terms, it may conjure the very value of ruins of textuality, especially that of the ruination of systematicity. One might say that there is a kind of systematicity even in the process of the ruination of systems, a formal incompleteness that is precisely the systematicity proper to fragmented composition. A fragment might share in the presentation of a ruined system or it might individuate itself as if it participated in no possible system. Interestingly, if there is a "fragmentary totality" it would have no nodal centre, for each fragment is "simultaneously in the whole and in the part", such that it presents both itself and the whole in which it participates but whose configuration reveals only indeterminate horizons. That is to say, if all fragments have an internal creative volatility expressed through the work of an individual self, then fragmented composition can be put to the systematic task of reconstructing the *ruination* of systems without merely offering another form of systematic discourse (LA: 40–50). Properly speaking, it is precisely the textual role of fragments to construct chaos, the already established ruination of systems, a role that must be itself chaotic prior to and wholly incommensurate with the construction of systems.

Nancy recovers this perspective in *The Sense of the World*, in which he notes that there are two kinds of extreme fragmentation. On the one hand, there is the fragment that exhibits fatigue and completion, of work having been exhausted as if there were nothing but ruins remaining from the labour of constructing and destroying. On the other hand, there is the fragment of the event of fragmentation that presents such fragmentation in its truth. In other words, if we can no longer assume that fragments are simply little shards of predetermined monumental visions or that a fragment can have all the force of such visions, then, Nancy wonders, what is left over that even the completion of fragmented composition cannot present? It is precisely the task of a free thinking inscribing itself into free composition to address this residuality of freedom in philosophical discourse.

However, it needs to be said that this is a book composed with the goal of elucidating Nancy's intriguingly timely thoughts and the finesse with which it is fragmentedly composed. Such a book is not mere mimicry of the consummate ability of its subject. A certain detachment is necessary, although one that implies only that this book cannot be read in the way that Nancy must be read. Strangely, commentary of this kind imposes the very conditions of the "book" Nancy himself tried to expurgate from his own composition. It does not do what it says must be done in order to appreciate its subject. And for that precise reason it should be treated as a mere preliminary guide to his thought, and not a replacement for reading his texts.

The literary "ethics" of writing

Nancy is not immediately interested in questions of philosophical methodology, yet often he does display a concern for matters of compositional protocol, as suggested in his approach to fragmentation. He maintains that all the discursive means by which singular meanings are appropriated or inscribed should be resisted through an "exposition" (a putting out of place, a supplanting of pre-position) or even an "exscription" (a writing that excludes from writing precisely what is appropriated by substantialist metaphysics) (IC: 19, 167).[10] Broadly speaking, to pursue meaning through his texts is to explore a variety of questions concerning appropriation–exposition and inscription–exscription, all of which keep open the future, the undecidable exigencies of discourse. What may one say or write of some topic? What may one write of "the topic"? When does a textual difficulty arise? What are the perimeters of a text and are these perimeters determined by intrinsic limits between conceptual tableaux? Most tenably, writing exhibits decisions of thought that answer to an "archi-ethics" of a commander-less command that singularizes its receiver (BP: 108). Inspired perhaps by Jacques Derrida, he is especially engaged by the authorial entitlements and duties of composition shaped in response to the exigencies of discourse itself. Indeed, he appears to wonder whether there are any textual protocols that regulate the authorial decisions and nodal points of texts, which is to ask whether there is an "ethics" of a text that determines the conditions its author must satisfy. Philosophy is, after all, a matter of style, of the *praxis* of thought and its writing (in the sense of the assumption of a responsibility for and to the "*ethos* of both thought and thinker") (SW: 19; see also R). To understand such protocols, however, it is necessary to examine the role writing plays as the guardian of sense, as the protector of the sharing of community of being from the formation of substantial community under political standards of appropriation. Hence, whatever protocols of "literary ethics" inform philosophical discourse, they must involve a hermeneutic of the unique nature of writing as the venue for the free thinking of the free circulation of sense.

One might summarize Nancy's position as follows. The imperative to write constitutes a protocol issuing from beyond philosophical discourse and haunts its effort to utilize its own criteria, fulfil its commitments and pursue its inherent interests. Obedience to it constitutes the interruption of the communitarian and political mission to seize speech and transform its content into the terms of a closed immanence. Philosophy is not only a process of healing the ruptures of discourse about truth. It is also a *praxis*, an incessant interruption of any practical attempt to subsume the interruptions of discourse themselves. Specifically, since it interrupts the desire to be practical with an "inoperative" or "useless" alternative irreducible to mimetic reflection, the production of meaning itself produces resistance that interrupts such production.[11] In other words, free writing poses incessant challenges to any philosophical or political means of appropriation. This is so not only because it presents ruptures of discourse that subvert the integrity of philosophical discourse, but also because it exposes a free communication that is always disruptive of philosophy's ability to maintain its own integrity. To write freely is to share singularly in community's sense, to shatter its substantial and conceptually accessible linkages and scatter them beyond the confines of discourses that promise only closed immanence. Moreover, free philosophical writing, expressive of its own inherent disruptions, dissipates the temptation to offer a politically inspired mythological vision of community and its world. Since writing itself is always available for political utility, the task of the philosopher is to keep its resources detached from any such appropriations. This requires that philosophical writing always inscribes its own sense of "literary ethics" in recognition of the non-philosophical imperatives and protocols that motivate it.

It is important to bear in mind that this "literary ethics" does not only possess existential relevance in the sense of the exscription of existence beyond appropriation as opposed to the inscription of individual meanings. As Francis Fisher has pointed out, writing is the exscription of existence in the inscription of sense, which is to say that "sense always happens to exposed existence and it happens as event, dispersion, brilliance or shard, punctuation: in short, writing".[12] Substantial community is everywhere in jeopardy and craves the security of immanence, but literature (including philosophy) always resists and suspends the attainment of this security by recognizing and enacting the sharing in (and of) sense. Given his fascination with the limits of philosophy, the edges where philosophical discourse exhausts itself, Nancy challenges the insistent distinction between philosophy and literature that this exscription of existence sustains. He deconstructs this "basic" distinction and evaluates the ramifications of free philosophical composition as an autonomous form of writing, as "literature", in terms of exscription of existence and inscription of sense. Such exscriptions expose the singularity of sense and expropriate it beyond the reach of political efforts to seize it. They are political because there is a "literature" of sharing in community, of "poetics of style", of modes of existence, of modulations of relation and retreat and so on (SW: 121).

But how does literary writing pose this resistance? He argues that literature is the "voice of interruption" of both myth and community. "Interruption" means that the literary and mythic effort to offer an immanential world view is *always already* fragmented or diverted. The drive to be "practical", to establish conceptual possibilities that are useful, is constantly interrupted by the *praxis* of dislocation and fragmentation of discourse. However, interruption does not merely follow from the insufficiencies of philosophical discourse. On the contrary, it always precedes the formation of the immanential worldview, which is to say that immanence is always disrupted *before* the terms of its formation crystallize. The organization of desire along, for example, political, artistic, psychoanalytic, humanistic and semiological lines (all of which serve as aspects of the "same general formation of signification") is intermittently suspended by the very condition of desire itself (GT: 32). In other words, the closed immanence of substantial community consisting of atomic individuals and the *mythos* that often holds community together is ruptured from within by this freely expressive voice necessary for the evocation of this very mythic immanence. The conditions of immanence (intelligibility, identity, representation) provide the means of the internal disruption of immanence itself. A community's passion for sharing singularities lends this voice and disrupts its own incessantly threatened immanence. This "literary" voice plays back mythic speech to a community without being mythic itself (which is not to say that modern literature is the purveyor of mythic immanence). Rather, it resonates without offering any originary message and anticipates the discourse of any myth that might scintillate the cohesion of a substantial community. Once mythic speech ceases, the literary voice persists in offering its own pre-originary or an-archic rendition of *mythos* that unremittingly counters the temptation of immanential thinking. Of course, "literature" might not be a substantial designation for the interruption posed by the voice of shared communal being, but it does benefit from the prior resonance of myth to whose exigencies it is never completely impervious. It might be seductive, then, to speak of "literature after myth", which, however, is to presuppose the "myth of the myth of mythless society" (that is, the very myth of a contemporary world without myth that nonetheless utilizes literature in its place). On the contrary, literature and myth cannot be interchangeable, and the former cannot serve the functional role of the latter. Where literature differs most dramatically from myth is in its incapacity to offer a revelation of a completed reality and an immanential community. Although myth necessarily consists in an immanential worldview, literature reveals nothing but its own vision of the possibility of sharing in that vision, a vision that is, again, always interrupted by resistance to metaphysical and political standards posed by the circulation of sense. Although each literary work is a writing of both myth and literature, the writing of literature interrupts the written mythic "speech" and forbids its crystallization. In so far as literature interrupts mythic discourse, but is itself a discontinuity that fails to reach fruition in immanence, it participates in the very "mythic invention" it interrupts. Even to read a work as if it wielded a mythic functional value is to read it in terms of a literary interruption of its own discourse.

To presuppose that there is a link between sharing in community and the free writing of freedom is to imply neither the "myth of communion through literature" nor the "myth of literary creation by the community". Nancy proposes the curious notion that the sharing that composes community "is" literature. In other words:

> It would designate that singular ontological quality that gives being in common, that does not hold it in reserve, before or after community, as an essence of man, of God, or of the State achieving its fulfillment in communion, but that rather makes for a being that is only when shared in common, or rather whose quality of being, whose nature and structure are shared (or exposed).
>
> (IC: 64)

Literature gives voice to the sharing of community and thereby expresses fragmented communion, the insubstantial condition of sharing that composes community. It is the common exposure of singular beings that each community demands in the absence of myth. Strictly speaking, there is a pre-philosophical imperative to write because there *are* others, or, more specifically, because it is philosophically necessary to address them or compose for them; if there were no others whose community is to share in the finitude of being, there would be no need for the free and interruptive voice that literature provides.

Such a speech of the interruption of the substantiation of community, Nancy maintains in *The Sense of the World*, is always in danger of being seized by politics. Indeed, politics itself is the "seizure of speech" and can be traced out as "testimonies of the existence of a world". Despite this never-ending threat of political appropriation, neither this world nor this speech can be subsumed by politics. Although each philosophical gesture of resistance is posed in as much as it is the gesture of a finite existence, each enunciation and reverberation of speech has *effects* that are seized by politics (which incorporates their concatenations and interrupts the circulation of sense in its own fashion). To change the figure, one might say that politics appropriates the singular knots of sense that compose communal discourse and attempts to untie them. The interwoven knot of singular forms of sense "gives a place to every event of sense" and is untied and laid out strand by strand as aspects of political discourse. However, this irreducibility of communal discourse is suggested by writing's resistance to political subsumptions, which becomes political (in another sense, as we shall see) precisely in this resistance (BP: 84; SW: 114–16).

Interpretative writing, then, exposes the limit of sharing in community, the "limit upon which communication takes place". Intervening in immanential discourse, the literary author suspends its mythic cadences and refuses to play them back to society in any resonating fashion. Specifically, although mythic founding speech in political discourse plays a society's myths back to itself, and thereby endeavours to establish closed immanence, literature offers an interruptive recitation in which the history of this endeavour is suspended. Literature is a free event of disruption by the circulation of sense, not the mythologization of an event voiced in and by a community, which is itself an event that instantiates a moment of communal sharing by singular beings (IC: 67–9). Writing is political in its essence, Nancy maintains, because it precedes political signification and offers a pure *praxis* resistant to mere communication of sense (C: 386). It conveys sense in so far as it establishes the possibility of messaging, of communication, not merely this or that message. If communities substantiate "around" or "under" particular messages (creeds, ideologies, etc.), then writing resists the "cutting up of world into exclusive worlds" by means of these messages. Indeed, he persists, free writing is the "task of sense" because it answers to the demand that ties not be established, even though the language of sharing in community among singularities is always threatened by political appropriation or subsumption. Literary writers should not give in to the temptation to think of themselves as producers of meaning. Instead, they should affirm themselves as those who both watch attentively as sense passes inexorably from the *future* and await the *futural* sense that does not pass. There is nothing resigned about this passivity in the face of uncertainty, because writing is an imperative that lends sense to all the voices and silences that are strictly exscribed, that receive no exposure in politically appropriable texts and their sense. The *praxis* of writing relays signification and communication across a plurality of singularities; it does not merely offer sense to the political seizure of speech (SW: 119, 121, 163). In this respect, it follows the trajectory of a "transimmanent" sense, as we shall see.

Writing is often appropriated by politics when it is defined in terms of the mythic status of the writer, who thus so easily becomes a figure of political discourse. Writers recite their own writing, as if they were not only tellers of a narrative but its heroes as well. A writer such as James Joyce is deemed to be not only a composer of myths, but also a participant in the myth of the composition of myths (as if the modern writer were exercising imagination in such a manner as to project a "primitive teller"). In other words, the subject of literature is both a "writer" inspired by literary evocations and an inspiring genius inscribed in dialogue with readers exscribed from literature. However, such a myth of the writer is no longer possible, since it has been interrupted and fragmented by the very nature of writing itself.

> The myth of the writer is interrupted: a certain scene, an attitude, and a creativity pertaining to the writer are no longer possible.

18

The task of what has been designated as *écriture* (writing) and the thinking of *écriture* has been, precisely, to render them impossible – and consequently to render impossible a certain type of foundation, utterance, and literary and communitarian fulfillment: in short, a politics. (IC: 69)

Generally speaking, then, philosophy addresses the exscribed sense of existence and inscribes its possible significations, thereby producing the undecidable conditions of philosophical inscription and political appropriation. In this context, Nancy promulgates the view that enquiry into the status of the philosopher (as well as the protocols it obeys that are definitive of philosophy) arises as an *ethical* question. Nowadays, it has become commonplace to ask "the ethical question", a query concerning the status and role (indeed, even the possibility) of writing "an ethics" and, moreover, the capacity of modern discourse to write "ethically". "Writing ethically" informs the very protocols of philosophical compositions: what is it necessary to write here? What ought one to say in response to this objection? What does one have a duty to address when surveying this subject?

Of course, the question of ethics proceeds from an anxiety about the lack of any ethics able to address the demands of the modern age and the deplorable vacuity of contemporary "ethical" thought. Indeed, Nancy wonders, might it not be the case that our demand for ethics is a symptom of a deeper cultural distress? Ethics is possible, he avers, but only on the condition that we are "deprived of rules, without being deprived of truth" and that we acknowledge that it is the possibility of a *future* emergence, "carried along by what we know about being". Thus, although our distress over the question of ethics is itself a presentiment of what ethics is, it can equally be accounted that "the restoration of existence to existence", without rules determined by the alleged superiority of the good, is possible in significations of ethical discourse (FT: 17–18). The question, then, is whether the philosopher who distressfully demands an ethics (or an answer to the question of ethics) is aware that the ethics required is part of the "distress of our world". The philosopher should bear in mind that ethics is a *futural* possibility available to the demands of philosophical discourse only by virtue of its present uncertainty.

In some sense, the "question of ethics" itself is a figure of discourse necessarily participating within the paradigm of a "finished" metaphysics. In brief, the very metaphysics whose end calls for an ethics is one in which the question of ethics is itself necessarily formulated. According to one of the many paradoxes one finds in Nancy's work, the "question of ethics" is self-defeating: it must be addressed within the context of a paradigm that cannot be sustained and that would, thus, efface the very possibility of the answer. Hence, Nancy requests that we consider the necessity of "withdrawing" from the question, of examining the perimeters and protocols that make this aporia so poignantly frustrating to contemporary thinking. Moreover, Nancy remarks, it is not clear what we could "know" about such protocols even if something must be "known" in order for the withdrawal to take place. After all, we do not "know" if we have the resources for querying such a withdrawal since the knowledge necessary to comprehend the unanswerable "question of ethics" is supplied by the very discourse about knowledge that participates in the metaphysics whose end demands ethics in the first place! We would need to "know" how things stand with our "ethical non-knowledge", which is itself a question of the limitations of a given protocol of reasoning and writing. At any rate, it is imperative that there "should" be an ethically pregnant domain from which ethics is born, but one that could not be thought to be "just another traditional ethics" nor one produced with a practical intention in mind.

Simply put (perhaps too simply put): to question protocols of philosophy would require a withdrawal from philosophical discourse, and there would need to be protocols for such a withdrawal that must not be traditionally philosophical. The "question of ethics" might demand a non-philosophical conception of non-philosophical protocols, or at least protocols, composed at the edge of philosophical knowledge, that were sensitive to their tenuous hold on philosophical ideals of discourse. Nevertheless, if it is not clear that one could "establish" protocols of reasoning and writing without being philosophical, what, then, is the "ethics" of the writing of the withdrawal from philosophical writing?

In reply, one might say that philosophy itself often complies with the protocol that "here" one necessarily must provide some rationale, and so on. Yet to insist that an ethics is necessary, that it is an *imperative* that the question of ethics should be answered, is to appeal to precisely the "necessity" of protocol that is under challenge. Indeed, behind every necessity of protocol is the "*Il faut*" or "It is necessary" that itself is the determinant of philosophical protocols *par excellence*. Even under challenge from political grasping at the sense of the world, the writer must still answer the traditional question of philosophical protocol: what is *your* ethics, the ethics that renders it possible for *you* to withdraw from the question of ethics? More specifically, what is *your* obligation to withdraw? What is it about the question and its aporia that requires that *you* withdraw from it "here"? Needless to say, to withdraw requires that one interrogate this necessity, to think and write in recognition of the fragility of this necessity. It calls for an "extra-discursive duty" that implies an "ethics" even if ethics itself is under interrogation. In many instances, we must simply surrender the demand for adherence to any protocol that could not fail to be similar to traditional philosophical methodologies. Not even philosophy, furthermore, could derive knowledge of a duty that would nullify the necessity of such knowledge.

Most generally, it could be said that it is impossible to get behind the philosophy–non-philosophy distinction in order to locate protocols, and yet it is precisely this withdrawal behind the distinction that is necessary for philosophy's deconstruction of its protocols. That is to say, there might very well be a non-theoretical duty behind this distinction that one must necessarily obey if one wishes to withdraw from the question. This might amount to an obligation to shirk philosophical duties informed by the Aristotelian model of philosophy: "*sophia* as supreme *praxis* of *theoria*". The duty to deconstruct philosophy (and its distinction from non-philosophy) might require answering to a non-philosophical duty that is itself philosophically demonstrated but non-philosophically accountable. It simply could not possibly produce an infinity of successive questions about ethics and post-ethics. It is a question, Nancy avers, of *maintaining* the question of the duty prior to any conception of ethics whatsoever. In other words, it is not as if one "knows" what ethics is, and then recognizes a duty to establish or explore it; rather, it is more a matter of answering a command to write the ethical question of ethics prior to any knowledge of what ethics is. "One must interrogate the duty of the question as to its propriety and its impropriety. The thought of writing has not written the ethics of this duty" (RP: 36, 41).

Specifically, Nancy suggests that there is an analogy between the haunting voice of conscience and the Kantian categorical imperative, which, despite its universal unconditionality, speaks only *to* singular beings in specific instances. Clearly, Nancy is intrigued by the non-ethical call that such an unconditional command represents. The command to which the author responds opens a gap that excludes the possibility of fusion between that command and that author. The law of freedom is received from no one, yet someone receives it and is singularized as such in this reception. If the imperative commands us to write of ethics, that might be because it is the free voice of the essentially free singular being. The essential freedom of the free person is not reduced by the conditionality of the silent, internal voice that "speaks" the imperative and thereby determines the freedom of the free man. However, it is utterly inconceivable that Kantian freedom could obtain, for there is no necessary imperative binding on a freedom that must discover its own conditions of possibility (this subject will be explored in greater detail below). The categorical imperative, he notes elsewhere, is akin to an uncanny voice that "haunts our thinking", a troubling peculiarity that disturbs only because it is so close, so immediate

21

in its estrangement. Any possible return to normalcy when haunted by this peculiarity would require precisely an ethics of this haunting that forbids normalcy (FT: 136).[13]

Ultimately, however, the non-localizable source of the silent voice of the imperative is obeyed by writing and in writing, in which the writer (and, indeed, "man") is called, singularized and effaced as an "individual as such" in answer to the command. The law of writing, the law to which all writing singularly responds and the law to which all writing is addressed, is received from an indeterminate source, without being heard; yet it is received as a singular presence that asks the question of finitude of each writer. As Nancy insightfully remarks, the question received is unanswerable, but it concerns the maintenance of the ethicity of writing on to which philosophical thought must hold but, paradoxically, cannot seize. To write of the writing of ethics, or even to write in obedience to the imperative to do so, is to obey, to do one's duty by exscribing humanity, philosophy and the self-effacement of man, as an end of discourse and of itself (RP: 51). It is precisely such a contextual imperative, obeyed in every instance of writing, that suggests the manner of addressing the question of ethics in terms of an inscription of the freedom of man that is always necessarily exscribed from the imperative to write. The demand that one must write freely issues uncertainly and the necessity to exscribe freedom from writing itself issues undecidably from beyond what is written of freedom.

Conclusion

Having surveyed a range of subjects in this chapter, I would hazard to offer a number of succinct conclusions.

- Nancy's philosophy is motivated by the commitment to explore and protect singularity from both a substantialist metaphysics (which treats it in terms of universals and essences) and politics (which would attempt to force its meaning to contribute to some expansive ideological vision).
- In conjunction with this point, it should also be emphasized that singularities are conceivable solely in pluralities. Nancy is fascinated by the ways that such singularities relate at the edge of philosophy: the circulation of sense through community, the intersection of experiential trajectories, the contact of bodies and so on.
- The proper mode of composition in approaching this question of "plural singularities" is a fragmented one. This is not to imply a

22

"fragmentation" or a ruination of a coherent whole, but an irreversible fragmentation that has a systematicity all its own. And one, it must be said, whose subjects philosophical writers should protect from substantialist metaphysics and political appropriation.

- Nancy emphasizes that discourse is not first formed and then "interrupted" by singularity, but is always already interrupted by its very own *praxis*. In other words, in so far as discourse is always "about" plural singularities that are irreducible to discursive themes, such singularities have already "interrupted" discourse from its very inception. Discourses are always open and incomplete in as much as they are incessantly interrupted by writing and thinking themselves.

- The discourses of ethics and the "question of ethics" are no exception. However, writing itself already obeys an imperative to write in response to its call. This imperative even inspires the "question of ethics" in the event that the very possibility of ethics is under interrogation. Roughly speaking, the question behind the question of ethics is one that addresses the ethical nature of the imperative to write of an ethics whose very possibility may be held in conceptual abeyance. The imperative does not confer an ethical meaning upon discourse; on the contrary, the imperative addresses the very limit conditions of ethics itself. Writing obeys an imperative, but not one that provides merely formal or universal conditions of obedience. Rather, each writer is singularized and called to write, and in doing so, provides the conditions of the incessant interruptions of discourses about ethics.

CHAPTER TWO

Nancy's influences

Occasionally it is insinuated that Nancy is a "French Nietzschean", a "post-Heideggerian" or even a "Derridean". This might imply that his achievement is nugatory, or at least derivative. Although only the least sensitive critic would dismiss it as mere commentary, it is understandable that some might regard it as an extrapolation from its sources. On this derogatory reading, Nancy is an occasionally impenitent philosophical exegete who selects influences and frames them with his own interrogative philosophical style.

Nevertheless, Nancy cannot be regarded as a disciple of any other thinker. Many philosophers meander through Nancy's texts (and are often present even when unnamed), but none has exerted an influence that would condition Nancy's achievement. Replete with unique textual styles and conceptual problems, his work demonstrates that he is very much his own philosopher. In fact, one might even say that there is often a certain impiety towards even those sources he praises, an impiety that comes in the form of a reading out of context, or a representation that cuts against the grain of the conventional readings of such sources. For instance, in *The Gravity of Thought*, Nancy rejects the notion that we should "return" to Enlightenment humanism, or that we should strive to make the principles of Kant or Hegel relevant to the contemporary age. Furthermore, castigating the despairing view that we have forgotten true philosophy, he insists that today we are entitled to say only that truth is as beleaguered as it ever has been and that we must think through our own times, not glorify any achievement of the past. He wishes to distance himself from "polemical interests and rigidities engendered by proper names" and to disregard as much as possible the difference of philosophical styles in the name of an effort to locate "something common" to them all (GT: 1, 7–8, 14). This is not the precept of a thinker dedicated to obsequiously championing the cause of any intellectual progenitor. Indeed, it would be surprising if a thinker who

24

emphasizes the importance of the sharing of being and the imperative of writing as a form of resistance to globalization and politics would be a fawning disciple of others who might not express such convictions.

Those thinkers whose role is perceived most vividly in Nancy's texts are: Rousseau, Kant, Hegel, Nietzsche, Heidegger, Bataille, Blanchot, Lacan and Derrida. These are presented here in convenient chronological order, not in order of precedence. What follows is an attempt to provide a gleaning of these relationships, not to offer detailed appraisal.

Jean-Jacques Rousseau

Nancy has a mixed impression of Rousseau's thoughts concerning political sovereignty. In *Retreating the Political*, this vacillation of interpretation forces him to offer a deconstructive reading of what can be learned about the origin of politics in communal activities. On the one hand, Rousseau is the primary source for examining the modern interplay between politics as it is known and the communal practices that constitute its vital sovereign force. The sovereignty of the general will is a startling proposal that suggests an understanding of the deeper and richer communal forces that compose political life. However, on the other hand, the dissolution of community into the general will provides sovereignty over it. Such a provision subsumes the community's interest beneath the standard of sovereignty or effaces the very communal conditions that warranted that general will at the outset. In yet other terms, Rousseau thinks of sovereignty as the crystallization of the interests of subjects who become autonomous citizens by virtue of exercising the general will. However, for Nancy, this might amount to a betrayal of the very notion of "sharing" in the intersections of singularities that compose sense and existence and that serve to define communities. What Nancy finds most objectionable is the thought that politics is the crystallization of the activities of isolated, atomic individuals who choose to recognize certain contractual limitations that are superimposed upon and purportedly reductive of the preceding community of being.

Immanuel Kant

Kant, in Nancy's view, is simply a force with which to be reckoned, primarily because his thought produced the various crises of nineteenth- and twentieth-century philosophy. This is certainly not to say that Nancy dismisses the "Kantian turn", but only that he does not regard it and its theoretical consequences as sufficient to address the "crises" of modern theory. In *The Gravity of Thought*, Nancy wonders whether Kant's philosophy is worthy of a re-inauguration given its various difficulties of signification (especially those pertaining to determinism and the categorical imperative). In his view, the Kantian schematic is intended to give content to concepts and perception to intuitions, but there is a certain obscurity in the thought that although signification is produced, it does not produce the meaning of its own production (GT: 21–3).

In "The *Kategorein* of Excess", in *A Finite Thinking*, he surveys the "absurd" incomprehensibility of the categorical imperative, which reveals a "pietist hypocrisy" competing with a "catatonic understanding" (FT: 133–4). In this vein, in *Retreating the Political*, he presents the notion that the categorical imperative is primarily the duty to write in resistance to political appropriations.

Striving to undermine the Kantian notion of freedom and its corollary of "radical evil" in *The Experience of Freedom*, Nancy challenges the notion that it is in the context of a schematic of rationality that freedom can be grasped as a "fact of reason". He maintains that it is not by means of rationally accessible self-legislation that the facticity of freedom is established, but by the spontaneous "burst" of freedom necessary for existence itself (EF: 21–5).

By extension, radical evil is a conceptual consequence of an undue emphasis upon freedom as a "fact of reason" informed by deontological criteria. Against the notion that evil should be conceived as an irrational transgression of the moral law (and thus is merely a perversion or malfunction of the exercise of freedom), Nancy proposes that we conceive of evil in a manner that is free from such constraints; in other words, to examine the possibility of evil as a pure positivity always latent in but potentially emergent from the very singular condition of freedom itself (EF: 124).

Generally speaking, Nancy offers myriad deconstructive readings of a Kantian schematic in order to show its vulnerability to the exigency of a finite thinking of singularity and its uncertain future.

Georg Wilhelm Friedrich Hegel

Although much of Nancy's work can be read as a critique of Hegel, it should not be overlooked that he praises him in *Hegel: The Restlessness of the Negative* as the "inaugural" thinker of the modern age who stresses the importance of the manner in which freedom facilitates our availability to the circulation of sense (HRN: 3–7). Elsewhere, Nancy notes that "the sole task of an ontology of community is, through thinking about difference, to radicalize or to aggravate Hegelian thinking about the Self until it caves in", a task that cannot be achieved or rendered intelligible by means of the Hegelian paradigm itself (BC: 3). Perhaps the Hegelian scheme is "inaugural" of the sense of freedom precisely because it cannot satisfy its own criteria or, hermeneutically speaking, cannot fulfil the terms of its own anticipations.

Furthermore, in *The Speculative Remark (One of Hegel's Bon Mots)*, Nancy interrogates Hegel's dismissal of a philosophical grammar, especially when the dialectic itself is predicated on the logic of sublation (which presumes the inherent transformation of the terms of logical identity). Nancy wonders whether there might be any place in the dialectic for undecidability, for meanings that ramble and are "lost". Again, one might say that Hegelian dialectics cannot determine the uncertain conditions of discourse it uniquely experiences.

In a similar vein, Nancy reads Hegel in "The Jurisdiction of the Hegelian Monarch" in *The Birth to Presence* as if his view of sovereignty were merely a "limit point" in the history of the concept (BP: 128, 110–42). The monarch does not figure in a dialectical sweep in which the differences of society are sublated into a more general teleological commitment. Rather, the sovereignty of the monarch is established only by the openness of the relations that compose sense. One might notice, here, that Nancy's reading runs counter to the many prevailing interpretations of Hegel and does not concede to the force of their conceptual possibilities.

This does not exhaust the many registers on which Hegel fascinates Nancy. For example, in "The Girl who Succeeds the Muses: The Hegelian Birth of the Arts" in *The Muses*, Nancy appreciates the Hegelian history of art and queries the necessity of an art that dissipates into "the arts", and then into artlessness.

As uncomfortable as Hegel's notions of freedom and historical totality might often make us, we must grant that, for Nancy, Hegel is the thinker of immanence *par excellence*. However, it should be obvious that it is the Hegel who explores negativity, becoming, and "good infinity", not the Hegel of the forms of the state and the progress of history, who fascinates Nancy most. Ultimately, Nancy presents captivating intuitions about singularity and sense, multiplicity and *praxis* that represent compelling engagements with Hegel, yet he does not identify his own proposals with Hegelian thought beyond this critical requisitioning.

Friedrich Nietzsche

Nietzsche's presence permeates Nancy's work in many ways. First, Nancy's emphasis upon finite thinking is a response to Nietzsche's demand for a seeking that demolishes the obstacles posed by universal and systematic schematics. Thus the very notion of a "philosophy of the future", which is perhaps the Nietzschean motif *par excellence*, assumes myriad forms in Nancy's work: the rethinking of sense, singularity, freedom, evil, community, sovereignty, politics and so on.

Secondly, one aspect of the challenge to the task of a contemporary "finite thinking" is the notorious "death of God", which Nancy insists in *The Inoperative Community*, *The Sense of the World* and *The Gravity of Thought* and nearly everywhere else is an unignorable cultural fact and philosophical datum. "The death of God is the final thought of philosophy, which thus proposes it as an end to religion: it is toward this thought that the West (which in this case excludes neither Islam nor Buddhism) will have ceaselessly tended." Indeed, Nancy suggests that there is something godlike about Nietzsche's gesture of simultaneously declaring the death of God and "madly" proclaiming himself a god. "God is resurrected a final time with Nietzsche, with the parodic and dizzying uttering of the inevitable 'I am God' of self-consciousness." Nancy remarks poignantly that "God gambles his own resurrection in the madness of Nietzsche", a "madness of derangement in an exhausted calling to the gods" (IC: 149–50). Nevertheless, in Nancy's work, there is none of the despairing gloom so often associated with this thought. In regarding theology's transcendental solution to questions of finite thinking of sense as positively illegitimate, he insinuates that the "death of God" has emancipated this thinking from theological requirements.

Thirdly, and perhaps most vital of all, is the presence of the Nietzsche of the "power quanta" and "power constellations", the fragmented metaphysics of the will to power. Reverberations of this thought are to be found in Nancy's stirring depictions in *Being Singular Plural*, *The Sense of the World* and *The Birth to Presence* of a plurality of singularities without any absolute (transcendental) point of reference. This metaphysical tableau is conceived most thoroughly at the intersections of singular events and the interstitial "between" of such singularities, as well as the "sharing" or "co-appearing" that is the creating origin of a circulating sense. Nancy extols a swirling constellation of singular events that cross one another and form further ephemeral events, each of which is a singularity indicative of the sense of the world itself. Every trajectory of value is curvilinear, offering myriad associations and flitting away from paradigmatic appropriation. "The singular exposes every time it is exposed and all of its sense resides

28

therein", he declares in *The Sense of the World*, and on each occasion it is attesting to itself in a groundless fashion (SW: 74). The world of sense in its sense, he says in *Being Singular Plural*, is an incessantly circulating sense in the "discontinuity of its discrete occurrences" (BSP: 5). At the very least, this has some affinity with Nietzsche's vision of plurality.

Martin Heidegger

There is hardly an aspect of Nancy's thought that is not endowed with some measure of the influence of Heidegger. Most broadly, Nancy is responding to the Heideggerian challenge to address the "ontological question".[1] For Heidegger, the question of being is one that queries the status and role of the individual being in a pre-existing Being. Nancy vituperates both the premise of a pre-existing Being into which the individual being is "thrown" or "fallen" and the precept that the question of the Being of the individual being can be approached as if it were wholly divorced from social relations. In *Being Singular Plural*, *The Experience of Freedom* and "The Decision of Existence" in *The Birth to Presence*, Nancy claims that the *Seinsfrage* (the question of being) must be posed in terms of the *Mitseinsfrage* (the question of being-with), in which the "between-ness" of social relation is primary. In general terms, the issue of social relations is the primary focus of the ontological question itself. This impels him to utilize Heidegger's "existential analytic" to challenge the Kantian notion of freedom; however, he then propels the discourse of freedom into the context of the *Mitseinsfrage* in such a way as to confront Heidegger as well. In addition, in "Sharing Voices" he offers a detailed appraisal of Heidegger's reading of the hermeneutic circle's pre-understanding of being, the anticipation of an answer to the question of being. Interpretation of the community of being, freedom and the social relation is not self-fulfilling or anticipatory of its own achievement, but is always open to the uncertain challenges the very activity of interpreting implies.

Of course, Nancy's perspective on the threat of alternative totalitarianisms is informed by the desire to minimize the seductions of Heidegger's view of community and history. In *A Finite Thinking* and *Retreating the Political*, the question of the essence of technology is examined in the context of Heidegger's view. Roughly speaking, he attempts to establish that, for all the risk of insidious misunderstandings, technology might also be able to provide linkages among persons that facilitate the open or insubstantial community he finds so fascinating.

Georges Bataille

Wherever the notions of surplus and sacrifice are at play in Nancy's critique of substantialist metaphysics, the presence of Georges Bataille is almost palpable. They are to be found in *A Finite Thinking*, *The Inoperative Community*, and nearly anywhere that community and religion are discussed in Nancy's work. Indeed, in Michel Surya's literary biography of Bataille, he remarks that Nancy's interpretation has become almost canonical. More specifically, Miguel de Beistegui has noted that "Nancy finds in Bataille the point of anchorage for his thinking and subscribes unreservedly to the Bataillean writing", although it must be acknowledged that the proximity between the two makes discernment between paraphrase, commentary and critique difficult.[2] Indeed, Bataille's notions provide Nancy with various templates by which a critique of substantialist metaphysics can be exposed. For example, to the extent that the Christian metaphysical vision of mediated self-sacrifice "through Christ" has informed the Western tradition, sacrifice is embedded in the very deconstructive possibilities engendered by the exploration of sense. This mediation is the indicator of a substantialist approach that he seeks to oppose by means of the possible affirmation of an open immanence of sense lacking precisely the mediation "Christ" provides.

Maurice Blanchot

Nancy's engagement with Blanchot figures most prominently as a debate over the (im)possibility of community. *The Inoperative Community* in particular can be interpreted as part of an ongoing dialogue with Blanchot. In his study of Blanchot, Gerald L. Bruns peruses the dialogue with Nancy as if it were mutually inseminatory of radical views of community. In many respects, Nancy's views of sharing and love are natural outgrowths from Blanchot's thought, although not aspects that the latter had himself cultivated.[3] Robert Bernasconi has queried whether Nancy has any right to claim that Blanchot accepted his own views of the "incompleteness" and "impossibility" of community. Nancy's final word in this dialogue, according to Bernasconi, is that a "community without exclusion" is not a form of reconstituted immanence that could open the possibility of totalitarianism. However, under the influence of the "ethical transcendentalism" of Emmanuel Levinas, Blanchot would insist that it is the alterity of the other, and not the sharing within open community, that enables community to remain safeguarded from totalitarian encroachments, a claim Nancy straightforwardly denies. Without a doubt, Nancy's thought is hostile to the transcendentalism of Levinas and its presence in Blanchot, but it is not clear that it is in any way flawed because of any neglect of its wisdom.[4]

Jacques Lacan

Nancy has had a love–hate relationship with the thought of Jacques Lacan. Perhaps no modern thinker has explored sense more vigorously, and none has offered a more enigmatic contribution to the hermeneutic thereof. Yet all the radical proposals Lacan offers suggest many of the tendencies of the substantialist metaphysics Nancy abhors. In the background of Nancy's reading of Lacan is a profound suspicion of subjectivity structured on an imaginary order fragmented and de-centred by the symbolic order, a transfiguration that plays into the hands of ideology. In *The Title of the Letter* (co-authored with Philippe Lacoue-Labarthe) Nancy explores Lacan's usurpation of Saussurean linguistics into a psychoanalytic theory that produces a subversion of the very notion of the sign. He surveys the implication of desire in the relationship between the letter of a text (or consciousness) and the truth (as revealed through psychoanalytic appraisals of the behaviour of signs). Moreover, Nancy objects to the philosophical simplicity of the presumption of the foundational viability of subjectivity and systematicity. Curiously, these enquiries elicited an umbrageous response from Lacan himself, who accused their authors of being little better than underlings (TL: 82).[5]

More generally, in *The Sense of the World*, Nancy regards psychoanalysis as a "severe punctuation of pure truth, that is, a pure privation of sense", ultimately to be regarded as a "necessary catharsis of an excess of sense, of an excessive demand for sense". He objects in particular to the Lacanian view that significations swarm around the "void of truth" masked by the "ego" (which is to say that the subject is taken for granted as the focal centre of signification). Such a view promulgates the theological excrescence that founds the notion of a "curable" world (SW: 46–7).[6] Under the inscrutably cold gaze of the analyst, the world itself is regarded as a Lacanian "Other" or "Law" within which there is a centre from which "sense arises this side of an opposition between insane and sane" (SW: 48–9; BSP: 45).

On a different register, in *Retreating the Political* Nancy questions the political commitments of Freudian psychoanalysis, especially those that involve panic over the dissolution of community ties. He criticizes Freud's ability to analyse the plurality of subjects presupposed by the very descriptive tableaux of the subconscious. Obviously, Lacanian perspectives are very much in Nancy's thought, but as a rejected polemical presence.

Jacques Derrida

Often thought to be a "Derridean", Nancy has proven that he merits this appellation only in a very general, and ultimately unhelpful, way. As surveyed in Chapter 1, Nancy has "deconstructive" commitments wherever he addresses the limitations of questioning, the demands of theory or the requirements of a given discourse. Deconstructive approaches to the restlessness of sense and the undecidability of language are of interest throughout Nancy's work. There is also the question of entitlements in compositional protocols: "what is to be done?" in the eventuality of a philosophical crisis is a question that presupposes the very absence of crisis, an undecidable state of theory, and one that may curtail our very "right" to ask this question. The thought that philosophy has "reserves", ethical or otherwise, from which to draw solutions and delineate alternative perspectives too comes under fire. There might be such reserves in the open and undecidable process of writing and reading, but not as latently redemptive states of a thought (RP: 33–9, 157).

In "Elliptical Sense" in *A Finite Thinking*, he also approaches the sense in which Derrida's philosophy opens the question of the lack of sense and the manner in which calling for sense always amounts to a call for yet more sense. Sense is in no sense given: "*Différance* is the demand, the call, the request, the seduction, the imprecation, the imperative, the supplication, the jubilation of writing" (FT: 95). One discerns the consequences of this claim for Nancy's thought in the scintillating notion of freedom and its discourse being free only in so far as there is "surprise" or "shock" at the very freeness of sense itself. In a sense, the "elliptical" movement of sense, whereby one addresses a discourse obliquely, inspires Nancy in his depictions of the circulation of sense along trajectories of sharing that compose community.

Separately, the problem of naming, of naming "God" or "Derrida", is also an essential aspect of Nancy's work: without presupposing "this" or "that" being beyond the name "God", one should name "properly" in the knowledge of an absence of names, as in "Borborygmi" in *A Finite Thinking* (FT: 113). This notion obviously plays a role in Nancy's almost dismissive approach to the naming of the god in "Of divine places" in *The Inoperative Community*.

And indeed, Nancy's notion of the future as the infinity of the "to-come" to which we should be open is grounded in his observations of the temporalizing of *différance*, that is, the "interior spacing of the very line of time", not merely a succession of temporal instances (SW: 35). Needless to say, Derridean motifs and interests are vital to Nancy's thought, but certainly less imperative for its comprehension than Nancy's own critical perspectives.

CHAPTER THREE

Immanentism

Nancy's dauntingly commodious exposition of "sense" is bound to his view of the multifarious nature of human experience. Offering a rousing critique of, on the one hand, any transcendental thinking that implies a source of sense "beyond" the world and, on the other, any immanential thinking that mimetically conceives of such a source within the world, he insists that all we can say of sense is that it is the world *itself*, or, alternatively, is constitutive of the very structure of the world. It is singular, material by virtue of its corporeal reticulations and coextensive with both thinking and world. If there is a singular sense "of" and "in" the world that is accessible to discourse, then by extension it is necessary to explore the multiplicities by which this sense is available at all to our finite thinking (a singular thought of a singular being, double genitive). However, the rigorous precept that this finite thinking has no access to the unthinkable "beyond" places ineradicable constraints on any exploration of sense. In this palimpsest notion of immanence, there is no inside–outside distinction at play, but only the very facticity of a world whose sense always collapses into an open, reticulated immanence without any recourse to transcendent (or transcendental) sources of meaning. Hence his critique of immanence is intended to approach its factical conditions, not to offer a panegyric for "the Other".[1] For Nancy, transcendence is merely what Western thought has customarily referred to as the untransgressible "beyond" of the horizon of immanence. Yet, again, there is nothing but "the world", an exposed and exposing sense of the world, a world that just is sense, nothing else.

There is another preliminary aspect of this critique of immanentism that merits preliminary scrutiny. Strictly understood, Nancy champions neither nihilism nor its philosophical alternatives. As one commentator outlines, there are three forms of immanence in Nancy's work: (a) the immanence of atomic individuals in closed association with one another; (b) the immanence of a group of individuals reflecting upon their cohesion as such; and

(c) the immanence of sense itself at the interstices of irreducibly open relations of sharing.[2] This last "sense", the focus of Nancy's ontological vision,
is at once lacking in the form of "absolute values", but also produced
within this lack in terms of relations between singularities. Given this
lacuna, it would appear to be impossible to speak of "the world" distinct
from sense at all. After all, this missing "sense" has now fragmented into a
multiplicity of *groundless* meanings; sense has never been completely missing and it always mistakenly has been assumed to possess the coherent
form of a *grounded* multiplicity of candidates of signification. Hence,
"sense" is to be found on the intrinsic limit, the singular interstice, of any
relation, not in the traditional dichotomies of metaphysics.

In the light of this notion of sense, then, one might speak of antipodal
notions of "reflective" and "open" immanence. "Reflective" immanence,
the "general horizon of our time, encompassing both democracies and
their fragile juridical parapets" (IC: 3), is that which is the "inside"
opposed to the "outside" of transcendence. It is an "immanence of mediation", in which there is a "here" and a "there", a "becoming-other of the
thing", the very formation of the subjective–objective dichotomy (BP:
182). Typified by the Hegelian "immanent synthesis a priori", the "self-
subsistent, self determined unity of distinct moments of becoming" (SR:
32), it involves *closure* of the terms of any relation and *reduction* of the
plural singularities of beings to a general or universal foundation (or
ground). In this way, "understanding is possible only by the anticipation of
meaning which creates meaning itself" (SV: 223). This immanence strives
to *appropriate* the fascinating exteriority of the conditions of the "inside"
by transgressing them. Finally, it creates *symbolic figures* of immanence
(mythic, communal, political, etc.) that are projected onto the horizon of
transgressibility, then reflected or played back mimetically for the purpose
of self-identification. (In this respect, it involves something akin to the
Hegelian notion of *Aufhebung*, the imaginative production of symbols and
allegories whose content is indeterminate (SR: 110–11) and the
Situationists' notion of "spectacle", the production of images that reflect
upon and provide a situation within which existence is intercalated (BSP:
50–56).) In particular, politics (including its henchman "myth") superimposes totalizing systems that estrange us from one another by drawing us
together under a "myth" that mimetically provides the means of individual
self-identity (NM: 296–304).[3] Totalitarianism, especially in respect of the
"kitsch" described so poignantly by Milan Kundera, is the most obvious
kind of "closed" immanence because all political questions and answers
alike are provided proleptically.[4] It establishes man in general as the
essence of community, but only in terms of the linkages between individuals provided by economics, technology and political will. The collapse of

totalitarian communism reawakened the ideal of liberal individualism, which seals each individual into an equally closed atomic subjectivity. Both totalitarianism and liberal individualism share this emphasis upon an immanential production and "playing back" of the essence of substantial community to itself (IC: 1–4).[5] One might conceive this immanence as being closed to transcendence altogether, but in actuality it is closed by means of the reference to a transcendent reserve of meaning.

Perhaps "closed" immanence is most discernible today in the possibility of living in a "spectacular" society in which "alternative" or "virtual" reality composes substantial reality. Such a notion has been approached by many thinkers, including Debord, Baudrillard and a host of postmodern theorists. Nancy himself addresses this problem in terms of a revision of the relation between symbols and reality.[6] He objects to the notion that social reality is determined by a "schema of an immense, spectacular, self-consumption". He insists that social being revolves on itself immanentially, not on the subject, the other or the same. The spectacle and communication are figures of symbolicity, not representative of it. If the relation between a social body and what it takes itself to be is a representation, then the *relation itself is the real in this representation*, and it is that real that composes social being. Such a "real" is the separated relation wherein "man" figures and by which it is identified and suppressed by totalizing politics (BSP: 56–8; P: 17). Although reflective immanence requires that a social body reflecting upon itself is representative of what it takes itself to be, this requirement presupposes a possible commensuration of a pre-existing substantial community and its own self-representation. But Nancy's anti-substantialist commitments rule out such a possibility, as noted in his emphasis upon the relationality of the "real" of social being.

"Open" immanence, on the contrary, is *monistic*, the single sense that is the world of material bodies and the singular events of their relation. Receptive to the coming of an undecidable future, it is *open* in so far as singularities never serve as individuals together in a closed "immanent reality", only as an irreducible plurality of singularities composing insubstantial communities. It suggests an "immanence of immediacy", the remaining of the thing in itself without symbolic mediation or comparison under universals. It is *affirmative* in the sense that its horizon is absolutely untransgressible and there is nothing beyond it to appropriate. However, immanence is closed upon itself precisely because existence itself is, for singular beings sharing in relations, exposed or open to sense. If society is the "network and cross-referencing of coexistence", then it knows itself (without exposing its knowledge) to be constituted in the open immanence of co-appearance (BSP: 32, 69; BP: 182). In other words, there is a plurality of "finite transcendences" within the closure of immanence, but these transcendences neither form a totality nor disrupt one. The world just consists of a plurality of singular "ones" that lack any exteriority from which their sense could originate and which are infinitely exposed to the sense of the world itself. The narrative of history, disavowed by Lyotardian postmodernism, may be suspended indefinitely, but it is conceivable as an open and insubstantial heterogeneity (or, more generally, as that which now lacks a closed and reflective immanential ideal) (BP: 144, 148, 163; C: 372). Perhaps Francis Fischer has this in mind when he discerns in Nancy the significance of an "ontology of being abandoned to the finite singularity of an existence" exposed as such without any "completed, closed sense".[7]

Some brief comparisons with other thinkers who engage with the problem of immanence might be illuminating. Ernst Bloch insists on the unfinished nature of the process of striving towards the not-yet-perfect utopia and the transcendence that is wholly within this open immanence. Nancy, on the contrary, demurs that we must think of "the end" *within* the uncertain ends of finite thought, not as the object of any unfinished striving, and that singularities are discernible within immanence solely as a lack whose sense creates no transcendental possibilities. And Theodor Adorno might establish the necessity of a critique of the immanence found in rationalist subsumptions and repetitions, political appropriations of the finite into a totality, and the mythic (media) epic of perfect mimetic reflection of cultural identity.[8] However, Nancy emphasizes the fragmented nature of the finite thinking of the lack of sense, such that he would be able to demonstrate that this three-tiered discourse of immanence is closed to undecidable futures and lacks the requisite unity of purpose that could resuscitate discourses of incertitude.

Baldly stated, much of what Nancy writes consists of a relentless exploration of the monistic value of the plural singularities of "open" immanence. His guiding question in this endeavour is: "*What is the sense of the plurality of singularities constitutive of the world?*" In answer, he struggles to formulate discourse of that about which there could be no discourse – a finite thinking of a singular "sense" circulating in a multiplicity of singularities or a thinking that is not a general thought subsumed under universals and available to reflective immanence, and that does not render the singularity accessible to political appropriations. This sense is discernible wherever there is fragmented contact between singularities producing a plurality of worlds that erupt into presence. Rather than permit the determination of singularities within a pre-conceived "Being", Nancy struggles to elucidate a social reality that just consists in *relations*. He is interested in the conceptual possibility of sense as the "absolute finitude" that lacks any "grounding" achievement and end (a "multiplication of singular bursts of sense resting on no unity or substance") but is nevertheless not an abyss of nothingness. The very presence of the existent, he insists, exhibits the absence of sense that is the sole sense of the life of such an existent (FT: 27). Sense circulates, experience of the world is always recreating itself, bodies enable thinking but resist thinking of their own singularity, and zones of sensing are unified only in the sense of a body's sensing of itself doing so. Ultimately, there is no transcendent origin of sense imposed upon a given world, but rather a sense that is constitutive of the world itself in a *transimmanent* fashion. In other words, sense may constitute the world, but it is accessible to thinking only in bursts of contact between singularities as it appears to divagate across their relations.

Humanism and the "return" of sense

Contemporary philosophy elicits by turns either defiance or resignation when it informs us that we live in an epoch defined by a "crisis of sense". Refreshingly, Nancy insists that this crisis demands a finite thinking of the problem, not conservative calls for return to (or renewal of) the sense of humanity, and its ideals of freedom and community. The insistent claims that history is no longer definitive of sense and that our time is a time of the suspension of history are now tantamount to a rejection of history as the context wherein such sense is determined (BP: 144, 149). All that we are entitled to suggest is that humanity is the "promise of itself" in a responsibility that is a sense for which we are, paradoxically, responsible (R: 3, 6). In other words, if there is sense in "humanity" and "history" today, it is in our responsibilities for the undecidability of responsibility itself. Properly speaking, "humanity" is not a property shared by human beings, yet it is discernible in the incessant surprising of the human condition and its exposure to an undecidable future.

From the vantage point of this (post-)*fin de siècle*, the twentieth century, he remarks, was a period of "innumerable destructions of sense, innumerable deviations, derelictions, weaknesses – in short, the century of its ultimate end" within which we may yearn for a rediscovery of sense, or at least a sense of direction in which to seek it. We have become desensitized by the scandals of the age to the extent that we present our history as a process of "planned savagery of a civilization at its limit", a civilization of extermination and destruction. This is so to the very extent that this "infinity of a senseless process" flashes incandescently across what we mistakenly understand to be a history that is either "senselessly" finite or "meaningfully" infinite. Even philosophy fails to inure itself to the "insanity" or "distress" of the destruction of sense, which is well attested in its obsession with its own end. It is haunted by its incapacity to recover the sense upon which it has been predicated from its origins. Since the eighteenth century, humanism has been aware of and reacted protectively against this loss of sense, thereby inadvertently producing the conditions of our contemporary distress (GT: 27). If nihilism today proclaims nonsense or the impossibility of sense, then, according to Nancy, that proclamation can only continue to have sense precisely as nonsense. Although it is necessary to concede that all sense has been abandoned by culture, this abandonment just is the venue of sense today. Sense, Nancy iterates, is its own constitutive loss. It presents itself in "the very opening of the abandonment of sense, as the opening of the world". The fact that there is a "there is", a world of existing singularities, testifies that thinking itself is the possible opening of sense (FT: 4, 8, 15; SW: 2–3, 80; GT: 10, 27). Within the exigencies of sense, nothing truly "has" sense, but everything in the nonsense of its being reveals sense to the opening of thought.

This intuition is sufficient, Nancy implies, to demand a "thinking through" of our times, not merely a response to 1775 or 1820, or the proper names and philosophical styles we associate with them (GT: 1, 14). Since history is suspended in a state torn between the dull platitudes of the Enlightenment and the potential exterminations of Romanticism dormant in contemporary market democracy (BSP: 63; BP: 144), the nostalgias of humanism (which received a devastating blow from the accusation of its implication in the global experiences of totalitarianism, national genocide and the failure of communism) are strictly inaccessible. After all, the last century witnessed the emergence of the phenomenon of anti-humanism, which denied the empowered autonomy of humanity at a time when "mankind" seemed especially helpless before the destruction of sense. With the death of God proclaimed, absolute values held to be mere conventions, and the very concepts of history, art, morality, philosophy and "man" thought to be at an "end", anti-humanism has come to dominate many sophisticated human discourses. For example, structuralism, post-structuralism, and postmodernism have been fragmented discourses that encouraged a seemingly frivolous circumvention of traditional problems. Most prominently, an entire tribe of "French Nietzscheans" have been competing to see who could strike the most tragic poses or utter the most evocative statements of "crisis".

In the very late twentieth century, Luc Ferry and Alain Renaut declared forcefully that anti-humanism lacks substance and is merely a trend that now serves as an obstacle to thinking of the woes of the contemporary age. In their dismissal of anti-humanism in the name of the renewal of the rich conceptual possibilities of the philosophical canon, they were themselves accused of irresponsibly ignoring the significance of what had transpired in

European thought since the Enlightenment. In particular, they vilified the notions of the "end of philosophy", the "genealogical" practice of questioning the external modes whereby a discourse is produced, the critique of truth as correspondence of "idea" and "reality", and the advocation of universal and historical discourses of categorization. These aspects of the "philosophy of 68", informed by post-Marxist and post-Heideggerian perspectives, presupposed a single and unitary history of subjectivity that, according to the authors, has never been written.[9]

Nancy has taken a very compelling stand against their call for renewal, although not one that benefits either side in the dispute between humanism and anti-humanism. For Nancy, we simply must take anti-humanism seriously, although it is irresponsible to give in to its despairing imposture. And humanism, despite being correct that a rethinking is essential, is mistaken to insist that only a return to something akin to Enlightenment principles could shake us out of our nihilistic stupor. He queries the value of any philosophy resulting from the seduction of a hermeneutics that would insist on the incessant possibility of "remanence", the return from or to an origin (SV: 214). Even though philosophy experiences periodic "crises" followed by a return of viable demands for sense, *sense is in the crises themselves*, not in the overcoming of the obstacles the crises purportedly pose. "The return thus first means that nothing had truly been lost and that neither the length of the crisis nor the abundance and intensity of its manifestation could have fundamentally altered a certain Idea (a schema, a paradigm, sometimes a norm) of Meaning" (GT: 13–15). In other words, when we demand a return to sense today, this demand often does little more than bracket the two centuries that have unfurled since Kant and the Enlightenment and "proclaim the return of a certain Reason – at once critical, ethical, juridical, regulative and humanistic" as if it had not been influenced by the philosophies in the intervening period. Those who champion this return, Nancy suggests, maintain that our forgetting of philosophy can be rectified by a remembrance of genuine philosophy. However, it would be truly bizarre to imagine that one could leap backward to the Enlightenment only to be able, then, to leap forward to a re-inaugurative moment. Perhaps a crime has been committed by anti-humanistic discourse. Yet to advocate a return to humanistic paradigms and rationalistic laws is not, he concludes, to think through the crimes of the ages.

But what can we do about the "crisis of sense" if recovery and renewal are impossible? Nancy establishes that, in order to think through our times, it is imperative to gaze critically at both the dismissal of post-Enlightenment thought and the demand for a re-inaugurative moment.

On the one hand, anti-humanism is often derided for offering nothing but extravagant paradigms, conceptual monstrosities, or deviations from

the sound meanings of tradition. It represents the "seductions of irration-
ality, the hunger for glamour or power, morbid or hermetic tendencies".
Nevertheless, despite some truth in all of these descriptions, it must still be
conceded that humanistic thought does not ask why weaknesses of
Enlightenment thought have been unveiled so easily, or why such spectacular causal bonds between "collective or individual pathologies and
phenomena" have had such a remarkable shelf life. The question "why has
theory taken such divergences?" is not answered by anti-humanism
because the crisis of post-Enlightenment thought is regarded as mere sickness. And in order to offer a diagnosis, it would be necessary to relinquish
the notions of crisis and return altogether.

On the other hand, Nancy notes that whenever there is the slightest
innovation in thought there is a subsequent summons back to the values
(and to value itself) as well as to the virtues necessary for their enactment.
Such values and virtues might be found in Kant, or Hegel, the Enlightenment, or, most surprisingly, medieval metaphysics. He notices that this
"call back" has several consequences.

First, the sense that is to return is one that consists of a "complete
collection" of ideals constitutive of truth. In order to overcome anti-
humanism, one would then have to select those ideals that constitute truth
(freedom, rationality, dignity, etc.) and their modalities of constitution.
However, Nancy demurs, this humanism of the return would be little more
than an ideology, a "thought that does not critique or think through its
own provenance and its relation to reality". Unpleasantly non-beneficial
to most of humanity, such ideals are useless if the "system of their closure"
is not elucidated. The very meanings humanism releases "necessarily
exceed the signification of humanism itself".

Secondly, humanism demands a "return to" an appropriate inaugural
moment rather than a "return of" its conditions. Nevertheless, if one were
to select Kant as the inaugural event to which we should return, then we
must ask what "law of history" justifies this limited choice and which conception of history would authorize such a law. If these questions are not
addressed, then there is no semblance of justification for neglecting the
passing of two centuries that would include Hegel, Nietzsche, Marxism
and, of course, Auschwitz.

Thirdly, humanists exhort us to return to a philosophy (perhaps Kant's)
that not only offered meanings prior to their mistaken dissolution during
the subsequent centuries, but also implied full confidence in the concept of
meaning itself. When such a humanistic meaning is taken for granted, our
thoughts are not empty of meaning, and our sensations are not blind to
reality. It is based on nothing other than a will to the presentation of sense,
a will to renew the presence of a meaningful essence of sense. If "man"

does not itself have a meaning, and the very fact that it must "will" itself to have one testifies that it does not, then it is solely in its willing that it acquires a meaning (or, more precisely, it is only the willing of man that has meaning). "This is how contemporary humanism defines itself: as the self-presentation of the will to meaning, or more exactly, as the self-presentation of the meaning of the will to meaning." When humanists insist peroratively on the "other meanings" beyond willing, they are themselves divesting philosophy of the means of bestowing meaning on such insistences. One might propose that there is nothing more to the humanistic demand for a richer meaning beyond what anti-humanism can provide, namely, a meaning of "man" that closes it off (in reflective immanence) from the very significations for which the demand calls. Humanism, then, is "the complete system of the auto-donation of meaning" that celebrates the will as the producer of meaning, and thus contributes to the production of the unsurprising inhumanity of this world.

In response to these three claims, Nancy's primary thesis is that humanism is mistaken to think that we have lost signification in such a manner that it is imperative to retrieve it. Always encountering our own strangeness as if for the first time, we yearn for a time when there was a sense that dispelled, or promised to dispel, this strangeness. It is in humanity's situation that existence is both exposed and exposing, which implies that humanity is often amazed by its own non-autonomous strangeness. Signification has never been lost to this strangeness because we are always newly implicated in it. In other words, we have never ceased to experience a certain disorientation that is as old as Western philosophy itself. In this disorientation, "the enterprise of meaning always begins by signifying the anterior or transcendent presence of a meaning that has been lost, forgotten, or altered, one that is, by definition to be recovered, restored, or revived". It is not as if sense were established and then lost, with its establishment serving nostalgically as a motivation to return to it or recover it into the present. On the contrary, the crisis of sense has always been concurrent with the establishment of orders of signification. More generally, "the thoughts of the return conceive of meaning as something whose essence has a structure of return, and as the re-orientation promised to the Occident". Indeed, the "end" of sense completes the history of nihilism, which is to say that nihilism accomplishes its own meaning; if this had not occurred, then the West as Occident, as global point of reference, would have been impossible. The "West" is not an establishment of sense, but rather the "exhaustion of the signification" that makes sense intelligible. It always accomplishes itself in incessantly creative returning to itself. The very notion of sense is one that has within its content the need for a return to meaning. Humanism is not the reappropriation of the sense of "man", but rather its exscription (its taking away or putting beyond writing by writing itself) from an impossible sense; it is "sacrificed to the super-humanity or to the inhumanity of the Subject of this ultimate significa-tion", which can take the form of ideals of nationality, science, technology, religion and so on (GT: 17–29, 48–52).

Even more generally, it is necessary to consider the possibility of a rethinking of sense, especially one that neither disavows it as anti-humanism has done nor nostalgically and irresponsibly pines for its "return" in the manner of humanism. Sense is now what it always has been, although it has never been more genuinely thought at any inaugural moment in the history of its exegesis. It is imperative upon us, Nancy avers, to address the daunting task the thinking of sense in "our" time represents and, indeed, has always represented.

"Open" immanence: the singularity of sense

The concept of "sense" is paramount in Nancy's voluminous works. No concept is more vital to their comprehension and none resists that compre-hension more vigorously. (Refusing to admit of any unitary interpretation, it is allegorically similar to the snow that falls on the living and the dead, in all their desires and jealousies, representing perhaps their mutual but fractious sharing in being, in James Joyce's "The Dead".) Any approach to sense must come in the form of an enquiry that considers the perimeters of the task of thinking it, which is to say that it provides the "very means of accessing sense". And wherever there is access to thought at all, there is sense (FT: 14).

What follows is admittedly a densely intertextual survey of Nancy's understanding of sense. However, it may be helpful to bear in mind that "sense" is not a mere "meaning" accessible to thinking and language, nor is it something that the world "has". On the contrary, sense is the coextensivity of thinking and world, the absolute contact that makes meaning possible but is not reducible to it. Thinking and world are the obverse and reverse of sense.

Despite its ubiquity in thought, sense cuts against the grain of all think-ing and its explicit discourses. Always "in permanent rebellion as much against any possibility of discourse, judgment, or signification as against intuition, evocation, or incantation", sense is already openly immanent to thinking, which is never orientated towards anything else (FT: 8). Nancy frequently maintains that thinking and existence are "coextensive", and the thinking of sense is a thinking of this coextensiveness. Rather than dismiss such circularity because it is irreducible to linguistic meanings, we should reject the notion that language itself is straightforwardly attuned to an adequated presentation of sense. It should not be (and indeed cannot be) the task of philosophy to *identify* sense in an intellectual doctrine; instead, sense should be permitted to be boundless and incessantly unique (R: 9–10).

What, then, is sense? Nancy insists that, on the one hand, it is singular and irreducible to comprehension of meaning, and thus requires a finite thinking, and, on the other, it does not consist in the significance "of" the event but "that" the event occurs at all ("what happens through the happening") (BP: 153). In so far as "singularity" presupposes a plurality of "ones", sense is the singularity of all the singular ones in three ways: first, a "distribution or disseminative sense of nonsubstantial unicity" (this thing here); secondly, the "transitive or transitional sense" of sharing out and in sense (a common finitude); and the "collective or worldly sense" of the infinite spacing within which the totality of the existent is determined as the "singular absolute of being" (SW: 68). In each case, the question of sense is bound to a multiply reticulated and irreducible singularity, not to any general or universal concepts that might make such a singularity intelligible (SV: 243–4). At any rate, generalizations about singularity must always be placed under intense scrutiny.

The word "sense" is vague because there is no "unity of sense, no original matrix of sense, not even a univocal etymological derivation", especially in the Latin, German and French. Indeed, he asserts, it lacks any definitive formal property, unless one emphasizes indication or reference, as in a "sense of orientation". He notes that such a sense implies "an Orient", a point of determination that is presupposed in acquiring such a sense. "Sense" suggests but does not exhaust the reason that calls for an orientation or the goal towards which it is directed. The "sense of sense" consists in an "unassignable unity of sensate sense and directional sense", in which the possibility of "making sense" is potential. In the "sense of orientation", "sensing" is necessary, and this requires an "absolute point of existence", a stance that one must take in the world. One must be "in" sense, in the sense of this world composed of the joining, playing, speaking, sharing, intersecting and communicating of itself. Articulating itself as such along the interstitial edges of such relations, the sense of the world is not something set over against the world, not a co-incidence of being with itself; it resides immanently in the articulations of all possible singular beings and events within it (SW: 78; M: 78; C: 383; BC: 5). Specifically, one is permitted only to speak of a world that is a totality completed by the openness of existence to itself. Again, one might say that the world is not a factual given ascribed with a sense, but rather that sense belongs coextensively to the very structure of the world itself.

Nancy utilizes the term *"transimmanent"* to describe this coextensivity of world and sense discernible in the incessant affirmation of singularity (SW: 55). As Francis Fischer remarks in explanation, the world itself is sense because it is "neither a completed totality nor a field of action for man, but the space of sense which belongs to existence" itself, an "exploded space" of singular existents.[10] In other words, there is nothing more to sense than the confines of the world within which "the self" takes a stand, and nothing more to this world than the confines of sense (SW: 76–8). Alternatively, to say that we exist "in" sense is to imply that sense is the "happening", the happening "through" happening, of existence itself (BP: 153). The fact that "the self" necessarily adopts a "sense of orientation" rules out the possibility that there could be an infinite regress towards senselessness or nihilism whenever the "absolute point of existence" is thought to be missing (SW: 79). For example, in Nancy's *Hegel: the Restlessness of the Negative*, he notices that subjectivity is the action of a self. It experiences consciousness of substance negatively, which is to say that the world loses structured reference in order to become an "immanent" world, always reflective of the "infinite work of negativity" which is the "restlessness" of sense (or "open" immanence). Having no exteriority or transcendence that could be sublated, such a world has no absent origin whose deferral produces only senselessness, nor does it move towards any end other than itself (HRN: 5–6). Disturbingly haunted by its own strangeness in such a world, mankind finds that the internal and finite reticulations of the openly immanential world itself are revealed in this very strangeness. Indeed, the world is nothing other than the sense of this erratic trajectory across being ("transimmanence") and it is only in this sense that one might speak of "transcendence", finite or otherwise (M: 69–72). In other words, sense and the world are coextensive in so far as the restlessness of sense, the incessant strangeness of the presentation of the "world", is constitutive of the open immanence of the world. This coextensive restlessness and strangeness of sense is the primary figure of immanence open to the uncertainty and undecidability of the future.

Obviously, Nancy is no champion of transcendence, in religious or other forms. If he criticizes a certain view of immanence, that is not for the purpose of exploring the possibility of a religiously accessible transcendence, as has been so common in the post-Heideggerian tradition represented by Emmanuel Levinas and Jean-Luc Marion, among others. I shall leave a discussion of the religious and post-secular theological aspects of Nancy's critique of such a stratagem for a later chapter. Here it may suffice to note that Nancy is suspicious of the West's "obsessive fear of the 'Outside' of finitude, however obscure and groundless this 'outside' may be". We should deconstruct the "closure of immanence", understood as a false infinity, that is, one which has never experienced a transcendent limit; rather, "what we used to call 'transcendence' would signify instead that appropriation is immanent". In other words, the appropriation of exteriority necessary for the exercise of the epistemological techniques of the West is, strictly speaking, the appropriation of a sense that is completely interior without exteriority (FT: 75–6). Hence it is the inside–outside distinction in the relationship between transcendence and immanence that worries at his notion of sense. Even so, the world does not "have" an exterior sense, he iterates frequently, but sense "belongs to its structure" as a constitutive "signifyingness" or "significance" of the world itself. The "there is", the happening of experience to existence itself, *is* the "constitutive" sense itself. The "end" or limit towards which purposive action is directed is that there is no longer any relation between a world and the sense it might "have"; rather, there is now merely a world, and it "is" sense. Again, "the totality of existences qua quality of signifyingness constitutes the being-here of being-there", which is to say that the world starts from a "here", and its sense begins and ends in the fact that there is this world "here" in its experienced materiality. The very notion that even the ideality of sense is indissociable from materiality, Nancy claims, is the "archi-thesis of philosophy" espoused by the tradition of atomistic thought but neglected by the canon as a result of transcendental preoccupations. After all, sense "needs a thickness, a density, a mass, and thus an opacity, a darkness by means of which it leaves itself open and lets itself be touched" as such (SW: 7–8, 57–58; GT: 79).

Sense, even in its apparent absence, is accessible to a thinking that is directed towards existence, whether that sense is one of life, man, world, history, or whatever else. Sense itself is something for which one (or the "we" composed of "ones") is always responsible precisely because sense cannot be divorced from responsibility for sense. To say that sense is implied in responsible thinking is to maintain that it is not produced from a pregnant reserve but instead is announced in the very *futural* promise of sense "to-come" in the openness to existence of each singularity (R: 6). It would not be possible to understand the role of man in history, for example, if thinking did not at once produce sense from thinking this role and if this role itself did not elicit sense. To think of existence is to think of the sense of existence, and without this thinking of existence there would be no sense; yet equally, the thinking of sense itself is necessary to think existence, and without the former the thinking of existence itself could not be possible (FT: 11). This incomplete accession to sense is reflected, for example, in painting, which exhibits the strangeness of humanity to itself. Emerging strange and frightened into history, into technology, from an opening without place which "refers all cohesion of ground and of totality", "we" encounter our own strangeness on the scene of existence. "Man" presents himself in art through this strangeness of his own sense, this sense whose "secret he wrested from the strangeness of his nature". Although art's ability to open the strangeness of singular things to us is threatened by technology, our finitude remains profoundly strange to us precisely in our very exposure to existence. Art reveals that finitude is not small and insignificant, but "infinitely finite, infinitely exposed to our existence as a nonessence, infinitely exposed to the otherness of our own 'being'" (FT: 126; M: 69; BP: 185, 155). Roughly speaking, open immanence is this intimate strangeness that haunts each self in a manner that scintillates artistic creativity and the sharing in being.

Furthermore, Nancy notes the difficulty of thinking the singularity of sense in the finitude of being. The "singularity of punctuations, of encounters and events" designates "this" thing or "this" person, which does not merely "have" an essence. In other words, singularities are instances in which specific things figure, but are not reducible to schemes of intelligibility accessing physical reality. Indeed, existence "has" nothing precisely because it has no essence other than that which stems from its "having" a relation to itself as sense. To write of a singular being as a mere thing is not to demonstrate any finite thinking, which of itself would guarantee that the thought of a singular being encompasses the notion that existence presupposes a lack of sense itself. On the contrary, sense consists precisely in the existential lack of sense itself, which is to say, according to Nancy, that to lack sense is to lack nothing (FT: 12).

Sense is intertwined in conceptual thinking to the extent that wherever there is thinking, there is sense. To enquire into the meaning of the word "sense" is to enquire about what sense "sense" has in the thinking of it. Indeed, philosophy gestures towards the "sense of sense", the inappropriable transcendence that just is sense devoid of the self-constitution of existence. However, "sense" is indeclinably singular in the sense of lacking unity or oneness: "it is (the) 'single' sense of a 'single' being because it is sense each time". Even so, it must be conceded that "sense" just is a concept, and thus to ask about "sense" is to utilize the very concept about which one is enquiring. It is in this sense that "sense" has the very structure of responsibility: it "precedes itself without end in the other", without end to this propagation, always expansively open to other *future* horizons (BC: 5; FT: 8; R: 7). That is to say that every concept "is" a sense, and thus to question a concept is to question sense openly.

"Sense" is most definitely not the same as linguistic meaning or signification. On the contrary, signification, understanding and meaning are varieties of the lack of sense, such that there is more to "the sense of life" than a mere meaning might evoke (FT: 5). For Nancy, the distinction between sense and meaning–signification is laboriously accommodated:

the latter is "located" as a specific bestowal of "this" meaning, while the former "resides perhaps only in the coming of a possible signification" (GT: 10). Meaning is merely the "meaning of" a particularity in collectivity, but sense is the signifyingness of existence itself in so far as there is a plurality of singularities (C: 383). In other terms, the very distinction between meaning–signification is the "presentation of meaning" in which the presence of a factual reality is established in an ideal mode, expressed in language alone. Sense, then, is the "element in which there can be significations, interpretations, representations" and is irreducible to a single meaning precisely because it already serves as the condition of possibility of their reduction (GT: 22, 59). Intriguingly, life would not have meanings–significations that compose its unified meaning if the very concept of life did not have a singular sense that permeates its discourses.

One might also approach "sense" in terms of relations. Every relation between singularities also relates to itself extrinsically, and its openness to itself is sense itself. Within each relation, there must be a spacing that possesses an ontological status as if it were relating to something extrinsically (FT: 7; SW: 3; BC: 7). However, speaking of this relation as "ontological" might seduce us into thinking that there is sense in the *terms* of the relation, and then *additional* sense in the relation itself. If being is itself openness within which singular entities relate, then there is "sense" only in the relation and not in any antecedent condition. In the case of desire, for example, the self is a relation between itself and the desired, but this desire is sense only in the desiring and the "sense" of the (sentient) sensing of desire itself. The sense of the "other" of desire is in the self's desire for what it cannot appropriate (a meaning of desire it cannot absorb, even though it can appropriate its sense in the relation to itself). The self lacks nothing and has no sense of lack; when desire is fulfilled, there is no sense lacking merely because the object of desire is appropriated. Rather, in all of the relations that transform the self there is no hypostasis of the self (as if all relations served to accrete meaningful states of existence). Given the open multiplicity of relations composing it, sense is produced in and through the openness of being to itself in which there is no closure of immanence (FT: 6–8).

Only a finite thinking that, on the one hand, did not generalize about the singularity of sense, and, on the other, was not a general kind of thought, could possibly approach sense. If sense is necessarily singular without unity or oneness, then the thought of sense is finite and groundless. Because "sense" is prior to any reductions to general thoughts about the unity of being, the singularity of being exhibiting itself to thinking in the essence-less finitude of existence does not lack anything when it is groundless. Finitude of being does not mean that the totality of sense is

lacking, as if there were something absent in singularity prior to appropriation. Being is rather non-substantive or intransitive "be-ing", although it
does not itself exist as such (which is to say that "being" is spoken of here
in the same way that "doing" or "eating" are). Strictly speaking, sense consists precisely in the "non-appropriability" of being into a mere entity.
Inappropriable being exhibits sense on each occurrence of its revelation, in
which sense is replayed, reopened and newly exposed. Thus we always
already come to presence and are exposed to the coming of presence of
sense on each of the plurality of singular occasions. Moreover, we are in a
position to understand non-appropriatively the finitude of being to which
we are always already exposed. To be born into a world coming to presence, a world in which we are coming strangely to presence, is to be born
sentient, sensing that we are sensing (FT: 9–11).

Finally, for Nancy the thought of finitude must always be open to the
undecidable future of a discourse about essence-less and groundless existential states. It would thereby possess sense for precisely the reason that it
possesses nothing appropriable. For a divided self relating to itself meaningfully and thereby producing sense in this relation, its own be-ing
requires responding to and from itself in this relation. Moreover, to be
finite means to share sense with other finite beings, that is, to share the
responsibility of sense in the response to finitude. To have community with
others is to share "out" one's own finitude with them and to share "in" the
infinitude of existence with them (FT: 13).

Incessant re-creations: "the wandering labour of sense"

Nowhere is this sharing "of" and "in" sense more impressively apparent
than in the presentation of the *circulation* of sense. Roughly speaking, in
grappling with the slippery strands of the notion of sense, the reader is
forced to circulate the very sense whose circulations are illustrated by the
fragmented texts themselves. The thrust of this hermeneutical endeavour
is not merely to comprehend some attenuated conceptualization of sense,
but, in enacting it as one gropes one's way to comprehension, to circulate
one's incomprehension meaningfully. It is appropriate that Nancy refers to
Jacques Rancière's notion of the "wandering labour of sense", in which
language speaks uncertainly to itself through its own communicability in
the relation, the "between", of singularities (SW: 115).

The reader is cursorily divested of the preconceptions that sense is
produced and that people, whether authors or readers, produce it. Nancy
wastes little time in delimiting the horizons of power that enable sense to be

produced. The traditional notion of sense is one in which the subjective mode involves self-representation, thereby becoming visible to itself as a "true *eidos* or idea" provided by history itself; however, such an idea is now lacking because history is no longer representative of sense itself (BP: 144, 148). Thinking can only circulate sense within the context of its own endeavour to capture figments of sense. Its interleaved relation with sense requires the necessarily incomplete assimilation of the sense it passively receives from textual communication. However, Nancy occasionally insinuates that since some sense is lost, or rather, passed around multi-directionally without purpose or fruition, it is never completely exposed transparently to the thinking of reflective immanence (CMM: 97–8). Sense cannot be completely open to reflective thinking because it circulates beyond thinking, coming from beyond it and passing beyond it within the world. Sense is "transimmanent". It "takes place" and "crosses through presence" in coexistences among singularities and their finite thinking (BSP: 5).

Nevertheless, sense itself cannot be "lost" completely, as if there were some pre-existing "space" of sense rendered inaccessible to the nostalgic wish for its return. "We" is the opening or common belonging wherein the sense of the world is suggested by circulating through all of the meanings that are accessible to singular beings. It is an eventual instance of the purposeless circulation of sense, each instance of which is strictly singular despite the repetition necessary for circulation (CMM: 33–5). The "co-appearance" (a common term in Nancy's work) to one another is not one in which, properly speaking, we share in being. Rather, being is the "sharing in" that precedes all produced and disclosed meaning: it is the sense revealed through the circulation of apparent meanings (GT: 61–2). In brief, sense, by virtue of its incessant circulations, is never possibly sub-ordinated to thinking's power or subsumed under the laws it devolves for the purpose of such subordination.

Moreover, the "we" is the "element" in which sense is incessantly created and through which it is circulated. "We" is not a being, but a hap-pening, the "essential otherness of existence" itself, which determines its strangeness in the statement "We ..." (BP: 156). It exists as an openness, an exposure, a responsibility for the sense that responsibility has and that, in the sense explored above, it is (R: 8). Communication within the "we" enables sense to circulate multidirectionally without being the "brute given" of either a pre-existing space of sense or the establishment of sense by rational operations. The forms of sharing (necessary for thought, art and writing) composing this "we" are:

> economic dependencies, the transformation of classes, of statutes, of generations, of families; the differences of the sexes, of cultures,

languages; the networks and disruptions of communication; the interaction of scientific and technical interactions; organ trans-plants and genetic and viral recombinations, contagions, pollution, ecological entanglements, the world system of geographers, the measuring of eight billion "human beings"; the interbreeding of plastic and musical designs; the tectonic slippage of public space, of cities, states, associations, sporting fields, spectacles and demonstrations, the blurring of war and truces ...   (C: 375)

In a richly evocative sense, for Nancy the "we" is a sharing in a plurality of voices, abandoned to this sharing without any subjective or transcendental reserve from which resistance might be posed (SV: 244). Sense is Being's sense shared within the "we" in a fashion that stimulates curiosity about the "explosion of presence in the original multiplicity of its divisions". The result is a "spacing" of existence that is composed of sense. Sense is being produced, not by the autonomous "self" that masters and dissimulates language, but by the disjointed presencings of Being itself. The "we" is the locus of sense because it is the "singularly plural coexistence" *in* which Being circulates and *as* which it circulates amongst such selves within the "we". Specifically, Nancy proposes that each self within the "we" is not a guardian of sense, but a participant in its inexorably multilinear circulation. It is both recipient of sense "in" the "we" and participant in its circulation of Being "as" sense through the "we". Wherever presence is spacing itself and thereby accessible to sense, "we" is said by the selves that compose it. Each self that says "we" enables Being to presence itself multifariously and facilitates the circulation of sense (BSP: 2–3; GT: 62).

The manner in which sense is not under the purview of the rational and autonomous agent should be apparent. It calls into question the thinking that makes this agency possible and enables it to address itself. Each self within the "we" is incessantly summoned to the necessity to reappropriate the thinking of sense that it practises on all other occasions of the repetitive circulation of sense within the "we". This summoning, in Nancy's view, promulgates a consistent need to reappropriate seemingly lost or opaque meanings. Since each instant of circulation is unique and does not allow reappropriation by thought, and all presencing of Being is multifaceted, the self is put out of synch within the "we". On each occasion that a self says something, the "we" says something in response to the self's thinking of its own address to sense. Thus it is implied that contiguous singularities remain detached from one another despite a continuous repetition of circulation across the interstitial space between them. Circulating sense within the "between" enables the singular self to be exposed to this origin (BSP: 4–7). In other words, the world speaks through the "we" when the "we" speaks in the place of the world (not merely "of" a world in which it takes a place).

Sense is the "passing" within the relation "between" us. It is within this "between" that sense, the "happening" of existence, takes a place and circulates. Of course, the circulation of sense is in and through the "we" and not among pre-existing individual selves within that "we". This suggests the possibility of "being-among, being-between, and being-against" as the a priori of being. If the world "is" sense, then without this "impalpable reticulation of contiguities and tangential contacts", the interstices and intervals of the social relation, there would be no world (SW: 59–61). Strictly speaking, the "world" is not a pre-existing womb of sense within which contiguous singularities touch. Instead, Nancy propounds, the origin of the world emanates from any contact composing a "we". Each singular self has access to the presence of the world, but it is only contiguity with other singular selves that enables it to have "access to an access". That is to say, there is a multiplicity of presences of the world within the "we", and each proximity provides a multiplicity of accesses to the presences. If each singularity is co-implicated within the world, then the originary existential state of all singularities is a sharing in the world, not any ontological divorce from it into a state of transcendence. The "world" is not merely some extrinsic horizon of singular existence, but the coexistence that enables existences to be exposed to the circulation of sense and the presences of a world. Indeed, Being itself is the incessant origination of the "punctual and discrete spacing between us" (BSP: 14, 19, 29).

If this is so, then such spacings are discernible solely in singular instances (plural) of sense. The singular, unlike the particular (which implies "togetherness"), is an incomparable "each one" that is "with" others but not "together" with them, such that the singular already implies plurality but does not compose it (BSP: 32).[11] "The singular exposes every time it is exposed and all of its sense resides therein", Nancy remarks tersely. "What is exposed in this way is thus a singular transitivity of being, and what every one engages in is an attestation of existence." In other words, on every occasion in which sense is exposed in the singular, the sense of the world itself is attested. Each singularity instantaneously discloses the complete spacing of "world" and enables new singularities to arise unendingly. Without general consistency, the singular instance of "each time" is both the discreteness of succession and the simultaneity of "each one". Each one is a one, any one, but there is no mere one (and no "other"); there are only ones, each one on each one occasion. Needless to say, this notion of the recurrence of the singular, or, to invert this priority correctly, the singularity of each occurrence, surfaces in myriad contexts throughout Nancy's work. For example, on each historical occasion, whatever happens does not stem from the "homogeneity of a temporal process or from the homogenous production of this process out of an origin", but from an absent (or impossible) and heterogeneous origin (BP: 57, 163, 179; BSP: 19, 65).

One might speak of this singularity, as Nancy himself does in *Being Singular Plural* and *The Muses*, as "creation". This is not a singular, temporally original event ("the Creation"), which is, in a sense, modelled on the incessant repetition of a circulation of sense in the contact of singularities. On the contrary, creation is continued in the "discontinuity of its discrete occurrences". Nancy is emphatic that there is incessant re-creation of a world, without origin or absolute point of reference. One can learn of the world as a dislocation into a plurality of worlds, or rather, the "irreducible plurality" of the world, an incessantly bursting creation of a heterogeneity of revelations touched in zones of sensibility. If a multiplicity of expressions of a single sense is repeatedly affirmed in order for a world to be originated at all, then, strictly speaking, creation means the unique unfurling of sense that repeatedly affirms itself without beginning and end. The world does not come from an origin, but rather the origin is the coming of a singular presence of the world in the contact between singularities. There is merely the fact of the world, as we have seen, the "being-the-there" of the "here of this world here", without any non-immanent creation at its origin. To speak of creation as the beginning of all things is merely to project a single instance of this re-creation onto a conceivable initial event. Rather, the creator is immanently embedded within the process of re-creation, not distinct or separated from it. When Nancy maintains that sense is not produced, it is implied that the world is not produced by an original creation, but rather production is the effect of the unremitting creation of singularities. The "nothing" from which the world is produced is an immanent burst of sense in the "infinite resolution of the finite" assuming myriad transformations, dissolutions and harmonies, not an original state of existence (BP: 5; M: 18, 27; BSP: 15–16; SW: 155).

In conclusion, one could understand Nancy to be saying that on each occasion the singular presences of the world are created in the interstices between singularities. The presence of the world that thrusts itself at the thinking of sense appears as something that stands out uniquely. If the circulation of sense is multidirectional, and the presencing of the world is multifaceted, then re-creation takes place everywhere and always. Existence itself is re-created in this way and each singular self figures in this incessant process.

The body's "dark reserve of sense"

A number of commentators have pointed out that there is a strong incarnational movement in Nancy's exploration of the body's material sense. For example, Graham Ward concludes that Nancy can assist mono-theology to rethink bodies and corporeality, although he concedes that such an appropriation would require that theological significance be "foregrounded" and reinvested. Gary Shapiro, who makes no demand for a rejuvenation of theological criteria, scents a whiff of incarnational values despite Nancy's overt effort to oppose the obscurantist mystification of the body.[12] Although it must be conceded that Nancy refers to the incarnation on several occasions, he is resolutely against any incarnational appropria-tion of the body in its variegated material modes. The incarnation, after all, is a concept in which the sense of the body is the result of an enigmatic gesture towards the transcendental source of value. Exemplifying the renunciation of incarnationism's substantialist metaphysics is his claim that literature and philosophy themselves are "sequels" to the "mystery of the Incarnation", and, presumably, it is precisely for this reason that West-ern philosophy struggles to think of the body at all. Although Christ's wounds had a spirituality in sacrifice, such sacrifice is now impossible: under the purview of the prevailing substantialist metaphysics, a body is just a body and can be thought only as such. However, Nancy makes his hostility to incarnationalist thinking apparent with the proposal that the thought of the suffering body can no longer be comprehended in terms of rich pathos-laden signs of sacrifice and an "obscure *jouissance*". Instead, contemporary discourses of the body can only gain access to the body as a broken, dislocated or decayed entity that is no longer sacrificed, either by or for Christ. Generally speaking, the Christian symbolics of the cross by which the metaphysics of suffering and sacrifice is enfigured has been disassembled. Patently, Nancy's work is not intended to contribute to incarnational perspectives and appears to be firmly against the substantial-ist and transcendentalist schemes of intelligibility they offer (BP: 273–4).

In brief, then, even if it is the case that Nancy has not evaded the allure of the Christian symbolics of the body, as Shapiro and Ward suggest, it is of prior significance to enquire into the very values that requisitely compose a finite thinking of the body. Ultimately, it is not the incarnational "sense of the body" that is of greatest significance to Nancy, or even the "body as sense"; rather, his emphasis is on the body as the untransgressible body of sense itself (double genitive), the body as the repository from which sense originates surprisingly. What is needed, as Francis Fischer has suggested, is a finite thinking of the infinite spacing and sharing out of bodies, thereby elucidating a "new world space".[13] The significance of the body should not be reduced to a body–soul incarnational paradigm. Instead, the materiality of the body should be thought to *be* sense itself. This entails that the incessantly re-created world is a world of bodies that come to presence in a circulation of sense through its contact with other bodies.

Nancy regards the body as both the *absolute* origin of thinking and something before which thinking is frustrated, even occasionally impossible. The impenetrability of all bodies makes access to the body difficult, but because language and thought stem from its fragmented states and activities, this impenetrability poses challenges to signification itself. Bodies have a density, an impenetrable hardness that can be defined "only through the distance, the distribution of its being this here", a finitude "liable to sense". Although there is a simulacrum of discourse about the body, authentic discourse is impossible without a corpus or catalogue of the "empirical logos" of bodies, their senses, and their contacts with other bodies. Nancy refers playfully to this corpus as an "ectopic topography, serial somatology, local geography" in which any part might encompass the whole of the body and its discourse. "There is no whole, no totality of the body – but its absolute separation and sharing out. There is no such thing as the body. There is no body." Why? Discourse cannot think singularities, especially the corporeity of the body from which discourse is evoked. That is, thinking that originates from the corpus of bodies cannot think "the body", cannot return to the "place" from which it "thoughtlessly" springs. Withdrawing from its own thinking, such that there is no "itself" when it touches itself, the body as "total signifier" is nothing other than an immanent "interlacing", mixing, (re)producing and absorbing of sense and the senses. In this way, the impenetrability of the body and the necessary interlacings with other bodies compose the relation of sense itself (SW: 62; BP: 189–98, 202–3). There can be no discourse of the body, yet every discourse is "from" the body that cannot speak about itself.

The body defies its own discourse because it disrupts the distinction between the "inside" and the "outside" of its own representation (which mirrors the paradigm of reflective immanence). In the interval of touching, the interstices of singularities, there is no subjectivity and objectivity, but merely a world that is itself, even if it consists of sites, places and distances (SW: 61). On the one hand, the body is the "inside" of representation and the representation of that "inside", understood in terms of an interiority of images. Sensation, perception, memory and conscience are formative projections in which the body appears to itself as "foreign", as something examined from the outside. On the other hand, the "outside" of the body appears as a "thick interiority", as an "organon" or repository of signification. In other words, the body is that "in which sense is given and out of which sense emerges". As such, the body provides a "dark reserve of sense

and the dark sign of this reserve", trapping it within both its own signification and its sense of the world. One might then understand why contradic-
tions of experience and imagination are bound to the opacity of the body's
relation to itself: the body is both something from which sense appears to
be produced and the locus into which sense incessantly rushes. The
impenetrable density of bodies is apparent when sense circulates through
touching, rending the body's effort to totalize itself and its activities.
Nancy extrapolates from this that "the self" itself is a surface of an
exposed corporeal mass. Specifically, the body reveals the self's topical
activities but conceals its utopic origins. This is intelligible, he insists, in
terms of a plurality of singular bodies, not by means of the presumption of
the existence of a body codetermined with the self in its "ipseity" (self-
representation from the "inside" as something external to representation).
The body is a challenge to thinking because it is a sign that produces and
projects signs, all of which refer back to its sense as the "empirical *logos*".
Ubiquitously, the body is both "sign of itself and being-itself of the sign". It
has "senses" that enable contact with the world: "sense" from which it
receives signification and to which it provides signification. Hence Nancy
reiterates the "material reunion and co-presence of sense with the senses,
the body of sense and the sense of the body" (BP: 192–4, 199).

This broaches the question of the absolute nature of the body's ipseity.
For Nancy, it is not merely the case that all of the self's values refer back to
the sense of the body's senses. When he maintains that the "body is the
absolute of sense" in the mode of being detached and shared out to the
world, it is entailed that the body uniquely and irrevocably permits a sense
that cannot be sacrificed or divorced from the body. If every body is absolutely singular in exposed, sentient contact with others and thereby circulates sense, then the absolute of the body is participation in the community
of bodies that pose impenetrable resistances to one another and dissolve
into one another's limitations. Curiously, if the contact of bodies is the
absolute of existence, then this untransgressible limit collapses into sense
at the instant of contact, such that there are no longer contacting entities
but merely a relation of singularities constitutive of sense itself. Nancy
supplements the various multiplicities surveyed above with a view of the
"auto-heterology of touch", which is both felt (as when one concentrates
upon the sensation of the nerves as one strokes something) and feeling (the
tracing of the contours or textures of what one is touching). The sense of
touch feels itself feeling itself and thus presents the proper moment of
"sensuous exteriority". It is both the interval between touching and
touched, and the heterogeneity of the ways this interval figures in contact
with the singularities of the world. As sensuous exteriority, the touched is
an intimate singularity removed at an approximate distance. Nancy

proposes that this "sensing-oneself-sense" is something akin to a sixth sense radically distinct from mere sensing. Even as one "makes" sense in sensing-oneself-sensing, one is detached from this "making", as if one sensed that sense has not been felt in passing along the contours of the moment of contact with the sensed (BP: 204–6; M: 17; SW: 163).

In alternative terms, since the concept of sense (any concept in its sense) has no fixed provenance, but is suggested in the very gesture of grasping at it, then sense is grasped wherever there is grasping at sense. On the one hand, one might say that the senses sense themselves sensing, and this grasp of its own sensing has a sense. On the other, it might be suggested that sensing senses that there is something that senses itself sensing, and this sensing too has a sense. To sense that there is sensing is to sense "sense" in its materiality, and to sense oneself as if one were producing sense. This "double aporia", in which "what senses in sense is the fact that it includes what it senses, and what produces sense in sense is the fact that it senses itself producing sense" is at its basis a revamped metaphysical distinction between the sensible and the intelligible. One might say that empiricism is at work in such a description, yet it should be borne in mind that empiricism is merely one form of enquiry into the relationship between the sensible and the intelligible (FT: 5–6).[14] Moreover, it is one that is not itself actively concerned with the question of the circulations of sense in the grasping of the senses.

Such claims are relevant to analysis of the (dis)unity of art and the heterogeneity of the aesthetic. What is of special interest for Nancy is the sense that art is an example of the dislocation of a world into a plurality of worlds, into the "irreducible plurality" of revelations of a world, each phenomenon of which is the production of a potential phenomenal world. A sense of "there being a world" is given in the plural dislocation of the five irreducible zones of the senses. It is art that makes the world phenomenally apparent in as much as sentience consists in nothing but the singular difference of touching and its zones. Art shows experience for what it is in so far as irreducible zones of sensing delimit one another, rendering a world as a unique unity.

More specifically, art demonstrates that, if the zones of sensing were not discrete, then there would be merely a disconnected bundle of sensations severed from complex sensed phenomena, not any possible synthesis of experience. Furthermore, if the zones were not discrete, then the very *aesthesis* of sensing-oneself-sensing would not be capable of producing the thickness, the fluidity, the figure, or even a movement, a flash of sound, a taste, or an odour associated with a sensed datum. In other words, although each sense has its "zone", it is only in reference to the sense of touch that complex associations of sensuous experience could be possible.

Most evocatively, the effect upon experience would be vitiating, gradually reducing the continuity of phenomenal experience to a nullity. The thing itself would not even be itself in the phenomenal experience in which zones of sensing were indiscrete. In order for the thing to have a disposition, to stand out as a singularity within the heterogeneity of zones of sensation, it must lend presence to a world and thus participate in the circulation of sense. At the point at which a self senses itself sensing according to the perimeters of zones of sensation, thereby letting a thing present itself to the circulation of meaning, a world is created. Since this creation takes place in revolution around the contact of self-sensing touch and thing in itself, it must be the incessant repetition of contact with the heterogeneous surfaces of singularities and the spacing of such phenomenal experiences. The "empirical" givenness of the thing in itself is not given to sensuousness; it is the "technics of the local, the presentation of place", a creative situation involving singularities in the magnitude of space-time. Sensing-oneself-sensing "disengages the world from signification" and extricates sensory perception from the inordinate demands of participation in the unified field of meaningful perception. The "sense of the world" itself is "in" the touch of singular bodies expressed in the plurality of arts that breaks down the "living unity of perception or action" and exposes another world of fragmented moments of singular instances of contact (M: 19–22).

Nancy's intoxicating depictions of sense and world might appear to obviate the necessity of an exploration of human sentience. He inverts the traditional priority of an original unity of experience within which an individual touch figures meaningfully. Rather, a "world" is evoked through the very intensity of the sense-of-sensing; it is not there to receive the touch as a contingent event of phenomenal experience whose meaning is predetermined. Thus it is illegitimate even to speak of aesthetic qualities being subversive or disruptive of patterns of meaning in perceptual experience. In conclusion, it might be possible to maintain that, in order for there to be unity of such experiences, there must be pre-originary "touches" of sense that incessantly re-create the revelations of the world of sense revolving around the contact of sensory zone and touched given.

The surprise in the event

Mulling Beethoven's "*Muss es sein? Es muss sein*" ("Must it be? It must be") Nancy conjectures that Being could not simply "be" (or otherwise, have a substantive ontological status as a state of affairs), for then nothing would ever happen and there could be no thinking. Being "is" could not mean merely that there is a "simple, immanent necessity". Rather, "necessity itself can only be the decided response of thinking to the suspense of Being wherein it is surprised" (BSP: 176). (It would be interesting to compare Nancy's treatment of this Beethovenian necessity with that of Milan Kundera's in *The Unbearable Lightness of Being*.[15])

This nodal concept of "surprise" figures prominently in many contexts. It serves to fragment the substantialist metaphysics of reflective immanence by opening a rupture in the thinking–event dichotomy. There are several examples of "surprise" in Nancy's work: for instance, Being is the "shock" of singular beings encountering each other; wickedness "surprises" the good even before it has occurred; to be exposed to existence is to be "surprised by the freedom of existence"; freedom is the "nothingness surprised by its fulguration"; and painting is the expression of man's surprise at himself as a stranger standing outside himself. What all of these claims about painting, freedom and evil share is encapsulated in Nancy's reference to a "multiplication of singular bursts of sense resting on no unity or substance" (BSP: 33; EF: 126, 95, 82; M: 69; FT: 27).

All events, however "necessary", are surprising to thought; even so, thought itself is an event, and thus thinking surprises itself when it tries to think of even the most "necessary" of events. Moreover, there is no (un)surprised and (un)surprising subject that simply reads off the surprises that come its way. One might say that the entire relationship between a subject, its thinking (an event) and the event about which it thinks is "surprising" in such a manner as to forbid any establishment of a privileged foundation from which to survey surprising events. After all, Nancy suggests, "surprise" is not merely an aspect of an event, but its being or essence. In so far as each event is always already a surprise to experience and thought, "the surprise of the event" or "the event is surprising" are tautologies. That events are surprising is itself a surprise to thinking that seeks to comprehend them; that events exhibit necessary patterns too is a surprise to a thinking that expects to be surprised. However, philosophy from Hegel, or even from Parmenides, has neglected this "surprising" aspect of the eventuality of the event. In other words, philosophy should concern itself with both "the truth of that which takes place" and a conception of "taking place as such". For Nancy (reading Hegel), "taking place" is the truth that takes place "beyond the true" itself. Convolution is unavoidable: "truth beyond truth" itself means that there is the truth exhibited by "what happens", and then there is the truth of the "taking place" beyond what is exhibited as true in this "taking place" (BSP: 160–67). The task of philosophy, then, is to think a very specific conceptual tableau:

Beyond the truth of what happens, what is happening, what is in the happening, what has happened, what has always already happened in the happening itself, it is a matter of thinking *that* it happens; it is a matter of the happening, or rather, the happening "itself," where "it" is not the "self" that "it was", since it has not happened. In other words, it is a matter of thinking sameness itself, as the same as nothing. (BSP: 162)

"That something happens" is the surprising truth beyond what is taken to be true in the temporal form of happening. But if there were nothing but anonymous existence, the monotony of mere happening, then there would be no singular events, just repetitions of a pattern of occurring. If a jarring surprise to thinking were impossible, then the wonder that Aristotle regarded as vital to thinking metaphysically about reality might also be impossible. Wonder is genuinely directed only at the fact that signification has had a completed history whose end is an event in which we exist (GT: 67). To think the event of occurring is to seize it as if no such wonder occurred, as if the event not only occurred inevitably, but was inevitably intelligible as well (BSP: 164). Thinking freely of the surprising event is not a matter of inventing new truths, but of undergoing the "shock of meaning" that opens its "possibility" (the capacity to be affected by it). In that opening, in which signifying systems are breached and threatened with ruination, sense is discernible to thought. This possibility, which suggests that sense is outside discourse, is vulnerable to the resistance existence poses, a resistance necessary for the thinking of sense. The impenetrable hardness of singular events presents thinking with a violent shock. Indeed, Nancy defines "thought" as "nothing other than that against which an infinite resistance is opposed and whose very object (or very subject) is this infinite resistance" (GT: 2, 70, 81). The self cannot think of the event, paradoxically, because whatever it seizes is still a surprise to thinking; and what has not been thought could not surprise and therefore is not an event.

To "think" the event requires that we think how thought can and must be surprised by the surprising event of thinking. "Thinking never stops catching itself in the act of seeing [surprise] coming". But, Nancy warns, even the concept of surprise would have to be surprised, and thus could not truly facilitate thinking of the surprise without being surprised. The surprise to the finite thinking of surprise would be essential to that thinking. Philosophical thinking that wonders at the surprise of each and every event would have to be surprised, which, in turn, would require being surprised that it had been surprised.

Thus, the surprise of the event would not only be a limit-situation for the knowledge of Being, it would also be its essential form and essential end. From the very beginning of philosophy to its end, where its beginning is replayed in new terms, this surprise is all that is at stake, a stake that is literally interminable.

(BSP: 166, see also 175)

The question is, then, how is one to retain the event without turning it into a mere object or moment of thinking? How could one think "within" the surprising event? Which is to ask: how could one be surprised in thinking by the surprise to thinking? Unfortunately, a surprise is not merely some newness in comparison with "given" events, but rather something that has always already leapt over a given event. Only a leap of finite thinking itself, a thought that would not be surprised by its own surprise, could proleptically encompass the surprise of the event. But if thinking itself is a surprising event, and no event could not be surprising, then such a leap could not occur. Baldly stated, there is nothing to leap, nowhere from which to leap, nowhere to which it can leap – the surprise of the event is a negativity in so far as there is no origin from which the surprise occurs.

In yet other words, there is a "disagreement" between Being and beings, a friction between Being's capacity to found the essentiality of beings, and the being's irreducibility (or what Nancy calls elsewhere the "unfounded-ness") to such founding. There is no coinciding or simultaneity of Being with itself except in the discordant shock of the unexpected spacing of singularities. The result of this disagreement is that no subject could ever be surprised by its surprise, since surprise does not belong to the order of representation necessitated by an agreement between Being and being. In explanation, Nancy notes that "the surprise is that the leap – or better the 'it', the 'someone' who occurs in the leap and, in short, occurs as the leap 'itself' – surprises itself". One might propose, then, that thinking surprises itself precisely because it neither represents itself nor its own surprise. The surprise of the event that is an unrepresentable and pure negativity is an intense affirmation of "ek-sistent tension". There is nothing to the event but surprise, and yet that surprise is nothing and comes from nowhere. There is, one might conjecture, a unique aporetic tension between the surprise of the "that there is" and the surprise of "there is thinking". There is nothing but a flux of eventuality bearing this tension along and dispersing surprise throughout eventuality and its thinking (BSP: 38, 172–5).

Nancy regards this irresolvable tension as what must be said and thought about sense, and moreover this is all there is to say and think about sense. There is a form of necessity in this sense, an unthinkable kind of sense that calls for confrontation and yet, paradoxically, cannot be confronted without any production of sense. The circulation of sense, in which a world of sense is recreated on each occasion, is suggested in the very surprise *to* the event of thinking posed *by* the surprise of thinking itself. The surprise essential to each singular event and the surprise of each finite thinking of such an event are equally groundless and irresolvable. Even so, Nancy maintains, they are vital to our efforts to think freely of the singular sense of each singularity.

Conclusion

- Nancy offers a critique of what I have called "closed" immanence, the composition and reflection of ideas of sense for the purpose of personal and communal identification. In this immanence, there are "individuals" together in a pre-existing Being who share an essence accessible to this reflection.
- Against "closed" immanence, Nancy poses a vision of what I have called "open" immanence, which is the circulation of a singular sense through empirical experiences of contact and social relations between bodies. Although closed immanence implies that the individual is at the centre of the being of community and its reflective activity, open immanence presupposes that the singular being itself is at the edge of the community of being and philosophical discourse. Each event surprises thinking, including the event of thinking itself. There is nothing that is not surprising in the circulation of sense through the reticulated relations of bodies.
- Thinking and the world do not "have" a sense. Rather, Nancy is emphatic that they "are" sense. Sense is no transcendental position from which thinking and world acquire meaning. In as much as existence is being exposed at the edge of the world, the world is coextensive with sense itself. And in so far as thinking is the modality of this exposure, sense is coextensive with thinking as well. Thinking and world, one might say, collapse into the open immanence of sense. The subject–object and immanence–transcendence dichotomies do not serve as the contexts for sense, but sense provides the open, disruptive context within which sense is neither of their terms.
- Along the way, Nancy proves to be singularly critical of the forms of transcendence, exteriority or otherness often presented by religious thought. He insists that there is no "beyond" of sense, no superlative source of sense from which meanings can be gleaned. Being incessantly surprised, "man" finds himself to be strange, and this strangeness alone is the crucial aspect of the internal openness of sense itself.

In another respect, sense is always incessantly creating itself in multiplicities of singularity, on which the transcendence of "the Creation" is modelled. Open immanence is the surprised exposure to the strangeness of existence itself.

- If sense cannot be comprehended in terms of a reflection upon its existential conditions, then humanism is flawed by its emphasis upon the necessity of a return to (or of) sense. The identity of "humanity" is neither one that returns nor one to which we can return. Such a notion is no longer accessible to the requirements of a finite thinking of sense. It is now imperative to understand that the sense of "humanity" arises on each occasion of the circulation of sense in social relationships. Humanity always "surprises" itself; to be human is to be incessantly surprised by the events of the world and of thinking itself.

CHAPTER 4

Libertarianism

Nancy's often poignant disquisition on freedom is perhaps the most robustly philosophical aspect of his expansive speculative vision. It strives to divest philosophy of recalcitrant notions of freedom that have been informed by ideological requirements. It offers two crucial arguments, each of which attempts to collapse the thinking of freedom into the open immanence of the circulation of sense.

- On the one hand, one cannot define freedom by theories such as those that originate in the presupposition of a "right" to freedom (libertarianism) or the rational intelligibility of the necessity of freedom (Kantianism). On the contrary, freedom can only be conceived in terms of the "finite thought" of a singular event free of theoretical constraints.
- On the other hand, freedom is intelligible as a "burst" that is not for the purpose of being free, does not stem from any antecedent condition or essential property of being free, and is not even a mode of comprehending oneself as free.

Generally speaking, in conjunction with his criticism of substantialist metaphysics and "closed" immanence, Nancy objects to ontological views of freedom discernible in works as diverse as those of Kant, Hegel and Sartre. Wherever freedom is understood to be a physical property of human being and/or an existential state of the human condition, in which the essence of human being is presumed or established, ontological views are in play. In this respect, ontological freedom presupposes substantialist selves that possess essential properties definitive of the human condition. For example, any claim to the effect that human beings are free to choose either to resign themselves to or to rebel against their condition is ontological in as much as this substantial self and its essential property of freedom are key to an understanding of the being of the existent itself. Yet in other respects, any view of freedom in terms of rational or juridical principles that can guarantee freedom as a "right" merely presupposes such substantiality and essentiality on another, equally ontological, register of thought. On the contrary, for Nancy freedom is not philosophy's rational "decision to decide", the volition of a moral self or "ontologically free" subject, but the very decision dictated by the open immanence of existence itself (BP: 82). And that openness is a singular, surprising "burst", irreducible to ontological presuppositions, that expresses the essence of freedom despite substantialist and immanentist efforts to ground it by other means. In alternative terms, free agency is a spontaneous movement that is inaccessible to reflective consciousness and thematic expropriation alike. It is expressed in the bursting of a multiplicity of banal decisions that surprise thinking (and philosophy), not in any heroic or tragic affirmations of human existence. One might conjecture that the difficulty of conceptualizing Nancy's notion of freedom is precisely the result of its rigorous finitude of thinking.

In a captivating but often abstruse fashion, Nancy endeavours to preserve freedom from what Howard Caygill refers to as the substantialist "metaphysics of the inaugural act".[1] By this act, freedom would be invested with substantialist and essentialist properties that purportedly establish the foundational conditions of its existence and its exercise: the self, volition, right, purpose, duty and so on. If theory has its way, then false notions of subjective agency will be inextirpably rooted in our comprehension of freedom. Nancy confronts traditional paradigms of this metaphysics, first among which would be the distinction between potentiality and actuality: he challenges the notion that freedom is either a latent but exercisable modality emerging from some transcendental reserve of intentional agency, or an intelligible property of the actions composing that agency. In brief, it is consequent upon Nancy's commitments that freedom is not a property of agents or of actions, actual or potential. Moreover, he objects to the conventional view that freedom is merely a rationally intuitable category of necessity or a transcendent consequence of subsumption under rational laws. In both cases, the presumptions are that freedom is a unified construct of a conceptual scheme accessible solely by means of that scheme. In the main, Nancy castigates equally the thought that freedom is just a concept among concepts and the more refined thought that it is a foundational concept of concepts established by reason.

As we shall see, he maintains that freedom, an intense affirmation of existence in engagement with a multiplicity of singularities, is "free" precisely in the sense that it is a spontaneous liberation from the constraints of cognition (which neither impels it motivationally nor incorporates it reflectively).

A finite thinking of freedom

Nancy vilifies the cant that accompanies so much discourse on human freedom today, especially that which regards it as a "right" exhaustive of sense. Bluntly put, Nancy is contemptuous of any effort to articulate views of freedom based on formal and conventional principles of rights under an ideal of justice (SW: 114).[2] A vigilant and circumspective "other thinking" of the singular experience of the "burst of freedom" is required. In general terms, philosophy is disbarred from approaching freedom because it thinks of it as a mere "problem", an unprivileged formal concept among concepts. The very finitude of freedom rules out its appropriation by generalizing philosophical paradigms. Philosophy, Nancy avers, is not a discipline on which freedom could be inaugurally founded, but a discourse that should express and preserve the freedom that "defines the *logos* in its access to its own essence". It should not adopt as its primary mission the task of producing, constructing, guaranteeing, or even defending freedom, although it can (and presumably must) keep open the access to the essence of the *logos*'s history, a process without which even logic in all its forms would be impossible. As thinking's reception of a freedom of existence, philosophy examines the fold in which thinking articulates freedom and freedom articulates thought. Logic is based on cognitions that are requisitely free; this freedom is irreducible to the terms and operations of this logic. If one grants that philosophy is itself a fragmented expression of finite freedom, not its tribunal, then one should scrutinize philosophy in terms of finite freedom, not vice versa.

Nancy offers a number of reasons why philosophy cannot proffer a discourse about freedom. On the one hand, even to conceive of philosophy as a "pure discipline of concepts" is to imply that there is a "preunderstanding that the order of the concept itself pertains, in origin and essence, to the element of freedom". It is the concept of freedom, and not the free thinking whereby that concept is accessible, that normally assumes the foreground of philosophical discourse. Apposite to this claim is the postulate that only freedom is that "through which the access to representation occurs". There would not even be philosophical discourse at all if there were not free thinking in play. Conversely, philosophy is initiated as a deployment of representing concepts, a deployment that could not be initiated at all if there were not a free activity of cognition. On the other hand, Nancy claims that to define "man" in rational terms already provides a false philosophical pathway to a comprehension of freedom. *Logos* designates a state of cognition prior to any coherentist or foundationalist schemes that promise to provide access to the "essence" of freedom.

65

The *logos* would never, for lack of this freedom, pose any question of the concept as concept, of the foundation as foundation, or of representation as representation (or any question of the logos as *logos*). Thus the *logos*, before any "logic", but in the very inauguration of its own logic, freely accedes to its own essence – even if this is in the mode of not properly acceding to any essence ... This amounts to saying that freedom offers or casts thought, in philosophy, always beyond "philosophy" conceived as the Concept or Foundation of the *logos*.   (EF: 61–3)

Nancy offers the intriguing thought that the logic of freedom merely passes along the surface of philosophy, striving to bestow meaning on "anarchic" states of existence, while the free circulation of sense prior to any "logic" is always already an exercise of freedom. From traditional epistemological perspectives, there is no "outside" of philosophy within which the *logos* of philosophy figures because concepts of "truth", "objectivity" and "knowledge" are understood to be founded in logic but not in the *logos* of freedom itself. In brief, freedom must be examined as both an expression of and an obstacle to cognition, not as an originary state founded and secured by logic. In consequence, without the cognitive endurance necessary for the singular resistance to thought, the thinking of freedom would lack meaning. Since the existential ground of freedom is necessary for thinking, thinking itself would altogether lack sense. Thus the "free thinking of freedom" is not merely an enquiry into the recognizability of freedom, but an imperative for the meaningful freedom of thinking as such.

What, then, is the difficulty in thinking freedom? Generally speaking, Nancy avers that it is no longer merely a question of considering freedom as a possession or right of property that determines human being as what it is. Rather, it is a question of *offering human being over to the very condition of free existence*, the "freedom of being", to its free exercise of existence divorced from theoretical constraints and paradigmatic commitments. Or as he remarks, it is a question of "liberating human freedom from the immanence of an infinite foundation or finality, and liberating it therefore from its own infinite projection to infinity ...". That is, *freedom is nothing other than existence itself*, divorced from any infinite horizon against which it may project itself in order to determine it and devoid of any transcendent condition within which its aspiration may be nurtured (EF: 13–14). If existence is a plurality of singular beings, and not any antecedent Being, then freedom is precisely the incessantly different experience of singularity itself, not any essence of substance by which this experience is intelligible.

It should be noted that this is not a firm affirmation but merely, thus far, the invocation of a goal, without any argument in favour of adopting such a goal. In order to provide such an argument, Nancy insists that the dominant Kantian and Hegelian proposals of freedom resonant in libertarianism (generally understood) stand in the way of a genuine free thinking of the very free conditions of thought. This generic libertarianism misguidedly conceives of freedom as a property of individual persons as such that can (and should) be rationally and juridically guaranteed, and, of course, protected. Bartered in the marketplace alongside equality, fraternity and community, this libertarian paradigm of liberation has become utterly divorced from philosophical orientations that stress freedom's existentiality. On a lower register, this divorce takes the form of a massive dichotomy between pragmatically established freedoms (rights and exemptions) and the very Idea of freedom philosophically presumed in "reflective" immanence. The prevailing assumption, Nancy implies, is that there is no such severance: the consoling Idea of freedom is in perfect concordance with the freedoms marketed so vigorously in political and economic discourse. However, according to libertarian hubris, it is unthinkably tactless to enquire too impenitently into the "moral self-evidence" of the common notion of freedom as endowed by a god or established by law, for this might lead to awesomely catastrophic consequences for civil society (especially in respect of the soothing self-evidence of its vision of market democracy). The commitment to this discourse of the "moral self-evidence" of freedom is pragmatic (bound to the interests of the market and the state) in nature: do not question "rights" to freedom, since without these nothing would work, nothing communal would be operable. Yet such self-evidence is always called into question by the consequences of the very *praxis* it promulgates. "In all the ways that we orient ourselves toward the exploitation of the resources of the 'Third World' or toward the management of automatic files and information banks, the rights of freedom today do not cease to complicate indefinitely their relations with the duties of the same freedom" (EF: 3). We are left then with a variegated discourse about freedom as a self-evident and unchallengeable common notion that lacks any philosophical content of its own. If the Idea of freedom is the reified given of the essence of human nature, then the common notion of freedom offers only verisimilitudinal depictions of human existence. Alternatively, such shallow depictions of freedom are so attractively packaged and displayed on the libertarians' shelves that they are given conditions that cannot be denied, not even through force (which every success over "Saddamite tyranny" and the "forces of terroristic evil" establishes). As Nancy maintains:

> But if freedom is to be verified as the essential fact of existence, and consequently as the fact of the very meaning of existence, then

this vacancy would be nothing other than the vacancy of meaning: not only the vacancy of the meanings of existence, whose entire metaphysical program our history has exhausted, but the vacancy of this freedom of meaning in which absence existence is only survival, history is only the course of things, and thinking, if there is still room to pronounce this word, remains only intellectual agitation. (EF: 2–3)

In other words, if freedom alone indicates facts of existence that may be taken for granted, and if meaning is engendered by the discourse in which freedom takes nothing for granted, then there can be no meaningful discourse replete with pre-established conventional meanings. Listing the self-evident rights to freedom eradicates the very possibility of thinking meaningfully of freedom, or indeed even thinking meaningfully at all. If simulations of freedom are bandied sufficiently, then meaning can be sold cheaply too.

In conclusion, Nancy maintains caustically that philosophical thought about freedom should back away from forms of thinking that are illegitimately self-evident or problematically foundational. That is to say, we should shy away from conceptions of freedom as an ontological property of either humanity as such or individual human subjects, or even as any formal view of freedom offered as an option to be chosen freely. Furthermore, philosophers should not represent themselves as unified subjects appearing freely to themselves. Every philosophical decision about how to approach the thinking of freedom, beginning with the decision for philosophy itself, indicates that thinking itself provides a place for the thinking of freedom. The thinking of freedom can only be seized or surprised by freedom itself, which enables freedom to assert itself beyond the epistemic limits of the logic and politics of "freedom". Yet philosophy itself is possible because freedom seizes thinking in a space of free play and thereby enables it to engage with freedom. Thinking this space, thinking about it and within it, is necessary to the vitality of any philosophy. Thinking is thinking that is free *for* philosophy, able to wander in the space of meaning with aplomb, and therefore free *for* freedom. In so far as thinking is accessible to philosophy, the very freedom that furtively resists thinking takes over thinking in order for the free space of meaning to be truly free.

Broadly speaking, Nancy attempts to think of freedom in terms of a self-engendering and multifaceted free space of meaning necessary for thinking itself, not an ontological venue from which thinking may issue. The "space" of free thinking that alone can receive sense is one in which freedom sets free the circulation of sense. Given the coextensivity of sense

with both thinking and world, the collapse of transcendence and immanence into sense, freedom is not merely available to thinking. It is a necessary condition of all thinking in which it is expressed. Indeed, neither
existence nor thinking could be said to be possible if freedom were
fettered. One might say that to enquire into the possibility of freedom at
all is to examine the absolute condition of existence in itself. The free play
of the sense of freedom is the element in which and by which existence
takes place and "accounts" for itself. Without the free play of freedom,
existence would simply not be, and without the free accountability of freedom, existence would be unintelligible. Nancy suggests that if this is the
case, then it is the necessarily ubiquitous presence of freedom in the thinking of existence that determine its status and value.

Kantian freedom as "fact of reason"

One might immediately discern the relevance of such a claim to the thought
of Kant. After all, Kant offered an exposition of the conditions by which
freedom is necessary and necessarily intelligible. It is widely acknowledged
that the fulcrum of Kant's vaunted deontological ethic is freedom founded
on practical reasoning. To prescribe duties to the self, it must first be established that the prescribed action could be performed. Without exception, all
events are causally determined according to laws of causal necessity. Yet, in
contradiction, this determinism is incompatible with the necessary sense of
self-causation in human agency. To be more specific, one might notice that,
on the one hand, the natural realm is bound by universal laws of causal
necessity, within which, on the other hand, there is a freely originating cause
of one's own action. Hence to say that one is free in a strictly causally
determined universe is to offer the contradictory view that there can be no
exception and that there is one exception to such universally binding laws
– the free moral agent. Although we can deny that we are free, it would be
unthinkable for practical reason to do so, since even to think and act
practically requires apodeictically that one has done so freely. Ultimately, the
"transcendentally" free self conceives itself under two aspects: it is at once
a self that appears to itself in the realm of causality, and a thing-in-itself
constrained by practical reason alone. A rational self must regard itself as
an "intelligence" belonging not merely to the world of sensation and causation (heteronomy), but to the world of freedom and practical reason
(autonomy) as well.[3] Being an exception to universal causation, we come
to know ourselves solely by means of the exercise of freedom in pure
practical reasoning. All morality, indeed all practical thinking of any kind,

is dependent upon the presumption of the apodeictic necessity of transcendental freedom.

Nancy lauds much in the Kantian analysis, but deems it flawed by excessive reliance on the notion of "facts" of reason (that serve as tribunals of facticity) at the expense of "facts" of existence. The interrogation of the necessity of "pure practical reason" as the "keystone" of the overall Kantian system requires an emphasis upon the established facticity of freedom. This implies that freedom is neither a property determining human essence nor a property of necessity whose legitimacy must be deduced if freedom is to be categorically necessary. For Kant, "it is not impossible to think of a law that serves only for the subjective form of principles as yet a determining ground through the objective form of a law as such", consciousness of which is a "fact of reason" because one cannot "reason it out from antecedent data of reason" and because it is a non-intuitional "synthetic a priori presupposition".[4] According to a peculiar logic of self-referential justification, phenomenal experience can only be established as such by the "fact of reason", and this will be so only if freedom itself is deemed a "fact of reason". Claims about experience (and by extension, about freedom) are logically derived from the facticity of reason, as when freedom is comprehended as the rationally factual experience of the obligation to be free. It is apodeictically necessary to take the "reality of freedom" as a "categorical modality of necessity", which is to claim, in the rough, that nothing can be established as necessary as such until the reality of freedom is necessarily determined. "Freedom as fact of reason" would be unintelligible if it could not "prove" itself to reason. Nancy remarks that "existence as its own essence is nothing other than the freedom of being", which is to say that factical determination of freedom enables existence as such to be intelligible as a fact of self-legislating reason (EF: 22–3). In other words, the very fact that one can think freely about freedom indicates that it is a fact of reason that can (or indeed must) be taken as such. But this neither presupposes a categorical imperative to do so, Nancy maintains, nor that there is a determinate reason at work in the conditions of freedom itself.

Nancy interrogates the precision of the relationship between the vaunted categorical imperative and freedom, both of which are "anterior to all morality". The imperative opens an unbridgeable gap between the agent and the commander, which is not a "who" but the law of freedom itself. Ontologically speaking, a moral agent as a "*some*one" received the command from "*no* one" and thereby is defined as an agent (BP: 79). Maintaining that freedom is a "fact of reason" does not imply that freedom is solely founded by rational self-legislation answerable to an unconditional command of the moral law. There is a blatant mismatch between the absolute sovereignty of the moral law and the exercise of freedom. This mismatch produces a disjuncture that no "fact of reason" could close nor any act of freedom bridge. Since the categorical imperative (which both facilitates freedom and requires its subsumption under law) suppresses freedom of initiative and deliberation, freedom proves its facticity only as a withdrawal from external commands that impose upon it. Nevertheless, even a free thinking of freedom would be haunted by the intimate enigma of a command that must be answered. Since this imperative to be free cannot be "domesticated" by reason or as reason in the Kantian manner, then, Nancy remarks, it should be our task to consider the "imperative's insistence for a thinking" that does not come in the form of a promise, but demands obedience out of duty and a respect for the law itself, that is, for the sake of the duty itself. The rational self-legislation of duty does not have the motivational force to order us to perform some action, but rather obliges us to do our duty as such. It effectively prescribes a *praxis* that is its own end, without primary commitment or content, the imperative that impels specific actions. However, this prescription is not a "pre-inscription", as if it were written that some specific action would represent fulfilment of the command of the moral law, but rather an enjoinment that issues irreversibly from beyond reason. That is why it can be said that it is as a "fact of reason" that freedom erupts in response to the unconditional command. If it is the case that the categorical imperative is exhibited to reason as a fact that depends upon no antecedent fact (which means perhaps that there is a moral prescription endowed in the very non-rational nature of such a command), then Nancy suggests that it can only be said to "befall" reason, not to stem from it (FT: 131–6, 141–4). Thus it neither sublates the conditions of possibility of freedom nor is itself sublated by reason. Exceeding such relationships between the conditions of freedom and reason itself, it is irreducible to the command of an action and whichever action is prescribed. Possessing motivational force precisely because there is a separation between the free being enjoined to act and the enjoinment to act as commanded, the categorical imperative is an "excess" precisely because of this incommensurability that obliges us (not because we are obliged despite this incommensurability). "We are obliged by and toward what obliges us, by and toward this obligation's injunction. Not because such an injunction has the power to command us but because it is incommensurable with any power of constraint or propensity" (FT: 144–6). Properly speaking, for Nancy it obliges us (a) to respect the law from which it issues and to which it is incommensurate; (b) to respect the very law that obliges us to perform an action; and (c) to be bound to the law of obligation itself, the law of law, as it were.

Nancy demarcates the moral from the rational law that purportedly founds it. In doing so, he will establish the consequences of their mismatch by noting that the moral law "withdraws" from the rational law that exceeds it (which implies that it obliges *praxis* motivated by submission to the moral law). Ultimately, subsumption under the *moral* law merely destines us to a submission to the *rational* law from which *both* the moral law and the subject *withdraw*. Divested of its own freedom, but given a formal self-legislating freedom in compensation, the free subject is abandoned by the moral law and in turn abandons the rational laws that are incommensurate with its freedom (FT: 148–9). It might very well be sufficient to say that the model of autonomous freedom offers little more than a simulation of freedom because of the withdrawals and abandonments that constitute its existential condition. And this is very pertinent to any coherent account of the relation between self-legislation and its moral and rational laws. An "individual person's freedom" is not established through self-legislation; on the contrary, the injunction addresses the very possibility of being addressed by it. It affirms the freedom of the individual, without recognizing any existential conditions that make this address possible.

> The imperative categorizes its addressee; it affirms the freedom of the addressee, imputes evil to it, and intends or abandons it to the law. In this way, the imperative categorizes the essence or nature of man, doing so in excess of every category, in excess of what is proper to man. (FT: 151)

The imperative does not delineate and signify the freedom of the respondent; on the contrary, it suppresses existential freedom in the very moment the respondent "freely" answers to its command. In other words, at the moment of address and response, an enormous gap is opened between the "fact of existence", in which the existential conditions of possibility of freedom are delineated and exercised in *praxis* by an individual person, and the "fact of reason", which is reason's address to its own conception of what freedom is and to that which is free. Nancy's point might be that this is not to establish that the individual is "rational" by virtue of its submission in the face of both the rational laws that withdraw from it and the moral laws before which it withdraws. In other words, this perspective simply does not even explore the existential facticity of being free, but offers only an "ontological" view of the necessity of freedom and the obligation to be free. It does not entertain the thought that there might be antecedent conditions of freedom that are purely given by the existence of the individual itself. Intriguingly, freedom is truly a "fact of reason", not because it can be called freely into question, but because it can call into question even its own affirmation of itself (EF: 23). It is not merely an "object of knowing", an object about which there is thought, nor is it even a purely given "subject of action". In tentative outline, the freedom of the act is apodeictically necessary for the comprehension of the free status of the subject performing the action. More generally, Nancy offers the pertinent observation that there is a self-referential inconsistency in Kant's scheme, for it is debatable whether the keystone of the necessity of "pure practical reason" is, on the one hand, the free subject performing actions, or, on the other, the "fact of reason" of its freedom.

It might be helpful to back away from the details of the critique of Kant to examine its broader consequences within Nancy's metaphysical vision. Obviously, the critique figures as an identification of an unappealing contortion in the Kantian logic. To say that the "fact of freedom cannot receive, in a rigorous Kantian logic, its status as fact" is to claim that Kant has not established the "free space of meaning" into which the meaning of freedom can be received (EF: 25). And yet it is precisely this establishment that Kant's stress upon apodeictic necessity is presumed to achieve. Kant, then, has not actually offered a "thinking" of freedom and its meaning, but merely a treatise on freedom that entails precisely the errors that such treatises cannot overcome.

Nancy examines Heidegger's sustained rebuttal to the Kantian understanding of the relation between freedom and causality. Heidegger inverts this subordination and insists that the will to do one's duty is fundamentally the willing of a duty "to be-there". Duty is not merely supervened upon existential facts, but rather the duty to exist, "having-to-exist", is a primary duty that necessitates all obligation to "will" being free. A self that is always calling into question the affirmation of its own freedom would be offering itself as the "ungrounding" of its own existence in an "anarchic", not a legislating, fashion. Existence is always already the ungrounding of the duty to be free to which it is always legislatively handed over. If there were anything factual about the freedom of an existent, it would not be discerned in any property of a rationally motivated action or any consequence of wilful behaviour. In the absence of referential or constitutive benchmarks by which to determine its essence, the wilful existent is always throwing itself against the limit of its own self-legislation in order to transcend legislation's limitations. For Nancy, all one can say of the essence of the existence of the wilful existent is that it consists in "being-taken-to-the-edge" of the law that delineates a limit to agency. But since it is the law that in its very presence permits all transgressions, the only law that any autonomous agent must impose upon itself for the purpose of self-legislation is untransgressible (on the grounds that the law of transgression that establishes the limits of agency cannot be transgressed). In other words, there is no pre-existing ontological framework or benchmark, no epistemological nodal points by which the factuality of freedom could be determined because such grounds are themselves determined by the factuality of wilful freedom. That is to say, freedom is a self-referential and self-constitutive facticity of willing itself (EF: 27–8). If it has an essence, that essence consists in its always singularized transgressions of its own existentiality, not in its self-legislation.

There is a convoluted but rigorous paralogic at work in the notion that the self-referentiality of each willing consists in a willing of an obligation to "will" the "effectivity" of willing. "The will" wills its own affirmation at "the edge" of its own self-legislation, transgressing it despite the absence of any (apodeictic) necessity that the willing existent's essence might provide. Willing already and always implies an obligation to exist to which obligations of reason must answer. All "facts of reason" pertaining to freedom must comply with "facts of existence" that express this freedom's efficaciousness. In willing, the sense of freedom as a fact of reason collapses into the open immanence of existence itself, for without it, there could be no calculations of choice or subsumption under normative laws. If the condition of experiencing wilfully enables the experience of freedom to take a place in the indeterminate spacing of existence, beings are singularized by the experience of freedom in the very exercise of freedom itself. Thus freedom is privileged as the experience of existence (which implies that experience itself is the foundation of all the foundations that freedom requires). Although this might appear in the form of an empirical given, Nancy insists that freedom is "anterior to every empirical certitude" without being indeclinably transcendent. Instead, freedom is "the transcendental that is experience", not the transcendental condition *of* experience (EF: 87). There would not be "empirical experience" at all if singular freedom were not incessantly transgressing its own limits of self-legislation.

Freedom, then, is not the consequence of, but an exception to, the deployment of laws of self-legislation, Nancy insists. It is a consequence of the will's necessary evasion of law, or alternatively, of the deployment of law and the law of deployed obligation. It is not a result of the bestowal of value by the self-legislating will. In a sense, the autonomous self furtively ducks beneath the very obligations it "sovereignly" confers upon itself. Not only is there no necessarily rational condition of freedom, there is also no logically necessary bond between facts of reason and facts of freedom. Only the self-referentiality of willing, irreducible even to the law it gives itself, can possibly preserve the sense of the wilful existent's freedom. Freedom is the irreducible and disruptive resistance against the very necessity of self-legislation. It is in the "an-archic" deliverance of itself to existence, and not in subordination to facts of reason, that it is essentially free. Even for the self-legislating existent, it is the "disgrounding" and "an-archic" resistance to the rational obligation to be free that determines that it is free. As Nancy writes:

> The fact of freedom, or the practical fact, thus absolutely and radically "established" without any establishing procedure being able to produce this fact as a theoretical object, is the fact of what is to be done in this sense, or rather, it is the fact *that there is* something to be done, or is even the fact that there is the *to be done*, or that there is the affair of existence. Freedom is factual in that it is the *affair* of existence. It is a fact, in that it is not an acquired fact any more than it is a "natural" right, since it is the law without law of an inessentiality.
> (EF: 31–2)

If the essence of existence would then consist in the lack of any essence that might guide the will of a self-legislating existent, then no external facts of existence (such as possessing "natural rights") establish freedom. Paradoxically, it appears that it is freedom's "disgrounding" resistance to its own establishment that establishes its facticity and its law.

Once freedom's essence has been rendered inaccessible to theory, it is still necessary to approach the question of our temptation to claim to comprehend it. Nancy, again addressing Heidegger, insists that we should open a space within which the meaning of freedom can be approached. To apply rational or other concepts to a given view of freedom does not facilitate comprehension of it; rather, any comprehended freedom is not the disgrounding freedom that enabled this comprehension to take place. Nancy exhorts us to nullify the danger of thinking beyond freedom without even having reached it. Since self-knowledge cannot be taken for granted, or even predetermined as the primary framework within which freedom can be thought, then the "free domain of freedom" must be respected and preserved. In particular, freedom should not be comprehended as a causation that produces effects, nor should it be modelled on any notion of "lawful succession" as such. If free thinking can only "know" that its own causal efficacy is incomprehensible, then knowledge cannot accommodate the power of effectuation that is the necessary condition of freedom. Specifically, there is a surplus of expended freedom that even the notion of causality cannot survey. "Freedom holds the secret of causality since it is defined as the power of being by itself a cause, or as the power of causing, absolutely. Fundamentally, freedom is causality that has achieved self-knowledge" (EF: 44–5).

The thought of the incomprehensibility of freedom in the context of the questioning of freedom's affirmation of itself involves a paradoxical logic of the limits necessary for philosophy to realize its freedom of thought.

Nancy notes precisely that "comprehending that something is comprehensible cannot signify simply that comprehension would come to a halt with the discovery of one of its limits". Although knowledge of the obstacle is not knowledge of what the obstacle obstructs, the fact *that* there is something obstructed is comprehensible through the obstacle, even if, again, *what* is incomprehensible is not comprehended by virtue of knowledge of the obstacle. "Comprehending that something is incomprehensible is certainly not comprehending the incomprehensible as such, but neither is it, if one can say this, purely and simply comprehending nothing about it." This is not to say that freedom has some exalted value beyond comprehension. Conversely, nothing would be comprehensible if the freedom that could enable comprehension were not irreducible to and transgressive of the limits of the comprehensible (EF: 48–9). The incomprehensible ungroundedness of freedom (and thence of philosophy) is the "supreme stage of the comprehension that attains knowledge of self-comprehension as self-realization". Comprehension can thus grasp the manner in which philosophy stretches towards its own limits, passing into active realization, always putting itself to the test, always testing itself against the intrinsic limits that are necessarily untransgressible. The free thinking self, in the free self-comprehension of the thought of freedom, can thus explore the self-comprehension of what is incomprehensible. Hence, in Nancy's view, freedom always asserts itself in the *praxis* of self-comprehension as the fundamental task of "free" thinking of freedom.

One might say in conclusion, then, that all free and finite thinking arises in thinking of freedom precisely on the limit of the comprehensibility of freedom itself, which is beyond theory. If all free thinking, including that of self-knowledge, takes place within this limit, for this limit and about this limit, then neither causal necessity nor rational self-legislation facilitates an understanding of this free thinking.

"Black fulguration": the surprising "burst" of freedom

Freedom, Nancy informs us, has no origin and is delivered to the world in a spontaneous burst that surprises thinking on each occasion. Freedom is nothing other than the prodigal expenditure of existence in an irreducible burst necessary if there is to be cognition and agency at all. Broadly speaking, thinking has a tenuous hold on a freedom that is "more intimate and originary to it than every object of thought and every faculty of thinking". Freedom is an unsuccessful giving of itself to a finite thought; or rather, singular beings freely give themselves to be thought about, and thinking freely thinks them, without satisfactory commensuration. A radical and effusive singularity, freedom is not a substance that expends out of a "pregnant enclosure" of potentiality (EF: 55). Nancy is insistent that there is no pristine, untrammelled domain of interiority from which or to which freedom bursts. If it is expenditure that constitutes consciousness without being reducible to its essence, then it lacks any closed immanence that might homogenize the multiplicity of aspects of this bursting or the being from which freedom bursts.

Freedom is not to be understood in terms of properties, essences or grounds, but rather by means of a finite thinking of a multiplicity of banal and dissimulated expressions: "values of impulse, chance, luck, the unforeseen, the decided, the game, the discovery, conclusion, dazzlement, syncope, courage, reflection, rupture, terror, suture, abandonment, hope, caprice, rigor, the arbitrary", as well as "laughter, tears, scream, word, rapture, chill, shock, energy, sweetness ..." (EF: 56). In every such instance, there is a wanton ferality, an untamed spontaneity in all giving of itself to thought and all free expenditure in thinking. Each is composed of an "infinity of figures or modes of a unique freedom, but which in reality are offered as a prodigality of bursts whose 'freedom' is not their common substance but rather ... their bursting". In other words, one might understand that in order to think *of* a free singularity, or to think *as* a free singularity, it is necessary to examine freedom in terms of "heterogeneous disseminations" and not in terms of modes of a substance or as substances determined by some pre-established conceptual framework. Each "burst" of freedom is determined precisely by an expenditure in which freedom "withdraws" from determination. For Nancy, then, freedom is not itself determinate, as substance or essence, because its seemingly determinate features are themselves expenditures.

Obviously, Nancy is fixated by the *intensity* of the experience of freedom. Freedom, he avers, following Hegel, is a nothingness, but it is one that is affirmed in a "deepening and intensification of negativity". To say that it is nothingness is not to say that it is freed from the choice of necessity. "The intensification of the nothingness does not negate its nothing-ness: it concentrates it, accumulates the tension of the nothingness as nothingness [...] and carries it to the point of incandescence where it takes on the burst of an affirmation." Such a freedom, Nancy asserts, is not a "freedom from" the freedom to choose an appropriate necessity, nor is it a freedom to make such a choice. In an intensely spontaneous "burst", *it is free from and for freedom itself*, which always surprises the thought "about" freedom. The burst of freedom is an "iruption of existence" that surprises the thinking of freedom. Nancy writes of a "black fulguration", a dark flash of lightning, in which there is an intense burst without premonition, purpose or transparency. Nothing could be foreseen by the free thinking of freedom's burst, since only the objective contents of freedom could be reflected upon, and the modality of their expression would be indiscernible to the free thinking blinded by the incandescent burst of freedom. If all thinking is impossible without the "burst" of freedom, then there could be no cognitive limits upon the burst's efficaciousness. Nancy asserts that finite freedom is not the foundation of the transcendence of finitude itself, as if we could only rise above our existential condition through a surplus of freedom whose intensity would provide meaning to existence. Instead, on the grounds that there is no substance that could be exceeded, it is the lack of precisely the existential foundation that might make such an overflowing possible. If freedom is the foundation of all foundations (epistemic and metaphysical), then it is nothing other than an indeterminate spacing (which is not merely some indeterminate place, but the possibility of places, wherein freedom takes places and is nurtured). The experience of freedom, Nancy proposes, is incessantly deciding a limit and this decision takes place at each moment of fulguration (EF: 81–4, 86). It is not expressed within a decision, but rather stretches itself towards a decision that makes the freedom of existence and the existence of freedom arise simultaneously.

Nancy maintains that the thinking of freedom would require some scrutiny of the intensity of its own ungrounded affirmation as the *sina qua non* of self-consciousness. Needless to say, although freedom is pre-subjective, prior to the affirmation of self-representing subjectivity, there is nothing more to consciousness of one's existence than one's antecedent affirmation of experience. This is not to assert that freedom experiences itself, but rather that it grounds itself in such a way that it always eludes reflection and refuses to appear to itself as an object of its own representations. Nancy notes that freedom and subjectivity possess the same formal structure in the sense that each "appears to itself by making itself, and it makes itself by appearing to itself". However, there is a wide disjuncture here: that on which freedom reflects is not what it has made, and what it makes is not that which appears in reflection. Freedom releases itself in the intense burst of thinking, but thinking does not reflect adequately as it is released. Such a release is initially lacking in certitude precisely because of its intensity; what is released lacks any determinate features upon which thinking could reflect, or, to put it otherwise, whatever thinking reflects upon as the objective content of freedom is not that in which freedom itself consists. On the contrary, each intense release facilitates thinking of freedom in the sense that now thinking must be a decision for freedom in the experience of freedom, a resolve to appropriate the releasing subject and the objective contents of the released subject in a modality or formal means of releasing. If the burst of freedom comes from and passes over presence in a modality of releasing, then a free thought about freedom could never approach the freedom of this thought.

One might hazard to propose, then, that freedom "comes-to-presence" by withdrawing from mere being and affirming the existence of the singular being by means of a release in finite thinking. This affirmation takes the form of a liberation that is not a liberation from existential limitations but a release that discloses the sense of freedom to its own indeterminacy and incertitude. If freedom is released, and if it is the object of representation solely as a modality of expression, then it is limited only by its thrust towards presence (EF: 93). This coming-to-presence is free and reveals that there "is" something solely in the releasing of itself. This disclosure, being an intense affirmation of freedom, is an improbable surprise to any reflection upon it. That something is disclosed, that there is something to be released at all, is a "surprise". Generally speaking, existence itself is incessantly and singularly disclosed in freedom in such a way as to surprise reflection.

"Furious freedom": the possibility of the positivity of evil

In recent years it has become commonplace to question the traditional metaphysics of evil by deconstructing the philosophical notion of evil that has been dominated irrefragably by the pellucid ontological dichotomies of the Aristotelian excess/defect, Augustinian positivity/privation and Kantian proclivity/disposition schematics. Astute students of evil as different as Slavoj Žižek and François Flahault have enquired into the possibility of an alternative view. The former has examined the relevance of Catharism (or gnosticism generally) and the philosophy of Schelling to this task, whereas the latter has rejected both the post-Augustinian notion of *privatio boni* and the post-Enlightenment liberal notion of evil as the product of external factors.[5] Similarly, Nancy summons us to think the seemingly impossible notion of evil as a positive presence: a thinking that might require a deconstructive challenge to the meta-ethical prerequisites that the traditional notion of evil would preclude.

It is no longer even possible to read the newspapers' account of human greed, viciousness and callousness, Nancy remarks, without testing one's endurance. It is as if there were a will endowed in human nature that strives for self-destruction. It might even be the case that history itself, in its "crisis of sense", has been suspended by the experiences of total war, genocide, nuclear power and so on that serve as evident signs of a "self-destroying mankind" unredeemed by any transcendentality or negativity.

Indeed, such an evil might even have paralysed the narrative of history itself, rendering it incapable of overcoming this suspension. Very plausibly, Nancy writes that, as a result of our debilitating horror at the ubiquity of evil in the spectacle of war, genocide and hunger in an age proud of its enlightened civilization, it becomes ever more pressing to rethink the challenge of evil. Perhaps we live instead in a "culture of destruction" (which I shall survey in greater detail in a later chapter), but if so, then it is imperative to "consider the possibility that our culture has seized upon evil as an intrinsic possibility – neither accidental nor secondary – of being itself". Evil should be regarded as the primary exercise of an attempt to establish grounds for freedom. Indeed, as Peter Fenves has shrewdly remarked, such an effort could only divest freedom of what little rational or foundational equilibrium it might possess (FT: 16, 82; BP: 144–5).[6]

To "think" freedom, Nancy exhorts, we must take evil seriously by shaping a new knowledge of its singular, positive facticity. In other words, it is necessary to think of it as a "constitutive decay", a corruption positively inherent in human existence, reflected in the incessant distortion of the exercise of freedom. If evil is a seemingly insurmountable obstacle to finite thinking, then there is no justificatory or redemptive reserve into which we can retreat from the indeclinable disruption of evil (especially that of the Holocaust). If so, then evil cannot be trivialized as a mere lack of goodness, as many traditional moral and religious paradigms explicate. In other words, posing a challenge to the meta-ethics of "good over evil" would entail a rejection of the age-old presumption that evil is a "negativity", a perversion of genuine exercises of freedom. A thinking of the positivity of evil requires that one must confront the thought that it may be inscribed in freedom itself. Following Bataille, Nancy suggests that evil might be regarded as an "extreme horror that keeps reason awake", which is to say that truth is illuminated in the "awakening of horror" whose extremity would of course be genocide. Bluntly put, the evil of extermination, refracted into contemporary values through the camps, is not reducible to some "sickness" appearing on the surface of the world in which the "normativity of the norm" is confirmed in the act of rupturing it (SW: 150; EF: 122–3; FT: 16, 69). Instead, it might be the very instantiation of an evil that is positively present in freedom itself.

Nancy clearly disparages any shallow descriptive view of wickedness as a weakness, distortion or malfunction of human disposition reflecting (or resulting from) a perverse denial of the rational nature of freedom. Kant's (re)theologization of wickedness takes us away from the problem of wilful perpetration and seduces us into thinking in terms of dispositions and proclivities composing a congeries of claims about the moral law, autonomous imposition of maxims, and esoteric theological fluff about the "perversity of the heart" or the "corrupt root" of human nature. In other words, Nancy comprehends the positivity of wickedness in terms of a burst of freedom irreducible to Kant's propensity to "will" maxims that "neglect the incentives springing from the moral law in favor of others which are not moral".[7] Hence, even the Kantian typology of radical evil – frailty, depravity and impurity of motivations – merely superimposes theological values upon the "positivity" of the burst of freedom in wickedness. Although Kant does note that even the misanthrope might wish humanity well but nonetheless find nothing estimable in human beings as it knows them,[8] he implies that even such a person is not exscribed or abandoned by the moral law as long as it has a moral "sentiment". However, the most significant problem is whether all wicked perpetration of gratuitous harm is motivated by malice towards morality itself, or even existence, not merely some suspension of moral sentiment towards individual human beings. As Peter Fenves has noted, the difference between Kant and Nancy might be that the former deems radical evil to be action "in spite of" the moral law, while the latter regards it as an affirmative action "to spite" the moral law.[9]

What, then, does Nancy project as conceptual perimeters for the thinking of the sense of positive evil? He argues that if evil is a positive wickedness, then the evil of genocide in particular is strictly unpardonable by theodicy. If freedom is mysterious because a fathomless capacity for wickedness is its spontaneous expression, then wickedness is no longer conceivable, Nancy proposes, as a "fact of nonfreedom" dragged along by the depreciable "mechanics of the sensible" (EF: 123–5). In brief, the evil of wickedness cannot be underestimated by any dismissive perspective on its negativity, but must be considered in terms of the possibility of its positivity.

Nancy proposes that this positivity should not be tainted by the traditional notion that the finality of an act is always represented in terms of "the good", even when the person strives to do evil for evil's sake. It is not as if goodness serves as both the ideal of conduct and the mediation within the affirmation of evil. Nancy appears to be suggesting that evil, especially the intense wickedness of genocide, is no longer merely a "moment or mediation" in the exercise of goodness. More radically, evil as such "ruins" the good absolutely, contaminating its "purity". To insist that the good no longer possesses a privileged value over an evil that is merely its privation is not to reverse the order of precedence. It is simply to affirm the possibility that if evil cannot be conceived as a corruption of goodness, then neither can goodness be thought as the redemption of evil. It is to say, moreover, that "freedom alone precedes and succeeds and surprises itself in a decision that can be for the one or the other, but only insofar as the one and the other exist by the decision that is also, fully and positively, for evil as much as for the good". In more general terms, thinking the positivity of evil entails that one acknowledge its inability to be resolved into the good, either theodesically or soteriologically: for if sense "turns into salvation, in one way or another, then it has lost the sense of sense, the sense of the world of existence that is and that is only toward this world". One might then be in a position to accept that redemption or salvation should not be permitted to be a discrete presupposition of any analysis of wickedness. Evil affirms itself as if "existence can grasp its own being as the essence" as the senseless insanity that closes off the aspect of existence that opens onto the need for sense. This is nowhere more obvious than in the example of the evil of extermination that erases the victims' distress from collective memory and renounces the possibility of each death having a sense. The question of the evil of sacrificing victims is reflexive: the sacrificers in the camps sacrificed themselves to evil, and in doing so, annulled the very thought of the sacrifice of sacrifice itself. The very rational operations of annihilation (the bureaucracy and technology of the camps) sacrificed freedom in the name of the affirmation of destruction (SW: 146; FT: 17, 69–70).

Unequivocally, Nancy maintains that one cannot dismiss evil's positivity as if it were merely a distortion of a decision about what is good. Nancy proposes that we think of "good and evil" as an equipollent polarity in which neither is the negation of the other, and this equipollence will inform every such decision about "good and evil". To "decide" for good over evil, then, is to deliberate over good and evil in such a manner as to decide for the scheme of good and evil as a means for assessing intentions and actions. But the traditional scheme of "good versus evil" already prioritizes the good of choosing the good, which locks the decision into a form of reflective immanence. Moreover, if one were to "decide for" evil, one would not merely "decide against" the good, as if the choice of evil were itself already determined to be evil, to ruin the very possibility of the good. "Wickedness causes evil by withdrawing from the good its possibility *in statu nascendi*", that is, it would "surprise" the good before its occurrence.[10] The rejected good is "stillborn", a good that was never fully open to sense. Devoid of any intentional meaning or consistency, wickedness rends the very promise of the good with an "infinite tenacity" (EF: 126). Terrible as this association is, it is one possible consequence of the finite thinking of the sense of evil's positivity.

Nancy refers to this "infinite tenacity" in wickedness as a "furious freedom", the "empirico-transcendental unleashing of freedom and fury". Freedom, in the wicked surprise of a quiescent good, unleashes itself against its own promise, against itself. Such a wicked freedom would necessarily need to hate itself (although in striving resolutely to negate itself it would merely affirm itself at the cost of the good). Almost shockingly, Nancy asserts that "being wicked is the first discernible positivity of freedom" because the fury of a wicked freedom and the grace of a good freedom are not equal if fury ruins the quiescent good. Endeavouring to realize itself as a Hegelian "pure freedom" in which there is an "unmediated passage into objectivity", it "annihilates" itself by devastating its own condition of freedom. In other words, the inveterate fury of wicked freedom removes the possibility of the choice between good and evil, since this fury is tenaciously self-annihilating of the very conditions of freedom that would make that choice possible. Freedom is at once the freedom from the necessity of choosing between good and evil; it is freedom for the relentless fury of total devastation. Indeed, it cannot be a "free choice" between good and evil, because every such choice implies that everything is good but that "evil" is merely a negative distortion of what is good, which further entails that freedom would be as incomprehensible as evil itself (EF: 133; FT: 139).

Finally, it should be obvious that Nancy is dismissive of theological concepts of evil that express a hatred of the world and a yearning to recreate a lost world. In more precise terms, wickedness is purely destructive of the very scheme by which the real and ideal worlds are opposed, not merely a "refusal of existence", real or ideal. It does not merely hate itself as singularity of freedom. It hates singularity as such, existence in all its singular aspects – freedom, equality and fraternity. If it is true that freedom can never be thought more genuinely than in the furious and ruinous choice of freedom, and freedom is implicated in the hatred of all singular existence, then "evil belongs to the essence or structure of freedom such as it has been freed and surprised in our history, as our history". If human history is a voracious ruination of the good, then the thought of the good is merely one of an indifferent negation of evil, a reserve of morality behind ethics, which could offer little moral consolation because it cannot obstruct the fury of historical evil. In such a history, every wicked perpetrator is an "outlaw", someone who has made a choice *against* the categorical imperative and thereby been abandoned by the moral law (EF: 128–30; SW: 145; FT: 140). Hence human wickedness expresses a hatred of existence as such by those whom the moral law has abandoned.

Conclusion

- Freedom, Nancy maintains, cannot be understood in terms of a "right" established rationally or juridically. Such an establishment would presuppose only strictly formal generalities about properties possessed by individuals. It cannot address the pure singularity of the thinking of freedom itself. To think of freedom in such terms is not to think freely, but to be bound by substantialist and immanentist criteria. Only a thinking that kept itself free for the thinking of freedom could possibly approach the radical singularity of freedom itself.

- This is especially true of Kant's notion of freedom as a "fact of reason", which produces only such general ontological conditions of the necessity of freedom in the very rational conception of freedom itself. Quite the contrary, Nancy remarks there would not be "facts of reason" at all, not even that of freedom, if freedom itself were not a "fact of existence" irreducible to but necessary for the establishment of reason. In other words, it is not reason that guarantees that reason itself must be the condition of freedom, but rather freedom that affirms itself despite any guarantees reason might make. Any such rationalist conception of freedom would suppress the singularity of freedom, not secure it; freedom itself would consist in the rebellion of existence against such suppression.

- Freedom should be comprehended as a singular "burst" in which singular beings express their existence, or rather, in which existence just is this expression. Such a burst will be completely anterior to any rational determinations of free selfhood and volition. It will also incessantly transgress all limits established rationally and juridically. Freedom, then, would not be an initiative of rationally inspired agency in control of its own exercises. Instead, it would be a surprising event of thinking the surprise of thinking in every free expression. Thinking would be a free burst of being surprised by the very surprising event of being free.

- Evil is not to be understood as a mere negativity, but rather as an aspect of singular existence that has a positivity all its own in its experience of a hatred of existence, of all singularities, indeed, even of morality. Such evil is not merely a distortion or perversion of the good, as if it were the good that were solely positive. On the contrary, wickedness shows its positive vitality when the singular being completely ruins goodness in its effort to affirm its own will against an anonymous existence. In order to understand the evils that surprise and horrify our history, we must bring ourselves to consider the possibility of evil's positive presence in the very affirmation of freedom itself.

CHAPTER 5

Post-secular theology

Nancy: atheist?

Nancy's position concerning contemporary religion and post-secular theology is unequivocal. He attacks not only the resurgence of religion in the social and political discourse of the West, but also the post-secular effort to show that religion has never been vanquished by secularization and retains all its vital significance in Western culture (albeit somewhat discordant and fragmentary in nature). He categorically dismisses post-secular theology's gesture of refusing secularization and awaiting the coming of a god as merely an activity of reflective immanence that closes us off from the undecidability of the future. Moreover, unremitting efforts to render divinity un-representable by fragmenting its signification through all cultural discourse (philosophy, ethics, legality, poetry, etc.) have served only to corrode the very nature of representation and disseminate "the god" into every "spiritual" activity culture entertains.

Generally speaking, Nancy rarely looks to religion for respectable addresses of discourse and, moreover, suggests that Christianity is especially deserving of deconstruction. Although Nancy speaks of Christianity as "empty", and deserving of further emptying, he does remark that the future of Christianity will be "the West coming out from the self-deconstruction of Christianity", a "to-come" that will not resemble traditional or contemporary versions of this faith (SDC: 5). We should be open to whichever form of "coming" comes, but that is not to say that this awaiting should be eschatologically charged with redemptive values. It would be difficult to ignore the rebuke in his claim that a "sickening traffic has grown up around a so-called return of the spiritual and of the religious", typified by the triumph of religion in post-Communist Poland, the demise of Communism, the emergence of Islam as a geopolitical force and so on (and one could add the religious revival at US universities). Elsewhere, Nancy refers to the "detestable effects of the sacralization of discourse", in which the names of the god remain "prey to sacerdotal arrogance, ecclesiastical love of power, not to mention clerical stupidity", even "prophetic bombast" that finds its way into political discourse. Furthermore, "all gods are odious", all sacrality oppressive, primarily because they "saturate the universe and exhaust mankind" by "closing off his humanity". Nancy pulls no punches when he writes that even St Paul plagiarized the "language of Hellenistic mystery religions", conveying a *"ressentiment* against the world, servility, and organization of weakness", and an "imperial" morality that should not be equated with "spirituality". Even the lapidary fashion of speaking of the "Other" blinds the singular mode of desire or hatred that makes "the other" divine or evil, a "mad desire" whose correlative is this "other" exclusive of the "originary interest" in the others of open community (IC: 122, 130, 138; BSP: 21, 135–6). In other words, worship and genocidal extermination are the obverse and reverse sides of this mad desire.

In more general reference to the "resurgence" of Western spirituality, Nancy exclaims witheringly that it is as if nothing at all has been learned from the relentless movement of reflective immanential thinking. With ideologies moribund, a fatuous spirituality is trumpeted stridently as the new cultural value for a "jaded" Western world. However, the return of religion, motivated by "stupidity or cunning", continues to be rendered "derisory" by the proclamation of the "death of God". To forget this "death" is to irreversibly vitiate the very conditions of thought available to us today; this forgetting has had an especially corrosive effect upon the finite thinking of singularities. Quite palpably, Nancy deplores the glutinous quality of religious discourse harmful to the human sciences. Ultimately, "we must not be blind to the danger today of a certain spiritual posturing, of a particular bland or sublime tone with which a 'sacred dimension' is 'rediscovered': it is one of the best signs of the absence of the gods" (IC: 122, 130). The dangerous vacuity of theological speculation has the merit of offering consolations at the expense of free enquiry into the sense of freedom and community in particular.

One of the most significant aspects of this refusal of the resurgence of the spiritual is, for Nancy, the necessary comprehension of the impossibility of the *sacrifice* necessary for ritual worship and faith in redemption. Religious sacrifice no longer involves anything more than the figure of the sacrificial victim, which is meaningful only in reference to an impossible exteriority. To insist either that "primitive" sacrifice (that of animals or other votive offerings) has been sublimated into the Christian consciousness of ritual is to continue the fallacy that we know what primitive sacrifice was. Nancy is adamant, however, that we have no knowledge of what an ancient Greek or even an early Christian regarded their sacrifices

to signify. He insists that pre-Christian sacrifice was not a "previous imita-
tion, a crude image of what transfigured sacrifice will henceforth bring
about" through the sacrifice-less sublimation of sacrifice itself. One might
surmise that the Christian transfiguration of sacrifice amounts to little
more than a *sacrifice of sacrifice itself*, that is, an unintelligible and
irresolvable aporia outrageously inadequate even for the rejuvenation of
"the spiritual". The figurative "sacrifice" of Christ is purportedly open to
all Christians as a uniquely universal spiritual transfiguration. Yet, despite
this universal accessibility, the very sacrifice definitive of Christian liturgy
is lacking, unknown – indeed, even impossible (FT: 51–9; BSP: 25). If one
grants that contemporary Christian "sacrifice" does not offer any opening
to an exteriority, then it is possible to conceive of it as nothing other than a
reflective immanential exercise in creating and playing back the figure of
sacrifice itself in a manner that forbids the finite thinking of the sense of
freedom and community.[1]

Conversely, in order to avoid lapsing into a weary humanism, Nancy repudiates any effort to divinize mankind. To situate man in the place of the
dead "God" is merely to offer another species of odious god. Humanism
repudiates the god/man relation that theology conceives, only then to base
itself on this repudiation: the god abandons us and then we abandon it.
Given the failures of both traditional theism and atheism, the only question remaining is one that is neither strictly theistic nor atheistic: how do
the figures of gods and man "appear" to one another and what are the
"spaces" that are the local figurative presences one might call "gods"? This
question reveals that Nancy is an atheist in the sense that he regards this as
the only question that could be addressed, and a very unconvincing theist
in discussing the behaviour of gods as suggestive motifs for comprehension
of the circulation of sense.

Nancy rejects metaphysical atheism on the grounds that it merely denies
the coherence of theistic affirmations and shares in its misconceptions.
Based on the "ontology of the Other and the Same" (BSP: 53), theistic and
atheistic argumentation offers only equipollently dubitable appropriations
of sense. One might speak of Nancy's position as "critical atheistic" in that
it is as critical of atheism's interplay with theism as it is of theistic schematics themselves. It deconstructs the conditions of the atheism–theism
dispute without lending a voice within it. The question is not whether a
god exists, or what essential properties it possesses, but rather *how* it
figures in empty sacred places. The result is that Nancy offers something
like a "natural history of religion", in which he writes of gods having
places and times, histories and geographies, or in other words, of idealities
figuring "religiously" in the plurality of human existence. Indeed, in one of
his most explicitly atheistic claims, he notes that atheism is "a matter of

opening the sense of the world" and getting rid of "demiurges and crea-
tors". In other words, to be atheistic, we must be committed to thinking of
sense in a manner that is stripped of the transcendental values of theistic
affirmations. However, it is precisely the finite thinking of the open immanence of the sense of the world that Nancy is advocating, and thus, by
extension, atheistic concatenations and consequences reverberate through
his work. Such reverberations preclude that Nancy's thought could play
into the hands of the theist and enable a religious critique of atheistic
discourse. Critical atheism implies that atheism has made its point effectively but has not divested itself of theistic presuppositions. Nothing
friendly to a religious apologetics is to be found in the notion that abandonment of and by the gods leaves behind little but devastation. Indeed,
the untenability of the faith–reason dichotomy can be taken right to the
point that faith in mystery itself has withdrawn along with the mystery of
faith. With mysterious and mystical revelations having withdrawn from
the possible, there is only "zero mystery", the mystery that there is no
mystery (SW: 158; IC: 132–3, 141). And sense must be thought in the context of such devastation, not, again, in reference to some transcendental
nexus of value.

Nancy's critical atheism consists in a demonstration of a paradox: on
the one hand, religion cannot speak the name of god without defiling it,
and thus it sacralizes discourse (thereby eradicating its ability to speak of
the unnameability of the god); and yet, on the other hand, there could be
no religious belief in a god who is undefiled by naming. Moreover, to insist
on the dissemination of divinity through culture and experience, as "post-
secular theology" does, leads to more complexly irresolvable paradoxes.
The foremost among these paradoxes involves salvation and redemption,
the need for which is categorically excluded by a finite thinking of the
sense of the world in open immanence. Nancy castigates salvation as a
symptom of the loss of the sense of the world itself that abrades the
integrity of finite thinking. He claims that one cannot save oneself or live
in a "saved" world if that requires adopting belief in the transcendental
condition of meaning. The suffering of the body of Christ cannot serve as
this originary condition, for it is now merely a figure of dislocation and
decay, a fragmented body whose particularization has none of the signification necessary for redemption. Hence the cross has been "disassembled", leaving us in our silent pity before the deposition of Christ's
suffering body (SW: 146–9). Again, it should be noted that this is no
friendly call for a refurbishment of the theological furnishings of the house
of a god, in the manner of post-secular thinkers. This is a wholesale
dismissal of the transcendentalist paradigm that salvation and redemption
ineluctably imply.

The lack of pronounceable names for an infinitely dying God

In post-Nietzschean thought, the "death of God" has become a denial that a god could ever possibly be what "God" has been thought to be. "Death of God" theology and other forms of post-secular thought have usurped this proclamation in order to reinforce the imperative of faith and the equally pressing need to explore the conditions of that faith. However, for Nancy, this demonstrates only an incomplete comprehension of the absolute epistemological and moral foundation that "God" allegedly provides. He insists that the proclamation of the "death of God" is the genuine recognition that the god is locked into an "ontological paralysis" in which it cannot be born into life and, since death is an absolute event, cannot be resurrected (BP: 51, 55; BSP: 150). One might surmise, then, that the celebration of its "numinosity" or "alterity", its saccharine "spirituality", is the result of its own ineradicable absurdity: it is underdetermined in the sense that it lacks basic properties of life and death, and overdetermined in the sense that this lack produces a plethora of outrageous claims about divinity. An irresolvable difficulty, monotheism continues to be the crystallization of certain divine abandonments in collective wisdom that linger despite the devastation of "the spiritual". It must be acknowledged that 'the death of God is the final thought of philosophy, which thus proposes it as an end to religion', a notion ceaselessly thought by the West but now achieving an ineradicable poignancy. This recognition entails that there can be no going back to any idyllic age of acceptance of this abandonment, nor even a more recent age in which there must be belief precisely despite this abandonment. There is now no single divine voice, but a plurality of differentiated voices that compose the "divine voice", the sharing "of" and "in" that composes community and the very condition of interpretation (IC: 128; SV: 237). And that is no suitable "divinity" at all.

Confidence that religion is indefatigable, that it always offers spiritual resources and consolations to make its own abandonment bearable, is now shaken. Religion has exhausted all its options, and thus can no longer put off the question of divinity with rhetorical convolutions and conceptual permutations. All that is left is "destitution before the empty temples", in which the god died because of the inseminating power of the West's reason, poetry, cupidity, generosity and even the "love of God" itself. The idols in those temples are not even subject(ible) to criticism, since they no longer correspond to any intelligible idea: the idols are no longer idols; there is nothing left but the "serene and secret, the unmoving smile of the gods". Of course, nothing is now sacrificed on their altars, and yet contemporary religion functions on the impossible presupposition that, in some loosely figurative sense, the altars represent sacrifice themselves. This is a sacrifice, it bears repeating, that we can no longer even conceive (IC: 141, 148; FT: 51–2). It might be concluded, then, that religion no longer has the ability to appease and console in the face of abandonment; it no longer possesses resources to palliate the consequences of this abandonment.

The very religious meaning of divine abandonment has often been posited as compensation for its unintelligibility. The incomprehensibility of a god's essence and existence is often deemed a uniquely self-evident argument in favour of theism: fideism requires that the god be incomprehensible because the god loses its meaning by virtue of the appropriation of its name into the paradigm of intelligibility (MMT: 95). However, Nancy recognizes a remarkable paradox in this conception. One might avoid the question of a god's existence by mulling potential descriptions of what it is; however, this avoidance presupposes the very solution to this question whose answer is not available to thought. On the one hand, we must say *that* a god exists, knowing that we may not be able to comprehend *what* it is; on the other hand, not knowing *what* it is calls into question our ability to say *that* it is. The inpredicability of a god's existence cannot lead us onwards to any recondite claim to the effect that a god is an "essence above all essence" or the very fact of its own being, each of which merely "defies the question, submerges it, and in that way satisfies it". Thus, "the divine is precisely what manifests itself and is recognizable outside of all knowledge about its 'being'" (IC: 110–15). In Nancy's terms, this question-begging reasoning satisfies its own conditions precisely because it is merely an incomprehensible answer that consolingly succumbs to this rebarbative demand. Specifically, "the god is incomprehensibly incomprehensible" is hardly an achievement of either faith or reason.

What value, then, does the name of 'God' have? Generally speaking, divine names fail in the exscriptive way that all names fail in the face of things. Instead of presupposing some wondrous "this" or "that" beyond all naming, we should recognize that for all things there is merely a 'deprivation' of names in the ungrounded "fragility of being" (BP: 175; FT: 113). Under Nancy's anti-fideistic purview, on the one hand, if a god is not a singular being, then "God" is not a proper name; on the other, if it is incomprehensible, it cannot possess the properties that it must possess if "God" is to be a common name. In either case, to name the god is to anticipate the very insufficiently determinate essence under enquiry. Instead, Nancy proposes that the name suggests only a self-referential operation of naming. What a god is, and indeed even that it is, is implied indeterminately within the very operation of naming it. There is obvious circularity here as well: "God" designates the very propositional property of divinity that makes it possible to designate a "God", a property, it is worth repeating, that is indeterminate and therefore calls for the question; but if it were not inerrable, it would remove the very need for that question. Tradition, then, has cleverly espoused a scandalously improper convention in which the proper name designates the unnameable. To name "God" is merely to provide a common name that properly serves as a proper noun when the object of devotion lacks reference. Such a being can be understood as singular in so far as it is precisely the being whose name cannot be pronounced. Hence, again, the operation of naming the God is "proper" when doing so implies the intention of naming only the unnameable. To say "My God" is to designate the operation of naming according to one's own pronouncement. This utterance is a singular operation in which one singular being (the subject of the utterance) stands in a privileged relationship with the very singular being upon which it calls. The resurgent question, then, is whether even the singular being that prostrates itself before the unnameable one has the right or even the ability to make this utterance. But of course, yet again, it is controversial whether one can know this about the name of a god without implying that something of the unnameable one's essence is intelligible. Although Nancy does not explicitly propose it, one might say that the necessarily improper naming of the unnameable singular entity is a scandal to the very minimal reason implied in uttering such a name.

Much of this revolves on the traditional monotheistic preconception of a god as being singular precisely because it defies the logic of singularity. "God" is often presented as an entity whose origin is uniquely in itself (as with the lazy thought of *causa sui*), external to the created order, in an existence in which it creates itself without merely being created. However, Nancy notes that there is proof of a god's nonexistence: "the originarity of the origin is not a propensity that would distinguish a being from all others, because this being would then have to be something other than itself in order to have its origin in its own turn" (BSP: 11). In other words, the absolute self-referentiality of a god's existence is determined by what one can and cannot say about it: the entity that "God" denotes is neither singular nor universal, but acquires a universal significance when its unnameability determines it as a uniquely singular being. That is, it is the only being that is singularized precisely because it is unnameable, or rather, its name is necessarily inadequate in the operation of calling on it.

Theology has always been ready to bear the impossible thought of a representation of the non-representable, as post-secular thought will attest. Theologically speaking, Nancy observes, the Other implies its non-representability, which gives rise to an interdiction of representation of the sacred itself; but given atheological commitments, this is a "denial of representation", an Other that oppresses the possibility of representation itself (BSP: 48). In so far as the Christian "God" retreats from representation because it does not present itself, it creates a "double bind", in which constraint on the very order of representation itself is produced (SDC: 4–5). The divine "other" is equivalent to its own being, to Being itself, not equipollent to its properties (qualities, functions or actions). Such a mono-theistic god is not merely a single god among gods, with whom it would share divinity (no matter in what infinitely more exalted fashion it might possess it). On the contrary, monotheism, implying the ontotheology of the pre-eminence of "God" *qua* being, establishes only that "divinity is equiva-lent to being, and its qualities and actions depend upon the fact of being". It is radically distinct from quixotic polytheism, which, in its innocence, posits no pre-eminence among gods or between gods and other beings. Although a divinity is not coterminous with any (or all) of its properties, immortality would be the property shared by gods, and thus divinity is shared among beings. Such gods "do not make up a group of figures of one divine. They do all partake together of divine immortality, but this divine quality does not exist by itself" (IC: 112). Hence to ask "Who?" a god is is to ask which one it is, to pick out its distinctness among similar beings and not its pre-eminence among beings.

Most broadly, Nancy identifies an unsavoury paradox in the thought that an appearing god would propose itself in such a way as to eliminate the very possibility of the question "what is God?" Such a question has significance only if there is nothing left of the divinity of "God", nothing that proposes itself as divine any longer. But, as we shall see, the divinity of the god has been not only buried beneath the rubble of the Western tradi-tion, but also fragmented and disseminated, rendered indistinguishable from multifarious cultural forms (poetry, subject, etc.), as post-secular thought propounds. Nonetheless, it is not even clear how it would be possible to ask the question, since the question whose solution we are seek-ing has so many opaque formulations. Hence, bizarrely, we can ask what a god is only when it would be impossible to answer; but if we were to know that it exists (proposes itself), it would be impossible even to ask what it is.

More generally, although it is often believed that one can simply not say enough about a god that is incomprehensible, Nancy conjectures that "there is nothing more to be said about God", because its theme or ques-tion "no longer means anything to us". Perhaps Nancy is submitting that, within the limits of contemporary discourse, "God" has been exhausted through inordinate dissemination. According to a desperate theistic strata-gem of post-secular thought, represented by thinkers as disparate as Emmanuel Levinas and Jean-Luc Marion,[2] the concept of god has dissi-pated into a plethora of forms, such as "infinity", "Other", "Being", "Enigma" and so on. Curiously, such thinking implies that "death of God" philosophy has done religion a favour: the old concept was always inadequate, and thus easily dissipated into myriad forms, and this "death" has provided an opportunity to discover what the god has always genuinely been (BSP: 19, 77, 199). Efforts such as Levinas's to conjoin the "Otherness" of the god with the otherness of a "common, indifferent and interchangeable" other are untenable on the grounds that they do not reflect an appreciation of the depth of the challenge the "death of God" ineluctably poses (FT: 124). Nancy addresses the capacity of this rethinking to satisfy its own requirements.

> What the theme of God might mean to us has already moved or been carried entirely outside of him. Is there any statement about the divine that can henceforth be distinguished, strictly speaking, from another about "the subject" (or its "absence"), "desire," "history," "others" (*autrui*), "the Other," "being," "speech" (*la parole*), "the sublime," "community," and so on and so forth? It is as if "God" were in fragments, an Osiris dismembered throughout all our discourse (indeed there are those who will now continue to speak of the divine in terms of explosion, dispersal, suspension, etc.). As if the divine, God, or the gods formed the common name or place – common and as such erasable, insignificant – of every question, every exigency of thought: wherever thought comes up against the furthest extreme, the limit, against truth, or ordeal (*l'épreuve*), in short wherever it thinks, it encounters something that once bore, or seems to have borne, at one time or another, a divine name.   (IC: 112)

In other words, Nancy rejects the notion that, although the singular thoughts of a god's existence and essence are impossible, one might celebrate a divinity that is saturated throughout thinking and language (as if a fragmented god were revealing itself as such in the variegated forms of its own absence). In yet other terms, for Nancy the god and its divinity are now merely corrosive aspects of thinking and language. For example, Nancy challenges Jean-Luc Marion's thought, in which difference among beings is all that the "modern" mind might think precisely because of the lack of an absent divinity against whose incomprehensibility one might think the "fullness of metaphysical being". However, Nancy insists that "God disappears even more surely and definitively through bearing all the names of a generalized and multiplied difference" (IC: 113).

Broadly construed, post-secular thought dissolves monotheism into a *polyatheism*, in which all forms of a god are diluted into ontological and anthropological schemes, saying nothing about the god and leaving nothing about it to be said. The temptation to find divinity "traced" in human experience, as if the god left a trace of itself (or a "trace of a trace") in passing (as in Levinas's famous formula) is one that Nancy insists must be avoided.[3] Even if each trace were representative of an absent name, the resulting overdetermination would be more than credulity could bear. Since the unnameability of a god is not merely a matter of being inaccessible to naming, dispersing divinity in this fashionable manner does not surmount the difficulty of naming the unnameable. Specifically, although tradition implies that divinity is the surplus reserve of the meaning of religious belief, Nancy maintains that the proper name of "God" does not function like a sign, as if there were a metaphysical excess of reality beyond the name itself. Today the problem is that names are lacking sense, which is not to say that the names are insufficiently potent, but actually that they are no longer *names of divinity*. There is no divinity hidden behind names and appearance, only the manifestation of a lack of meaningful names, by which one can no longer offer praise and against which one can no longer even blaspheme. The scheme in which the revealed conceals the real remains unthinkable in the absence of names for divinity. "The lack of sacred names is not a surface lack concealing and manifesting the depths of a sacred held in reserve. It bars the way to the sacred, the sacred as such no longer comes (*advient*), and the divine is withdrawn from itself." In other words, one cannot assume that the lack of names changes nothing; on the contrary, the collapse of sense into immanence entails that the lack of names indicates a lack of the sacred altogether. Furthermore, the very practice of religion and the value of faith are at stake in this problem of signification. To pray is to name a singular god, but if names are lacking, then this prayer is "suspended": to recite prayers is, in the absence of a name, merely an address of a "lack of prayer to a lack of a sacred name, it is a litany laid bare". Genuflection being impossible because of the lack of sacred names, the believer now merely quotes a prayer in a non-sanctified language (IC: 118–21, 141, 148). For post-secular theology, this suggests that all discourse about love, the beautiful or nature itself is sanctified in the tracing of the god's absence. But, Nancy interjects:

> Why not recognize, on the contrary, that thought in this age of ours is in the process of wrestling from so-called theology the prerogative of talking about the Other, the Infinitely-other, the Other-Infinite. It is taking away from theology the privilege of expressing the absconditum of experience and discourse.
>
> (IC: 113)

Discourses about forms of transcendence are no longer the exclusive property of theology, precisely because theology was forced to redefine transcendence in such a secularly accessible fashion that it has lost hegemony over them. Even to speak of a god is to risk "the detestable effects of the sacralization of discourse". If the fragmented and absent god is discernible in, say, poetry, that does not enable the theologian to cling to a desperate faith in this god, but rather *enables the secularist to wrest poetry's transcendent value from the theologians*. One might suggest, then, that theology must relinquish the claim that *anything* "transcendent" is indicative of the absence of a once-present god. Nancy is emphatic in his pronouncement that it is no longer possible to name every lack of sense "God" because that would provide some absolute foundation and even, by theological lights, to blaspheme against a god by imposing an inappropriate predicate onto its subjectivity. Moreover, Nancy proposes rhetorically, there must be something illicit in the constant movement of debaptizing and rebaptizing forms of divinity: now it is, and now it is not, the subject; now it is, and now it is not, the sublime, and so on and so on.

If a god has become every exigency or limit of thought, then it is quite justifiable to ask whether it has a place within the discourse about the sense of the world. Only in such a context would it be worthwhile to designate it with the name "God". Unfortunately, Nancy continues, answers to the question of whether a god exists and what it is that exists cannot specify the place within which something would be worthy of this name. Since there appear to be many "places" within which it would be discernible (each of which is one in which there appears to be no means for distinguishing the god from something else), one needs to extricate oneself from the tangle of competing loci in order to address the question. If creation is merely the "brilliance" in which the god comes to presence, then even if one speaks of it as a transcendental figure of this unique creation, one must still enquire about the singularity of the local tracing, of places as "divine" spacings. Nancy offers the interesting suggestion that there are many places in which gods could be named (although it is not apparent that they merit names at all): those they have abandoned and those where they hide, those bound to hearth and home, and those that are nomadic; gods common to all places and a god with a common place and so on. There is, after all, a "desire for the Position", a "desire to fix the origin, or to give the origin to itself", in such a manner that the other is identified as Other (God). But if traces are singular, local places, if each divinity is merely a spacing composing a place, then this desire for a fixed Position is necessarily unrequited (IC: 114; BSP: 17, 21). "God", it must be said, is merely the name of an absence that floats through cultural discourses and practices. It no longer signifies anything at all, not even the sense of absence itself.

With considerable eloquence, Nancy describes godless "divine places" as approachably open and ubiquitously generous with divinity. Providing transcendentalist means by which the world's sense is spaced, they are no longer mere temples, but spacings that exhibit only destitution in the absence of a god. The temples have become "divine spaces", beyond which and within which there is no "reserve" of the divinity of a god. They nurture no "sacred enclosures" within which that reserve could be protected. Their spacings merely call us to find our own pathways, not to orient ourselves around the numinous divinity they no longer enfold (IC: 150; SV: 237). Once we understand that there is no surplus or reserve of transcendence beyond these spacings, it is possible to enquire into the sense of the world in which the destitute sacred places figure. Moreover, it would also be necessary to enquire into the finite sense of that world and the commensurately finite thinking that renders it accessible to cognition.

Transimmanence: Nancy's naturalistic thesis

Although it might prove ultimately unedifying, one might recognize that there is a naturalistic strain throughout Nancy's critique of religion, especially in his view of the "transimmanence" of the sense of the world and in his emphasis on the linguistic inability to utter anything meaningful about transcendence. Given that monotheism merely effaces the very divinity it proposes incomprehensibly (BSP: 15), we must seriously consider the possibility that the world is all there is, and nothing more need be conceived. After all, it is coextensive with the plural singularity of the coming to presence of sense, within which all things come to presence. One might refer to this as Nancy's naturalistic thesis: there is neither transcendence, present or traced, nor any need for discourse of it.

The vertiginous seductiveness of monotheism's transcendence may be the result of a hermeneutic prerequisite for the symbolic in terms of an expansive religious sentiment (SV: 214). Indeed, theology itself, he proposes critically, presupposes the biblical figures of trace and passage, as described so vividly by Emmanuel Levinas. "God" passes, leaving a trace of itself, a trace that does not efface it in the vestige of spirituality left behind this passage. For instance, Nancy suggests that art, even religious iconography, is merely a "vestige without God", not a (re)presentation of an Idea beyond the iconic figure itself. Religious art, then, is not "image-art", art that presents an image through which the divine exterior shines. Neither is it any "vestige-art" believed to let such exteriority shine immanently. In the absence of sense, religious art is now atheistic because it presents only the sensible divorced from its divine aura (M: 96–9; MMT: 96). If "art" is produced from the conditions of open community and retains something of its evocations (C: 387), then a "religious" art is now strictly an impossibility.

96

Both of these affirmations – of a trace of a god and a vestige of this trace in iconography – are standard stratagems of the post-secular thought rejected by Nancy.

Generally speaking, the introduction of the notion of traces of divinity does not rectify traditional theological limitations. It merely extends them into contexts in which they serve as figures of absurdity. Nancy argues that a necessarily existing being could be no "supplement" to the world, which has no supplement other than itself and "its" origin (which, if the world is "everything", is *the* origin) (BSP: 11; SW: 148–9). Elsewhere, he maintains that the "constantly recurring error" of post-secular thinking that being itself is God must be expurgated. A god is not "the god" of being, he insists, but merely a being that is the god of man. Such a god is in no way supreme among beings, but merely the being we are not, a being which is no longer available to discourse and which merely "appears or disappears before the face of the existing, mortal beings we are". Since creation is the incessant re-creation of sense in the experience of singular beings, "God" is no singular creator or source of sense. If this is the case, then there is nothing more to the divine than the lack of sacred names beyond knowledge, "visible and legible everywhere" precisely as such complete and irreversible destitution. Perhaps Nancy is suggesting that it is only the strangeness of the god as a "singular, bare presence" that could make sense of the strangeness of each singular being surprised by its own freedom (IC: 115, 120, 125–31). Here Nancy's naturalism reaches its zenith: the existence of the world discounts the existence of a god, which is to say that "there is" does not include the god and the sense of this world is available only when the notion of the god does not mediate in thinking of the sense of the world. "There is" means there is a world, the "there" designating the whole of the world, such that "there is" that there is. There is no Other, he insists, nor is the "there is" an Other, just the "punctual and discrete spacing between us". Moreover, there is no mysterious quality or spiritual dimension that would add itself to the plurality of bodies and things in which the material spatialization of a world consists. "Spatialization – space and time – first of all makes up, or entrances, existence qua liability to meaning." There is no reference for the thought of a singular creator of a single instance of creation (the origin or absolute matrix of the world cannot also be the senseless origin of sense). Creation is an excess of creative potency within the world itself, Nancy remarks; the physical fluctuations and constants of the universe are themselves the universe's creation (BSP: 19, 181–2; SW: 156–7). Against the transcendentalist commitments of theology and post-secular theology, Nancy insists that sense is produced from and in a world, or in other words, meaning adheres to the things of the world themselves, and cannot be divorced from the plurality of singular bodies. Indeed, Nancy propounds, meaning itself could only be thought naturalistically, which is to say without a "metaphysical surfeit" outside the world.

> In truth, if one understands by world a "totality of signifyingness or significance (*signifiance*)," no doubt there is no philosophy that has thought a beyond of the world. The appearance of such a thought and of the contradiction it entails comes from the Christian sense of world as that which precisely lacks all sense and has its sense beyond itself. In this sense, moreover, sense itself is a specifically Christian determination or postulation that supposes a step beyond the cosmos to which *agathon* still belongs. To this very degree, that which we have to think henceforth under the title of sense can consist only in the abandonment of Christian sense or in an abandoned sense. Which one can also put like this: sense – if it is still or finally necessary to do justice to the obstinate request of this word – can proceed only from a deconstruction of Christianity. (SW: 54–5)

In other words, it is necessary to deconstruct the conditions in which Christianity colours discourse of sense. In particular, the tendency to understand all interpretation as modelled on biblical interpretation, and thus to determine the dependence of all discourse on religious values, is especially needful of deconstruction. The problem is that, traditionally speaking, sense is a "Christian determination" of a surplus of meaning outside the cosmos, yet there is "only" a world. Thinking finitely of sense demands that no such otherworldly surplus be implied. The deconstruction of Christianity would require that thinking be maintained along the elliptical trajectory of the collapse of sense; that is, to look truth in the face, the truth that there is only the world. Although all of the great motifs of Christian dogma necessarily require deconstruction, especially the Christian determination of truth that God is infinitely perfect, Christianity itself provides the means by which this deconstruction is possible. Christianity is not a religion, but an "exit from religion", for primarily this reason: it demands its own deconstruction with the question "What does this mean?" (SV: 213; SW: 32, 148; BSP: 200; DC: 512–13; SDC: 3–4).

The task of a deconstruction of Christianity, then, would be to discern the constitutive sense of a world despite the accretions of monotheistic values. It would require that we think of "transimmanence", the sense that circulates across the world and surfaces whenever the fact that there is a world is addressed. Art, through which the trajectory of sense is discernible despite the lack of sacrality it exhibits, possesses the sense of sacrality precisely when it is not at the service of worship. However, Nancy enquires mischievously, would we not need to "have done with the divine" if art itself is the exclusive domain of "sacrality"? This suggests that the primary role or operation for art is to manifest the divine in a polyatheistic fashion (gods come and go, reveal and conceal themselves, yet their sacrality is bound strictly to the manifestations of art). It is important to notice the shift from singular god to plural "gods". The transimmanent trajectory of sense opens the possibility of a "sense the absence of which makes no sense" (IC: 129–31; FT: 52; SW: 131). Obviously, Nancy will have no truck with the notion that the absence of a god is a trace of its absent presence, although he does laud the notion of divinity only in so far as its transimmanent sense reveals the multiple reticulations of the circulation of sense.

The impossibility of theology's usurpation of Nancy

It has become commonplace for some theologians, especially those who describe themselves as "radical", to strive to usurp the perspectives of atheistic, or at least alternative, perspectives on gods, religion and mankind. Thinkers whose thought is in no way friendly to religious perspectives have been utilized in an effort to rejuvenate religious philosophy. For example, Graham Ward has remarked that Nancy's critical atheism can assist post-secular thought.

> His critical thinking could help Christian theologians then to reconsider the nature and function of the ecclesial body – made up as it is of so many diversely located and temporally dislocated physical bodies, working in, through and beyond local, national and institutional bodies to figure forth the global body of Christ. Nancy could help theology to rethink bodies and corporeality, notions fundamental to Jewish and Christian forms of incarnationism.[4]

However, co-opting Nancy in this way would be the result of a rather serious miscontextualization. His notion of the symbol excludes the possibility of any multiplicity of bodies "figuring forth" any global body of Christ, which could only surge up from a pregnant enclosure beyond the open immanence of insubstantial community. In other words, a Christian symbolics could only inform us of the sense of the body, but the task of a finite thinking is to approach the question of the singularity of the body as origin of sense itself. In *The Birth to Presence*, Nancy confesses some distaste for the mystical and/or negative theological notion of a scandalously impenetrable "glorious body". He insists that "I did not deduce the discourse of these fragments from the thought of a glorious body. On the contrary, the phrase from the Gospels [*Noli me tangere*] came first, alone, to my ear." For Nancy, the "ecclesial" body is "capable of becoming horrifying, massive, destructive of its members and itself, a society burned at the stake by its Church, its Myth, or its Spirit". Although such a community can regard itself as standing in the place of the god, to be present for a god in reflective immanence, an open and insubstantial community is without communion, mediation by divine countenance or the corrupting values of its institutional religion. Hence, if theology were to be "helped" by Nancy's critical thinking of singularity, it would necessarily overlook the various deconstructions that facilitated that critique. Since Christianity as a system of assurances of an "other" world is finished (see interview), it is Christianity alone that can help philosophy to understand the prevailing onto-theologic that fosters technology and globalization (BSP: 273–4; IC: 143–4; SDC: 1–5). But philosophy is not available to a Christian reading that might help rejuvenate theology, since Christianity itself provides, on the one hand, the problems of presence and representation philosophy has inherited, and, on the other, the deconstructive means by which to approach them. More generally, for Nancy the point is to "empty" Christianity even further, to facilitate its self-deconstruction to the point of reducing it to the philosophical. Ward continues:

> Furthermore, Nancy's thinking (its insights and dangers), which is ultimately monistic, requires theology to give an account of the analogy whereby difference is accepted, celebrated and allowed to stand within commonality such that the pluralizing of difference does not lead to indifference. This is the danger of Nancy's thinking, for if "we know that it is all for nothing, to no other purpose than to exist", the celebration of difference can become a celebration of indifference. A new construal of the analogy of being is required, based upon a new construal of presence as both communion and communication. Nancy points a way ahead but the Christian symbolics of his discourse need to be foregrounded and reinvested with a theological content.[5]

However, there is no such "symbolics" capable of being divorced non-violently from Nancy's deconstruction. In *The Muses*, Nancy makes it clear that he will have no truck with any "symbolics" in which art offers a figure of transcendence whose vestige alone remains in the wake of a god's passing. On the contrary, such a "symbolics" would now lack the privilege of this openness to exteriority. It no longer makes the invisible visible in a figure, no longer suggests a trace of exteriority or the passing of a transcendent god. Elsewhere, Nancy observes that symbols do not represent social relations, as a Christian "ecclesial body" implies, but instead compose the singularities constitutive of social realities (M: 89; BSP: 57–9). Ultimately, such a Christian symbolics offers no potential finite thinking of the sense of the world.

Indeed, even if there were a Christian symbolics in Nancy's thought, there would be no obvious compatibility with Christianity's theoretical constraints. After all, Nancy maintains that although Christ is the prototype of mediation, what is needed is an immanence of immediacy, "mediation without a mediator", in which there would be a "crossing" between singularities but no "cross". Obviously, deconstruction of Christianity would entail some highly nuanced challenge to Christology and the "theology of the cross" as well as the creationist paradigm that Christianity generally, and incarnationism specifically, requires. Although Ward warns that Nancy celebrates "indifference", it is precisely in institutional religion that Nancy vituperates the indifference of communion that composes the "ecclesial" body of faith. In addition, to superimpose a "Christian symbolics" on to a thought that has endeavoured to deconstruct any symbolics of religious commitment would be to ignore the coruscating tone that so frequently resonates in Nancy's alternative atheistic and naturalistic perspectives. On an earlier occasion, Ward refers to a "nihilism" in Nancy from which "theology has little to fear" because "out of nothing God did and does create something" (BSP: 57–9, 94–5; BP: 182; CMM: 56; SW: 149; IC: 113). Yet, as we have seen, Nancy denies that Ward could use the name of God so casually, or that the problem of an original creation could be so patently ignored. After all, Nancy's critical atheism is unequivocal in its insistence that there is but destitution in the wake of the gods: empty temples shorn of sanctity, idols that merely smile imperturbably, recitations of desacralized prayers to no longer even unnameable gods, the impossibility of faith in vanished gods, the mysterious lack of mystery and theological obscurantism.

In brief, theology would need to violate Nancy's thought, to ignore its "nihilistic" tones and to make ostensible appropriations in order to render it pertinent. And what would be chosen would be less interesting, or at least less genuinely Nancean, than what would be overlooked.

Conclusion

- Nancy could be said to offer an "atheistic" thought, but this should be understood in terms of an effort to disrupt the traditional theism–

atheism dichotomy by deconstructing religion itself. Atheism being indebted to theistic paradigms, it can only be said that the condition of the erasure of Christian values is not only possible in itself, but necessary for any finite thinking open to the future of sense.

- The very concept of "the god" has emptied itself of signification by virtue of its multifaceted but vacuous roles in discourse and the absence of any "reality" beyond its significations. It now merely plays a role in the reflective immanence of religion, an immanence that is possible precisely because of its vacuity.

- Post-secular efforts to fragment the notion of "God" and disseminate its meaning through "traces" in "secular" discourse and practice results only in a polyatheism, a lack of reference for the many empty names of the "god".

- "Transimmanence" is Nancy's term referring to the movement of sense across discourses about "the god", a movement that occurs even when the notion of "God" is emptied of significance. When there is nothing but "open" immanence, that is, when there is no exteriority beyond the circulation of sense, then all the various references to divinity serve only to refer to a vacancy of sense that itself has sense without being reducible to any religious paradigm.

- Although Nancy's thought is (non-traditionally) atheistic, it is not a stance that religious discourse can appropriate or undermine. Nancy is not merely offering yet another secular discourse of "the body" that can be taken up and put to religious use. On the contrary, it is precisely such an appropriation that Nancy insists would forbid any enquiry into the singularity of the sense of the body in plurality, or into the sense of the body's singularity.

CHAPTER 6

Communitarianism

Jean-Luc Nancy identifies a major anxiety definitive of modern identity in this (post-)*fin de siècle*: the dissolution of community at a time when it is thought to be formative of certain democratic institutions and, by extension, political resistance to the overweening State, a voracious capital and nefarious forms of globalization. He is clearly ambivalent about communitarianism, which is, roughly speaking, an effort to revitalize ideals of social and communal relationships against the onslaught of the kinds of 'liberal' notions of freedoms and rights addressed in Chapter 4. In other words, Nancy is critical of *both* communitarianism and its liberal targets: he rejects the essential nature of, on the one hand, "liberal" notions of universal "rights" and the "liberty" to pursue one's own good and, on the other, communitarian notions of culturally informed relationships revolving around basic social goods. Moreover, he is suspicious of the notion of "the State" as it figures essentially on both sides of this dichotomy. Indeed, he regards communitarianism's stress upon an equilibrium between social forces and the individual, or specifically between the responsibilities the former requires and the rights the latter must demand, as a *symptom* of a profound and prevailing misconception about community.

What he finds especially objectionable about all contemporary notions of community is the effort to comprehend it as a *substantial* entity consisting of *substantial* individuals who reflect *immanently* upon themselves in order to fashion traditions of symbolic order that define "community" as such. In brief, Nancy rarely responds point for point to the communitarianism (however individually reluctant and collectively disparate) of Charles Taylor, Michael Walzer, Michael Sandel, Amitai Etzioni, or, of course, Alasdair MacIntyre.[1] Instead, Nancy is aiming at the substantialist metaphysics and closed immanence that contemporary conceptions of community (including those of the communitarians) imply, not at specific dimensions of relationship, social cohesion, tradition and so on. It might be said that Nancy's critiques of communitarian nostalgias, myths and social reality are epiphenomenal, or at least subordinate to his more profound concern with the "crisis of sense".

The guiding lights of communitarianism are, by differing accounts, Aristotle and Hegel, yet the substantialist, essentialist and teleological commitments of these thinkers are placed under rather intense critical scrutiny in Nancy's work. Above all, perhaps, reading Nancy on community might leave the reader with a lingering sense that community is understood in less formal terms than in the fashionable communitarian theories. For example, Nancy is most captivated by an inversion of the Heideggerian emphasis on the *Seinsfrage* (the question of being) over the *Mitseinsfrage* (the question of being-with), understood in terms of, most specifically, sharing, contact, singularity and the circulation of sense. These are concepts, it must be said, that are not easily appropriated into communitarian discourse, nor even compared with its more empirical orientations. At any rate, although there might be a glimmering of similarity between, say, Nancy's notion of sharing and the communitarian conception of social ties, ultimately there is an incommensurability between them, a lack of translatability and coextensivity in their descriptions. This is not to say that there are no conceivable points of engagement between Nancy and communitarian theory. After all, he is insistent that, despite the ubiquitous distress about the vertiginous expressions of its disintegration in the crisis of sense, many issues worthy of philosophical prodding (such as sense, myth, freedom and personal identity) are interleaved in the meshes of the crisis of community's fragmentation. However, it must be emphasized that such points of contact are not immediately edifying since they require a radical re-contextualization that is not always beneficial to an understanding of Nancy's thought of "the community of being".

For Nancy, the question of community is posed on many social registers of thought, especially those involving social being, being-many, being-with-one-another and so on. Nancy's intuition, strictly speaking, is that although the metaphysics of *substantial* "community" that communitarianism presupposes is now discreditable (and in many respects impossible), certain communal phenomena provide conditions of thought that are prefigured in the notion of an "inoperative" community: an open, circulating space of sharing which cannot be politically appropriated.[2] It is tempting, but ultimately facile, to try to thrust this into a communitarian context. Generally speaking, he maintains that the contemporary ontological question appertains to the open "community of being", not to the communitarian "being of community" (BC: 1). An open or insubstantial community is one composed of a welter of instantaneous creations of new spacings of the world. It consists of the "common" or "banal" linkages of sharing that compose being in everyday life. Such linkages, it merits emphasizing, are not reducible to substantialist and immanentialist paradigms, but are precisely disruptive or interruptive of them (C: 384–5). Perhaps it is here that the increasing divergence between Nancy and communitarianism takes place. If such a condition of banal sharing is necessary for the intelligibility of community and the condition of communication, then the very status of thinking today is enmeshed in the question of community. But this thinking must be finite, that is to say, it must give rise to singular thoughts about singular events that do not merely give way to the universalist values that the very communitarian notions of "community" ineluctably produce. Although communitarians are perhaps misguided to assume that philosophical revisions can simply "think" community and its elusive meaning in terms of traditional perspectives (e.g. Aristotle and Hegel), contemporary thinking itself is intersected at vital points by this problem of the "others" and the "we". As Ignaas Devisch has pointed out, for Nancy it is now necessary to conceive of a "community of finitude" in terms of the "dissemination" of "original presence", which is to say that such "insubstantial community" is a conceptual possibility within the circulation of sense (BSP: 77).[3] Yet communitarianism, to be sure, does not acknowledge any such dissemination or insubstantiality.

Communitarianism has inherited both this anxiety and many of the traditional paradigms that, according to Nancy, fail even to address the question of the essence of insubstantial community. Notoriously difficult to define, communitarianism rejects the prevailing liberal theories that imply a vision of separated "atomic" individuals divorced from any communal or traditional context. It often insists that communities are configured by collective memories that determine their responses to specific communal difficulties as well as by a language that provides resources for doing so.[4] There are also shared constitutive or definitive characteristics, expressive of preferences and aversions that shape an individual's appraisal of its community's formation and the role of an individual within it. However, we have addressed enough of Nancy's thought in the preceding chapters to be able to acknowledge that he inverts these priorities. Community does not consist of a collection of individuals and their personal dispositions. Instead, all of the linkages of sharing that interrupt such collectivization and reject its substantial and operative cohesion constitute the "sense" of community. Community, in other words, is not an aggregation of individuals, but, rather crudely, something very much like a "feeling" at the moments of sharing in contact between irreducibly singular beings who do not even share the property of "belonging together" in a cohesive group.

On a separate register of thought, Nancy disavows the communitarian hermeneutic of the "lost" community to which we can return or which can be regained (although the return to the origin is always possible if one acknowledges the threat of closure of the hermeneutic circle of under-standing and belief itself). Living in an age in which the fact–fiction dichotomy is always destructively superimposed upon mythic discourse, we lack the means to form cohesive substantial communities in which one's personal identity is clearly delineated on the inside of reflective immanence. However, he insists that it must be admitted that community of the closed immanential kind has always been an impossible myth. "There is no communion of singularities in a totality superior to them and immanent to their common being", only the communicability that precludes the possibility of mimetically reflective myth. Even though communion of this kind is inaccessible to the modern mind, community itself has not dissipated. Indeed, community today is precisely what it has always been: a sharing in the vulnerabilities, fragilities, sufferings and mis-fortunes of human existence. Community is an open spacing of others that excludes the possibility of foundation, even the foundation seemingly created from the exclusion of others. It is this sharing, this "being-with" or co-appearance to one another as such vulnerable beings, that constitutes insubstantial community. Community is this shared but always irreducible and unavowable experience that consists of fragmented singular selves related to one another along trajectories of existence (SV: 214; IC: 28; C: 392).[5] This sharing serves as the groundlessness that singularizes and differentiates beings as such. Conceiving of singular resistances (such as death) that disrupt the ever-threatening closure of substantial communities under given conventions and that open singular beings to the circulation of sense is both necessary for, and frustrating of, any contemporary concep-tion of community. It is in the very condition of plurality, or more specifi-cally, of the voices that serve as interruptions of the sharing of the *logos* itself, that a notion of social reality can take shape (SV: 247).

Therefore, "substantial" community consists in the coming together of predetermined and autonomous individuals that reflect upon themselves in terms of a cultural symbolics. Since Nancy wishes to avoid such "a With or a We as a Great Subject that swallows the individual up", in Ignaas Devisch's phrase,[6] "insubstantial" community is nothing other than the various trajectories of relationships that finite individuals share among themselves. It is the task of "finite thinking" to address the conceptual pos-sibilities of the latter and resist the temptations of the former, especially in the terms communitarianism so frequently expounds.

Nostalgia for lost community

Nancy takes special umbrage at the communitarian implication that community has been or is being "lost", that only individuals result from this disintegration, and that there is some justification for nostalgia for the glorious past of community.[7] He maintains that communitarianism rests on unestablished yet unchallenged presumptions about the dialectic nature of history responsible for our inability to think community. The concepts it superimposes upon the thought of this formative experience devastate our ability to think its singularity. In particular, it obscures more basic singular events that constitute sharing among finite beings. It is no accident that its intellectual avatars are Aristotle, who offers insights about the kinds of immanence possessed by community, and Hegel, who demonstrates how this immanence was subverted and "lost" in a dialectical play of socialization and individualization. Both of these notions of community presuppose general reflective paradigms of community in which individual persons come together under common conventions. Ultimately, Nancy objects, we do not merely "have" reflective experiences of community in any masterful fashion; on the contrary, such experiences are always open to the uncertainty of the future. Given that it is necessary to conceive the unheard demands the impossibility of thinking community places upon us, community can no longer be modelled and celebrated in a communitarian fashion. Thinking of community is no longer a matter of intuiting essence, closure or sovereignty, nor even of comprehending an organization formed by decrees of a sovereign Other or established for a historical purpose. Instead, it is a matter of interrogating the sharing-in-and-of the circulation of sense. Community is historical in the sense that it is an infinitely finite happening, the "togetherness of otherness", and that is all that remains of history (BSP: 143, 155–7). Although communitarianism has arisen within the epochal crisis of the circulation of sense, it has not proven its ability to address either this sense of the nonsense of history, nor its own emergence as a cultural possibility within it.

In explanation, Nancy suggests that communitarian perspectives presuppose a measure of declinist nostalgia for the origin of genuine community in which there were "tight, harmonious, and infrangible bonds" and an "immanent unity, intimacy, and autonomy" that is "played back to itself" through cultural institutions and rituals. This "playing back" of immanence assumes the form of an "organic communion with its own essence", especially the form of personal identities that are shared, diffused and impregnated by such cultural forms that offer a "supplementary mediation of this identification with the living body of the community". Of course, we might wonder, as Robert Bernasconi does, whether a non-immanential community, in which singularities are not totalized by any reflective social consciousness, is even possible. However, the question is not whether it is possible, but whether the insubstantial sharing buried beneath but still active within the symbolic order can be liberated from the constraints that communitarianism offers. In other words, it is imperative to acknowledge that symbols do not mediate but rather serve as a modality of sharing. It is the communitarian ideal that cannot be actualized, given the non-representability of singularities (IC: 9; P: 16–17; BSP: 54–5).[8]

By communitarian lights, the communication constituting substantial cohesion and identity has been gradually sublated into a larger institutional phenomenon known as "society". Classical sociological theory bears this nostalgia: *Gesellschaft*, closely knit, family-based communities in which face-to-face relations were the norm of social interaction, gave way to impersonal *Gemeinschaft*: larger, more individualistic and industrial relationships mediated by legal schemes.[9] The cult of the community is effaced to make way for the social cult of the empowered individual, which is, by implication, merely the residual of the dissolution of community. Interestingly, for Nancy communitarianism implies that the formation of society necessitates that reflective immanence redounds on the individual, who is the figure of immanence taken as the origin of itself and of its own certainties. When communal immanence is sublated into society, such individuals are merely isolated fragments of a shattered community, atomic particles that are remote from one another and lack any aggregation other than the participation that is itself constitutive of community. The result, then, is that society consists in nothing other than constituent individuals, although there will be some, such as Rousseau's "solitary walker", who amble through nature in futile search for another form of pure immanence than their own interiority. Although he was not obviously a communitarian, Rousseau is the primary avatar of the thought of the "social bond" that is artificially imposed upon bondless (or abandoned) individuals.[10] In terms of the contractarian model (which I shall survey in greater detail below), individuals are at once brought together by the bond and separated from one another as individuals. Although Rousseau shared the communitarian nostalgia, he also demonstrated, according to Nancy, that there is an irresolvable tension in the notion that community has been lost, for it would have to precede itself in order to be constituted at all. That is, individuals would be erased at the very moment that the social contract was formed, a contract that would thus be subverted by this dissolution. Nancy appreciates Rousseau's point that substantial community would have been dissolved at the instant of creation, and thus no such thing has ever been eventuated in any form other than as a figure of the symbolic order of immanence.

Nancy maintains staunchly that this nostalgia is not endemic to philosophical discourse alone. Indeed, it is incessantly expressed in the millions of individuals willing to die for their vision of what their country has been or has shown itself capable of regaining. However, just as no one's individuality would be raised into a higher dialectical reality by the re-actualization of lost community, neither are such deaths given any higher signification by the symbolic order. In other words, the willingness to die for one's country precisely because of what it "represents" (which is the closed immanence of the symbolic order) is a symptom and not an antidote to the sickness of this active nostalgia. The meaninglessness of the life of the isolated individual in society is not tinged with a higher value by virtue of justification of its death in defence of this ideal.

The flaws and failings of communitarian discourse impel Nancy to object that we should be suspicious of this retrospective consciousness of any lost community for which we yearn, by which we desire to identify ourselves, and indeed, for which we are willing to die. We should ask a brutal question that might have devastating consequences for the symbolic order of immanence: *precisely when was this "lost" community?* Historically, the West has always looked back to a number of ideal communities as apexes of Western social and political life. Homer, Hesiod and Heraclitus reflect this debilitating nostalgia that permeates the history of the Western world, including even those cultural formations and epochs that moderns regard as worthy of veneration: the natural family, the Athenian city, the Roman Republic, the first Christian community, corporations, communes, brotherhoods. During each of these evocations of historical immanence, there was precisely the same nostalgia for a yet more "archaic community". In alternative terms, each zenith of Western culture itself played back its own immanence in terms of a mythic symbolic order inspired by a nostalgia for earlier, more utopic epochs that are actually representations of an impossible dystopia.[11]

In the main, there appears never to have been any idyllic moment that could be the glorious object of historical consciousness against which the modern individual might examine contemporary society and find it wanting. The myth of lost communal immanence presupposes that there was once a political space within which there was a free play of meaning, a pure space within which immanence was a pristine cultural transparency. The very notion that there is a past "foundation" of community, upon which the community we are "losing" has been built, has a vague metaphysical justification, or perhaps a psychological projectionist one. But there is no manner in which it is intelligible that an absent foundation could be the present ground on which community could be built. There is something outrageous in the myth of communal foundation, for no "free"

109

thinking of community could possibly be surprised in the endeavour to think of such origins. For example, we are "born free" into our societies, not in the sense that a natural or civic law (a pure "foundation") guarantees enjoyment of this privilege, but rather because each birth is a "releasing of being", abandoned to a singularity or to a trajectory of singularities (EF: 74, 84, 92). If that is the case, then it is the incessant re-creation of singularity in the circulation of sense and not living up to the standards of a nostalgic symbolic order that determines the sense of sharing in community.

Naturally, communitarian nostalgia is often conjured in the context of the contemporary Christian desire for a return to the original Christian community. Indeed, Nancy regards modern communitarian nostalgias as extensions of Christian eschatology.[12] Christianity has always explicated the "true consciousness of the loss of community" in the "heart of the mystical body of Christ" and a vision of what it would be like to partake of "divine life". Nevertheless, it would not be difficult to demonstrate that the original Christian community was itself prone to certain nostalgias pertaining to a god who had abandoned humanity. Being little different in its content, contemporary secular nostalgia may be nothing other than a response to the harshness of a reality abandoned by God and the perception of the impoverishment of secular alternatives of "deified" man. Both original Christian community and derivative modern nostalgias exhibit a transcendental illusion that is merely one of an "experience of concealed immanence" of the symbolic orders of substantial community. That is, nostalgic projections of lost Christian community never obtained; even if there had been such immanence in an original Christian community, it would not be the object of contemporary cultural reflection. One might propose, alternatively, that an original Christian community never existed in the fashion that communitarian nostalgia desires, but that even if it had existed in this way, nostalgia would immediately reduce it to the symbolic order and play it back immanentially. Even if a religious community once had a "sacred meaning", the modern reductive and appropriative symbolic nostalgias would not permit the sacralization of contemporary community. As a result, the insistence on the vitality of a kerygmatic calling from an original community merely entangles us in a nostalgia irrelevant to contemporary thought of community.

With his notion of incessant re-creation in mind, Nancy provides an alternative interpretation in which each nostalgia for a time when the "sacred" was imbued within community is actually an exercise of the passion resulting from the turmoil of sharing passivity, suffering and excess among singular beings. Such an exercise is unmediated by the symbolic order and does not endow its closed immanence with a sustained and discernible value. If there is nothing more to the "sacred" than this tumul-tuous sharing among singular beings, and if precisely this sharing consti-tutes insubstantial community, then the "transcendent" nature of the sacred has been abraded. Therefore, the kind of community its presence might engender is categorically unavailable to either Christian nostalgias or the concepts they represent. At best, one might say that all nostalgias for lost substantial community are riddled with the many banal transcend-ences that compose the finite sense of insubstantial community, but one cannot maintain that this composition provides any "sacred meaning". The conventional post-secularist doctrine that community is the space of transcendence attests to our inability to comprehend the sharings that constitute it. By those lights, each sharing traces a pathway of gods who have withdrawn, which might lead us to gather that the "sacred" is a reification of multiple representations of gods who have never existed but have served as figures of "sacrality" in the reflective immanence of substantial community.

Nothing, then, was lost in the purported historical movement from community to society. Rather, Nancy makes the ingenious proposal that community is all that remains of the eradication of society. This does not mean that Nancy simply inverts priorities from a continuum of commu-nity–society–individual to one of individual–society–community. Commu-nity does indeed "happen to us" in the wake of society, but what has been submerged is precisely what has always been constitutive of community – sharing among singularities, with sense circulating between them in their relations. Immanence of the symbolic order has not been "lost", for if immanence were actually to obtain, it would instantly suppress the sharing-in-and-of community, that is, community itself.

One important question worthy of scrutiny, then, might concern the symbolic order of this desire for immanence. Nancy explains that it is the fearful experience of death that brings about immanence, seals each individual off into its insular defensiveness, seemingly vulnerable only to the absolute event of death. However, the death of the individual is an irre-ducibly singular event and, as such, it disrupts community into a collection of continuously identified atoms that then reflect upon the community of death. This, he continues, is warranted in the notion that all political and collective enterprises that are "dominated by a will to absolute immanence have as their truth the truth of death". Echoing Bataille, Nancy avers that communities are communities of death or of the dead, if only because immanential community would require the complete realization of the potential of each individual, a realization that is possible only in death (IC: 11–12).[13] Death is neither an excess of finitude nor even an infinite fulfilment of existence. Although each self is immanently focused on the absolute event of death, this focus reflects back on the community only after its death. The community forms itself around this mimetically informed and symbolically endowed event, thereby bestowing communal significance upon death in order to render it intelligible. Death takes on a higher dialectical significance, an "operative" significance that appropriates it into the immanence of community. However, Nancy is adamant that death is neither a representable event in which we could share communally nor one that could have an operative significance. In other words, what each singular being shares is the very opacity and inoperability of its own death, a singular exposure to the singular event of death. This sharing is one of the trajectories of social reality that serves as an intersection of the existence of two singular beings. It is the affirmation of the sense of existence that serves as the singular response to the impending event of death that brings us into the presence of others as a "one" always coming to presence before death (IC: 13, 31, 35; EF: 95).

In conclusion, then, it might suffice to add only that community is singular in the sense that it assumes the impossibility of any closed immanence bearing the deaths of individuals by raising them up to a higher signification and/or putting them to work for that purpose. It presents the finitude and the irredeemable excess constitutive of finite being. In community infinite desires are finitely interrupted and finite desires are released in the surprising burst of interruptive freedom. Properly speaking, such consciousness may happen in and through a community, but not as a possession of the self. Rather, community is nothing other than this incessant encroachment of the truth of finitude into self-consciousness. Hence the sense of community would just consist in the collection of interruptions of the reflective immanence of self-consciousness. Needless to say, such interruptions sever the bonds between past and present, living and dead, in such a manner as to forbid the complete success of the symbolics of communitarian nostalgia.

The interruption of contemporary myth

Occasionally it has been hoped that one might be able to revitalize community by establishing new myths or by resuscitating the old. It has been believed that the archaic mythmaking scene of the bard enrapturing an audience by the fire should be given an innovatively modern form. However, according to Nancy on another register of his critique of the metaphysics of substantive community, the scene of mythmaking, which might be the "essential scene of scenes", is itself mythic and refers to yet more

112

archaic mythic scenes (Joyce's "Homer" recounting older tales). For Nancy any modern effort to re-enact the mythic scene could not succeed on two grounds: on the one hand, there appears to be an indefinite regression of modalities of reflection (technical, political, etc.) whereby myth is rendered operative, and on the other, contemporary thought cannot resist the temptation to filter myth through prevailing reductionist schemes. To devise new functions of myths, to treat them as if they represented the human condition, to posit myths as founding events around which communities could congregate, is merely to think in a *mythological* fashion, not to establish some truthful essence of myth. Moreover, the effort to do so is always based on an empowering nostalgia associated with horrifying modern phenomena such as totalitarianism. Myth is the mimetic instrument *par excellence*; it is the primary means of identification whereby "guiding myths" achieve totalitarian power. Mythic power brings people together and projects an image by which personal and social identity is possible. Yet, presumably the ancient myth-evoker had the advantage of living in a world in which myth permeated everything and possessed a coherent motivational force by which universal processes lent definition to a community; today, however, the fact/fiction dichotomy and the desire for a "mythic" meaning renders this "mythation" impossible (NM: 297–8, 301, 305).

Although myth provides a politically practical fabric of sense, and all ideological configurations provide only increasing homogenization, Nancy suggests that we may not even have any right to speak of myth as a cultural resource of value. Since it saturates a political society, threatens the openness and sharing of community and remains discrete in the exercise of theoretical *praxis*, we cannot assume that our modern reading of myth can inform us about the "sense of the world" in which mythically minded individuals lived. To treat myth as a variant of the sense of the world accessible to us today would be to broaden the notion of the sense of the world beyond intelligibility. Furthermore, the very notion of myth is based on a pretentious representation of the West's power to shape its own destiny by returning to a mythic origin for reserves of cultural value in the name of traditional ideals. If the West's very self-consciousness is enshrouded in this mythic ideal, then we can no longer have genuine access to any myth we might try to think. In consequence, then, the inauguration of myth would be always already suspended by the inability to mull myth outside of the West's effort to re-empower itself. The discourse of myth is one that calls for a suspension of the practice of theory and resistance to appropriation into the political discourse of myth itself. In yet other terms, every sharing of vulnerability or mortality, every ecstatic burst of freedom, has already suspended the tranquil communion that the community of myth implies. One might comprehend myth within the scheme of interruption (which implies that the scheme itself is comprehensible), but this comprehension itself is already interrupted at the limit of this scheme. When history itself is suspended, when our epoch is the time of this suspension, then inaccessible and already interrupted archaic myths cannot be revitalized. It is not even possible to invent new myths, since "mythation" is properly speaking not a process of invention of new myths but a recuperation of mythic values now necessarily inoperative despite our efforts to put them to a political agenda (IC: 25–6, 59; BP: 144; C: 372).[14] Since now we cannot know anything about this founding mythic scene, and must invent myths in order to understand it, contemporary myth is impossible. To insist that myth is interrupted is to maintain that the conditions whereby mythation is possible are dislocated and that any effort to recuperate mythic values is immediately reduced to political and mythological meanings.

Nancy remarks that it should not be forgotten that myth is not merely a datum of knowledge, but an *original form of speech*. In humanizing nature and naturalizing (or divinizing) man, *muthos* is the "act of language par excellence", in which a paradigm serving as the *logos* "fictions" this paradigm for the purpose of self-empowerment. Drawing our attention to *what* it says and to the *way* that it says it, mythic speech itself disseminates sense across human discourse and thereby reveals a "world". Unfortunately, the West has always reflected on its cultural identity in a manner that is orientated around "the Greeks" and their founding myths. For the Greeks, Nancy writes, *muthos* and *logos* were essentially the same given the reflective immanence of the symbolic order, in which the disruptive distinction between fact and fiction did not debilitate mythic speech as it does today. This sameness amounts to an uninterrupted link between the world and one's projected religious origin in it. That may be why thinkers of myth from Schelling to Lévi-Strauss have tried to understand humanity itself in terms of this ideal sameness, for mythic speech issues "live" from the origin that immanence posits reflectively. However, given that there is a founding mythic moment in which what is strictly figured as transcendent (reality, world, cosmos) is itself appropriated into the immanence of a culture, genuine mythic speech is an impossibly immanential figuration of transcendence as such (IC: 47–50; NM: 294, 301). Today, myth is, at least, furtively transimmanent and, as such, lacks any proclivity to empower culture mimetically.

For substantialist metaphysics, mythic speech and community are intertwined: speech arises solely within communities, and communities arise in accompaniment to this speech facilitating cohesion and a link with the world it conjures. Every form of mythic speech presupposes the communitarian myth of community-formation and perfect communion. "The totalization of myths goes hand in hand with the myth of totalization", and modern mythologies are simply efforts to repeat this totalization. Nevertheless, such modern mythologies have a grave disability: "we no longer live in mythic life, nor in a time of mythic invention or speech". For the Greeks, to speak of myth is to speak mythically of an immanential presence; to speak of myth today, however, is merely to invoke an absent, impossible world in which myth's immanentizing function is lacking. We cannot but think of myth as fiction, since the immanence of its speech is impossible; and, because we could not help but "mythologize" mythic speech, any effort to instil authenticity in mythic speech would itself be inauthentic (IC: 51–3).

Such critiques of myth, of course, are nothing new. Since Plato, myths have been regarded as dangerous fictions that offer only sacrilegious lies about divinity and encourage unethical behaviours (NM: 297). Today, we quite rationally subordinate this fictionality of *muthos* to the rationality of mind and conduct, in which myth always has a "deeper" meaning subject to psychological projection and cultural analysis. Nancy explains how the mythation of modern reality is suspended by the "fact–fiction" dichotomy incommensurate with the reflective immanence of substantial community. On the one hand, it is necessary to think of *mythic foundations as fictional*, which itself implies the lack of immanence necessary today for myth to have the kind of paradigmatic motivational force a modern mythation strives futilely to attain. On the other hand, it is necessary to think of *myths as fictions that serve as foundations*, which is a thought that lacks the requisite commitment to the ideal of a real and cosmic founding. In other words, even to distinguish between myth and reality is to imply that the latter is the "foundation" of the former, which is incompatible with the very intention of mythation. To speak of myth today in a "mythological" fashion is to expect that it would say something other than myth (which implies that it is not itself the truth, but some symbolic structure that reveals it). Myth is now understood to be strictly operative within a reflective immanence that is known to serve the purpose of group cohesion. "Myth represents multiple existences as immanent to its own unique fiction, which gathers them together and gives them their common figure in its speech and as speech." Community must be possible in order for mythation to make it actual; and myth must be possible in order for a community to make it actual. But there can be no substantial community outside mythic speech, and alternatively, no mythic speech divorced from substantial community. There are no new mythologies or communities, and no futural possibility of their conception (IC: 55–8).

In conclusion, mythation is impossible given the "ontological misfortune" or "disaster" of the dissolution of the ideal of operative community. Myth is inaccessible under conditions of communal self-effacement and substantial community is precluded by the impossible advent of mythic discourse. However, if open, insubstantial community consists of the singular events of contact along trajectories of sharing of finite existence, then a space within immanence is always already interrupting mythation despite this devastation of the communal ideal. Therefore there is a double interruption of myth: on the one hand, the interruption of mythic discourse by the lack of substantial community and, on the other, the interruption of substantial community by the lack of myth; one might say that interrupted myth reveals the hidden nature of community as a community of co-appearing singularities, and the incessant interruptions of the effort to substantialize community reveal the interruptions of the myth of community. Although reflective immanential knowledge of mythology and substantial community would eradicate this possibility of genuine mythation and open community, open community always tears open closed immanence through the circulation of sense that resists the political appropriations of mythation.

Being-with in common: the essence of community

The question of the possibility of the metaphysics of a non-substantial community or of the "philosophical dynamics of vectors and relations"[15] that compose it weaves throughout Nancy's work. A "coexistential analytic", in which the question of co-existence is the ontological question *par excellence*, is the paramount goal of Nancy's work on community. Inverting Heidegger's prioritization of the analysis of individual existence over the question of social relations, Nancy attempts to offer a provocatively new ontology of the "with" or the "in-common". Rather than interrogating the being of community, he proposes, we should be addressing the community of being itself (BSP: 61; BC: 1–2).[16] In other words, it is necessary to acknowledge that community is not merely a collection of selves, but the occurrence of singular events that relate individual selves. More roughly, it is not only what they share, but how they share in such relations, that constitutes community. Possessing no ground upon which to be established, community is articulated in the plurality of evocative sharings and voices, not in the substantial relations freely entered into by "atomic" or autonomous individuals.[17] Each exposure of singularity to singularity is an opening of existence to another sense of being in a manner that disrupts closed immanence.

The notion of community as insubstantial sharing is not easy to elucidate. Nancy offers a variety of definitions and descriptions that furtively elude theoretical grasp. He discloses a viable description of community in *The Birth to Presence*: "Community is not a gathering of individuals, posterior to the elaboration of individuality, for individuality as such can be given only within such a gathering." He lends voice to the notion that community and communication are constitutive of individuality, rather than the reverse, and individuality is perhaps, in the final analysis, only a boundary of community. Community is no longer an essence given prior to the existence of individuals, for it does not consist merely of the communication of separate "beings" (which exist as such only through communication), but also in the intersections of the lives of such beings that facilitate communicability. Elsewhere, he insists that autonomous freedom is contemporaneous and coexistent with the interlaced relations between individuals, much in the same way that "being-in-common" is contemporaneous with singular existence. Indeed, singular being has no determination outside such relations, yet is always capable of exempting itself from them (BP: 153–4; EF: 66). Strictly speaking, Nancy inverts subsumptions and then erases them: autonomous subjectivity is not subordinated to communal determinations (or vice versa), and each is intelligible solely within the relation between them, which is to say that the relation (the "between", "with", "being-in-common", etc.) must be addressed if the essences of freedom and community are to be intelligible. In fact, Nancy enjoins us to accept the truth of the notion that the "we" definitive of being-in-common is not merely "a being" among beings but "a happening". It is the essential otherness of existence given to the finitude of subjects who figure in "we". Indeed, taking this to greater lengths, Nancy affirms that each self figures only in the reticulated "happenings" of open community.

There is a contemporary imperative for a discourse in which the substantiality of community is exhausted and the pre-originary spacing of relations is exposed. What communal individuals "share" among themselves, Nancy proposes, is what their relations reveal to them, namely their existences outside themselves. The essence of community is the co-appearance of singular beings in, for example, their finitude before death. The thinking of community requires, not that we identify ourselves as a "we", but that we should dissociate ourselves from every kind of "we" that would be the subject of its own representation in reflective immanence. Again, Nancy warns against interpreting this as a sublation of exposed finitude, as if one's existence could be actively invested by community. Being "finite" does not mean being non-infinite, as if we were insignificant beings overwhelmed by the enormity of universal being; more precisely, we are infinitely finite in the sense of being infinitely exposed to our "strange" existence. There is simply no "work" that community could perform for the "end" of such an exposure: it cannot ever be overcome or put operatively to any social or political task. Rather, community is precisely this exposition of finitude, not a sublation producing a certain utility. Communities are infinitely finite, not infinite in dialectical potential, which is to say that communities consist of "inoperative" finitude. More specifically, singularization is not a process in which singularity is extracted, produced or derived in a dialectical fashion. "A singular being does not emerge or rise up against the background of a chaotic, undifferentiated identity of beings, or against the background of their unitary assumptions, or that of a becoming, or that of a will" (IC: 26–7). There is no ground anterior to the codetermination and co-originarity of finite beings in singular relations; on the contrary, "with-ness" is precisely the ground for all determination (although it is itself "unfounded"). In other words, "'with' does not add itself to Being, but rather creates the immanent and intrinsic condition of presentation in general". It is incoherent to presuppose that finite beings are singularized against such a ground and yet also sublated to fully realized selfhood by communal immanence. There are material and immaterial spaces of sharing in the "between" of any contact between them. Nevertheless, the self is a "reconquest" of its "irreducible alterity" despite the loss of self in death shared among singularities. In yet other terms, one might say that each "self" is an other, and each individual's otherness is not some substance it shares with other selves. It relates to other selves through the surprising strangeness that is the modality of sharing (BSP: 71; IC: 29; BP: 155).

Nancy insists firmly that communal "togetherness" consists in a sharing of singularity and a sharing among singularities, in which there are no singular beings divorced from other singular beings sharing in singularity. Sharing is not merely an accidental activity of atomic individuals; nor is it merely a "unique substance". It presupposes no encompassing totality, no communion of singularities that would make singularities what they are. The finitude of singular being is always presented communally, and is always exposed to the judgements of community formative of law. Co-appearance does not mean that there is any "bond" among them, as if something were superimposed upon them. There is merely the "between" and the "with" that singular beings share among themselves. The "origin" is not a ground of Being against which atomic individuals are determinate existents, but rather the "between", the "punctual and discrete spacing between us, as between us and the rest of the world, as between all beings". "With-ness" might then mean that the plurality of identities is codetermined through the singularity of each identity, a state of codetermination that does not take place within the world. Instead, it forms "the essence and the structure of the world" itself (BSP: 44, 78, 83; BP: 154–5).

Being-in-common means that being is nothing that we would have as common property, even though we are, or even though being is not common to us except in the mode of being shared. Not that a common and general substance would be distributed to us, but rather, being is only shared between existents and in existents. ... Consequently, on the one hand, there is no being between existents – the space of existences is their spacing and is not a tissue or a support belonging to everyone and no one and which would therefore belong to itself – and on the other hand, the being of each existence, that which it shares of being and by which it is, is nothing other – which is not "a thing" – than this very sharing.

(EF: 69)

In brief, community would consist in the finite totality of irreducibly infinite sharings among singularities, not some "being" or "ground" or "foundation" against which such singularities would be determined and by which sharing would be rendered possible. Precisely how such sharings in singular relationships figure in composing relationships, however, cannot be accommodated by the thought of intersubjectivity, of two singularities sharing the property of being subjects that interact. Instead, there should be some means of describing the *surprise* of each singular thought of freedom in the linkage between them as well as the strangeness of each "with" between them. The link between the "I" and the "you" assumes many permutations of co-appearance: you and I, you (plural) are I, the you is the I, and in each case, the you that is/are entirely other than the I. Indeed, given such permutations, it can be maintained that there are no such things as "human beings", for if they are not given to themselves as such, only relations between singularities could possible bestow them with "humanity". It is the surprising freedom of singular beings that gives humanity to singularities in relation. The relationship between the I and the you is one of asymmetrical resemblance: the I is not identified by any resemblance between itself and the you, which would imply that the death of the other enables the I to recognize something familiar in itself. On the contrary, the I resembles the other in a fashion that has no origin other than the limit by which selves are exposed to one another. If resemblance among beings is determined by the sharing of identity, then sharing with the you a desire for self-identity, the I does not recognize or rediscover itself in the other or in the other's death, but in the surprise and the strangeness of the event of its death. Since there is nothing other than this "between" the I and the you, the "with" that holds their being together, then people are strange to one another, and thus are strange in themselves. Moreover, the strangeness of others isolates the I in the world, which is in its own right "strange" because the world circulates its sense

119

through it. To be part of "the people" is to be strange among strangers, if only because each singular one is a participant in the "simultaneity of together-ness" and "disseminated singularity". Such simultaneity and dissemination come in the following form: whoever enunciates "we" cannot be identified by saying "we", which is to say that at best "one" says "we", and it is thus that "we" exists, "sharing the possibility that I say it at every moment" (EF: 72–3; IC: 29, 33; BSP: 7; M: 69–72).

In conclusion, Nancy's conceptualization of community exhibits a tendency to collapse immanence into the sharing relations that occur in a manner irreducible to determinations of entities, such as selves and groups of selves.

Globalization: the question of "total immanence"

Nancy takes an ambivalent position in relation to the dauntingly controver-sial notion of "globalization", which is, by the lights of the Hardt–Negri thesis with which Nancy's work shares some marked affinities, a decentred, deterritorialized, expansive form of sovereignty unlimited by the traditional nation-state.[18] Although he does not champion it with resolution, he does think that the "surface" phenomenon of globalization (in particular the man-ner in which it mediates social relations by technological means) does not exhaust globalization's role in the contemporary world. There is also a "deep" phenomenon in which the circulation of sense through such social relation-ships is expanded and in some respects refined by such mediations, without being merely reduced to the symbolicity they offer. In other words, the closed immanence of globalization cannot succeed in eradicating the sharing that composes community, but, in fact, can provide expansive opportunities for it. And this is nowhere more apparent than in the connection between "the West" and globalization itself. "The West" is at an end because it has been globalized in the very process of Westernizing the globe (MMT: 94).[19] Despite the "technological proliferation of the social spectacle and the social as spec-tacular, as well as in the proliferation of self-mediatized globalization and globalized mediatization", we struggle to understand ourselves as a "we". In a sense, this has been implied in the very destiny of the West, which has always held up the ideal of the "global nature of an *oikas*", a competition for natu-ral resources on a global scale (BSP: 70; P: 17). Nancy writes movingly:

> Our time is the time that, as it were, exposes exposure itself: the time for which all identifiable figures have become inconsistent (the gods, the *logoi*, the wise, knowledge), and which therefore works toward

120

(or which gives itself over to) the coming of a figure of the unidentifiable, the figures of opacity and of resistant consistency as such.
"Man" thus becomes opaque to himself, he grows thick and heavy
with the weight of an excessive thought of his humanity: eight billions
bodies in an ecotechnical whirlwind that no longer has any other end
than the infinity of an inappropriable meaning.   (GT: 83–4)

Despite the dismal quality of this denunciation of modernity, Nancy
insists that we have as little to fear from globalization as we have reason to
hope nostalgically for a return to lost community. Although humanity is
"strange" to itself and its apperceptions have become clouded, exposure of
finitude in the sharing in community could never be reduced to a closed
global immanence of the symbolic order. Nancy identifies two conceptual
trajectories on which globalization is unthreatening. On the one hand, the
very notion of a "global humanity" lies outside the models by which there
is an underlying purpose or "end" of humanity itself. On the other hand,
the total immanence that globalization requires would be as globally
impossible as it is locally so. Generally speaking, our current "ontological
situation" is one in which existence itself challenges any "globalness", even
one designated as "capital". A world that "played back" its symbolic or
mythic identity to itself in order to enhance its own dominion would be
incessantly disrupted by the specific sharings among singular beings that
are the sole bonds of communication and community in the political
realm. Playing on the duality of "*mondialization*", in which globalization
would mean both total reflective immanence and an open spacing of infinitely finite creation, Nancy emphasizes the irreducibility of the latter to
the appropriations of the former. Not merely a "surface" phenomenon,
globalization has two levels on which the world is evoked: globalization
has "emerged as the surface of what is at play in the depths: the essence of
being-with". The "bare web of the *com*" in communication suggests a
global exposure of our interconnections that exposes the humanity of the
human. Since such exposures are indicative of the circulation of sense
(through the singularities of each being's relation with others), then the
very sense of the world is inaccessible to the globalization of the circulation of capital (BSP: 28, 45, 131; CMM: 45–8).

The globalization taking place on the surface, which consists of social
relationships mediated by substantial forms of communication, is in some
respects the delivery of the promise of what Nancy calls "market democracy". When capitalism and democracy merge under the rubric of "freedom and rights" to the extent that "democratic values" come to represent
little more than the circulation of capital, then "market democracy" is a
distinct catalyst of surface globalization. Nancy writes:

121

At this very moment, when political subjectivity is doubtless to a great degree coming undone, and when substantial sovereignty is splitting up, are we not in the process of learning that the virtual advent, or in any case the almost universally desired advent, of a world citizenship (beginning with that of Europe) nonetheless risks corresponding to the triumph (itself without sharing or division) of what has been called "market democracy"?   (SW: 108)

With subjectivity and sovereignty themselves in process of corrosion, the circulation of capital is the remaining aspect of the democratic ideal that functions without compromise. Nancy asks whether democracy is exhausting itself in a dream of a "politics-without-or-against-the-State" while its absolute subject becomes, increasingly, the "global figure" of capital itself (SW: 109; CMM: 19–21). Nancy fears that capital will become a truly global figure of a market democracy that determines the manner in which individuals identify themselves and relate to one another. After all, there are signs that the global economy is exhausting "perspectives, hopes and ends" and that whatever is not economical in nature belongs to the timidity of humanitarian politics. However, Nancy suggests that globalization is simultaneously unravelling the fabric of its own totalizing web. He objects to the thought that globalization will rend our genuine social relationships and replace them with new, mediated forms of community, if not dissolve community altogether. Although multimedia technology stresses the ultimate efficiency of global communication, the notion that technological advancements will pull us apart is questionable on the grounds that we have never been "together" in the sense implied.

> Communication, in truth, is without limits, and the being that is in common communicates itself to the infinity of singularities. Instead of getting upset over the gigantic (or so they say) growth in our means of communication, and fearing through this the weakening of the message, we should rather rejoice over it, serenely: communication "itself" is infinite between finite beings. Provided these beings do not try to communicate to one another myths about their own infinity, for in such a case they instantly disconnect the communication. But communication takes place on the limit, or on the common limits where we are exposed and where it exposes us.   (IC: 67)

Rather than thinking of a single, monolithic "technology" and the pristinely immanential world it is feared might be its end, he encourages us to examine the plurality of relations that technology can promulgate. One might entertain the thought that technological means of communication only strengthen the bonds of sharing among singular beings and the ties of community (provided, of course, that the individual does not assume that its own powers are infinitely removed from those of the community in which it shares). Living in a world of technologies (plural) throws us up against the challenge of thinking of the finitude of sense in a fragmented world striving for immanence. Nancy interrogates the question of "global technicization" and wonders whether, all nightmares of a "reign of robots" aside, the end of technologization would expose the finite sense of freedom and community. However, this would require that we focus on the workings of the specific technologies (plural) that constitute a global economy. Although Nancy writes of "worldwide" enchainments in which an insubstantial and formless politics consists in gestures of tying together individuals, groups, nations and so on who have no unity apart from their common enchainments, he also maintains that the notion of a common humanity devoid of linkages of sovereignty is untenable on the grounds that this would have no political value. It would represent a "measureless" world, the loss of all measure, and existence as well, since existence is shaped by the sharings and intersections among singularities (FT: 24–6; SW: 112; BSP: 135, 183). One need not despair over such a worldwide enchainment because it does not reduce the sharing that such communication facilitates. After all, there might also be a circulation of meaning that ties and enchains itself without having or knowing any final, global accomplishment. This is to say that a globalized substantial community could never be created or even enlarged by enhancements of communication. It could only broaden the horizons of a communicability or sharing about which we need not even have knowledge.

Furthermore, communication of this global kind might even enable each writer to express ideas that interrupt the very myth of globalization that enables it to be produced. A global literature, presumably, would be one that drew from technologically enhanced means of communication, but would call the hypostatization of such means into question by interrupting its myths. Moreover, writing represents a "resistance to the closure of worlds within the world as well as resistance to the closure of worlds-beyond-the-world: the tracing out (*frayage*), in each instant, of this world here" (SW: 120). Even in a "globalized" world, each writer would take a specific stand as a singular being, using literary styles to interrupt the most contemporary myths and subvert the possibility of total immanentization that globalization allegedly threatens.

In conclusion, globalization would expand the conditions of communicability that constitute the sharing of community, infinitely extending the singular sharing of community, vulnerability and death. Although it does indeed threaten a closed ecotechnical immanence, it also provides conditions of community that unravel its entanglements.

Conclusion

- Communitarianism, in Nancy's view, is flawed by its presupposition of substantial groups composed of substantial individuals whose essence and being are ontologically predetermined (beings-as-such) as well as rationally, politically and juridically pre-established. He also rejects the communitarian presumption of tradition as a necessary and viable means of communal identification. For Nancy, community consists of the linkages of sharing among radically singular beings whose only essence is a common exposure to existence, especially the social relations wherein sense circulates through the sorts of reticulated sharings addressed in earlier chapters. Generally speaking, he proposes an enquiry into the "community of being" (an irreducible multiplicity of singular beings) not the conventional "being of community" (in which predetermined individuals come together in communion). Community is proposed in terms of an open and inoperative sharing of relations through which sense circulates. In other words, it is the multiply reticulated forms of sharing, not the mediatizations, that threaten to reduce them to social and political practices. Such relations of sharing are not predetermined.
- Nancy also objects to the thought that communities require myth for the purpose of determination. In other words, he regards the notion that a community necessarily reflects on itself in a myth-mediated fashion as now impossible because of the prevalence of the "fact–value" distinction and the necessity of a reductive appraisal ("mythology") of myth. However, most pertinent is the criticism that mythic discourse is always already interrupted by the very means by which the myth is conceived.
- Globalization has a "surface" and a "depth", one might say. On the surface, Nancy remarks, there are social relationships configured by technological means and that offer symbolic figures mediating in all social realities. Such technological means threaten to create a total, closed immanence that would dissolve all singularities of being and relation. Yet, given the irreducibility of singularity, globalization at its "deepest" also enables a more expansive form of communicative means for the sharing of community, which is perhaps to say that the circulation of sense will work its way through the trajectories of global technology and not be mediated by them.

124

CHAPTER 7

Social contractarianism

Nancy relentlessly interrogates our ability to address the question of the future of politics in terms of the prevailing paradigm(s) of the meaning and the value of "the political" as philosophers understand it. What Nancy seems to desire is a finite thinking of the condition of possibility of political discourse. He wants us to find a way to address the irreducibility of the political as a circulation of sense within the sharings of community. This necessitates that we query the incertitude and undecidability of the discourse of politics, which is to say that political criteria must be conceived as being devoid of the arrogations of rationality and tradition that inexorably establish dominance. It is precisely the notion of sovereignty and self-sufficiency that must be suspended in the name of an an-archic sovereignty that withdraws from, and does not establish, the multifarious forms of political domination. In other words, he challenges us to offer a philosophical approach to the essence of politics without deploying the criteria that guide the empirical practices of contemporary politics. Indeed, is it possible to interrogate the essence of the political without being political as one does so? More generally, is not discourse about politics already political discourse, in which case the reflective immanence of the discourse places ineradicable constraints on our ability to offer a rethinking of what we understand politics to be? Indeed, what is needed is an inscrutable view of the essence of the political that is not merely a "leftist" or "rightist" perspective, and does not pander to the interests and fears of a triumphant market democracy.

Roughly speaking, Nancy has discovered an intrinsic incommensuration within political discourse that divests us of the confidence to address its own sense. Often in collaboration with Philippe Lacoue-Labarthe, he writes of a viable distinction between *le politique*, or "the political" (the essential nature of political practices and ideologies) and *la politique*, or "politics" (which is the empirical practice of politics itself).[1] What intrigues Nancy is that, in an age in which "everything is believed to be political", the political reduction of everything to reflective immanence creates a knot of meaning in which it is difficult to think of the essence of the political other than in terms of the political determination of all essence. When it is said that "everything is political", does this mean that social reality is saturated with the values of a communal discourse about what politics is, or does it mean that all social realities participate in and are appropriated by the empirical practices of politics? However, he insists that "the political" as the non-totalizable openness of the sharing of community is completely incommensurable with political paradigms. In other words, thinking of politics solely in terms of its empirical practices renders impossible any point of vantage from which politics can be rethought deconstructively. The challenge is to locate such an orientation in the interrogation of "the political", which is possible only if one queries whether "the political" is retreating or withdrawing from politics. Has the essential nature of politics withdrawn beyond what political appropriation finds accessible? Is politics as it is practised now inaccessible to political paradigms? Alternatively, has the philosophical notion of "the political" moved beyond any interest of actual politics? It must be conceded that such a withdrawal is established by the reflective immanence that exscribes any form of circulating and irreducible sense as it may figure in "the political". That is, even the essence of the political is approachable solely through the thinking of essence provided by political determination. However, the very thinking of the divorce between politics and "the political" opens up a space within which the question of the spacing of "the political" itself can be addressed. "The political" thus comes to reveal itself as the circulation of sense despite the crisis of sense its discourse produces. If so, then contrary to political paradigms, sovereignty is no surplus of sense beyond community; it is the very insubstantiality of community itself, its openness to the future (P: 20–21; BSP: 36). It is necessary, then, to question "the political" with the end of thinking of its essence outside the prevailing political paradigms. We can only interrogate the question of "the political" when politics itself has withdrawn into a lacuna of sense, revealing the ties that bind the plurality of social relations. As such a lacuna, it is the very pre-originary *praxis* of politics itself, the unavailable ground of its paradigm and appropriations. Thus "the political" that Nancy queries is not merely a conceptual possibility of political discourse, but the essence of politics itself, an essence, it must be said, that is not one politics itself has determined. Contemporary politics, shaped by a post-1930s vacillation between fear that democracy is weak and trepidation about the risk of a resurgence of totalitarian forms similar to those that arose in the 1930s, can provide few insights on this line of interrogation. Of particular relevance to contemporary political theory is the proposal to deconstruct the notion of the social contract, which is the glue of the liberalism that has always already threatened to fall prey to totalitarianism.

Thinking the withdrawal of "the political"

"The metaphysics of our age", Nancy maintains forcefully, is "what one could call the metaphysics of the deconstruction of the essence, and of existence qua sense." He might be thinking here of the manner in which singular beings share in community in ways that are not transparent to theory. Essence, it might be averred, is now enclosed in the ideal of reflective immanence. Yet, if it is immanence itself that forbids any kind of enquiry into the essence of relationships composing the political, then it may be necessary to probe the question of precisely what kind of essence the political might have. By way of proposition, Nancy writes elsewhere of an "entire ontology of being as tying" and "politics of the tie as such" as necessary for an understanding of politics and the political. This tying is precisely the immanential bond that, when subsumed under political interests, obscures our ability to think the essence of the political. What is needed, on the contrary, is a politics of communicability possessing a value beyond traditional forms of communication between and among substantial citizen–subjects within a predetermined political space (SW: 92, 112–14). In brief, what is worthy of interrogation is the question of whether the sharing constitutive of the vectors of singular social events might not disclose (or even compose) the underlying value of the political.

It is not altogether clear how one might go about thinking this metaphysics, this politics, if politics itself is an insidious template of closed immanence. Nancy, working with Lacoue-Labarthe, proposes to examine the question of the retreat or withdrawal of the political (and all its sharings of communicability) from immanentist politics. There is an additional question of how this retreat would compel us to "displace, re-elaborate and replay" the concept of "political transcendence". If "the political" is not to be appropriated (or even abandoned) by the politics of power and of the "common subject", then it must be regained in terms of the essence of the sharing in being-in-common (RP: 130; C: 389–90). On a more considered view, the possibility of political transcendence is not determined by any fixation with the facticity of irreducible aspects of the political. Rather, what Nancy appears to require is that transcendence in political discourse is possible solely for the purpose of illustrating the limit conditions of an enquiry into the underlying determinations of "the political".

More specifically, Nancy proposes that we think of political discourse and the discourse of "the political" in terms of a tension between "questioning the essence of the political" and a "political determination of essence". The latter is the effectual condition of reducing all essence to a term of reflective imma-nence, whereas the former is what actually takes place in communal relations and what we might have called "politics" if only we were not blinded by the platitude that "everything is political". It might prove to be that everything is saturated with political values, to the extent that it is difficult, or even impossible, to think of the political itself. Even so, neither democracy nor totalitarianism offers insights into the question of this determination of the political: post-Enlightenment thought, for example, poses few modes of resistance to it. It leads only to the totalitarian phenomenon in which there is "social transparency", homogenization, management and "enlightened direction", that is, politics. Nancy notes that such thinking of the political, despite reduction to immanence, produces only "questions, obstacles and warnings encountered along the way" (RP: 108–11, 116). Regardless of whether the "question of the essence of the political" is answerable, one simply cannot continue to retreat from political appropriation of the politi-cal and its communal circulations into an innocuous philosophical realm of abstractions of liberality.

Of course, much of this means that the closure of politics entails the enclosure of the political, which is to say that the political bonds that tie us together prior to immanentization are thinkable solely within the confines of the immanence of politics itself. Simply put, one cannot easily wrest the possible configurations of "the political" from politics. One can only survey the extent to which the political does (or might) withdraw from immanentization, not the manner in which it obviously resists it. It should be noted, however, that this potential withdrawal is merely definitive of the open immanence of the circulation of sense among singular events. Given this ubiquity of immanence, it is so very obvious that "everything is political" that one can only question somewhat wistfully the essence of the political outside the domain regulated by the dichotomy. That is why enquiry into the irreducible essence of "the political" is a task that comes in the form of convoluted questions. We should be "dedicated to returning to the most archaic constitution of the political, and to exploring the essence of the political assignation of essence, and that is to say, to putting into question the concept and the value of the archaic in general: origin and primitiveness, authority, principles, etc.". Merely finding new grounds or rationale for "the political" would be insufficient, for that would be to think of the very origins that support (or are supported by) the nostalgia of politics for lost community. Moreover, it simply cannot be a matter of inverting priorities by "confirming the domination and the *principiat* of the political" over politics, for that, again, is merely the stratagem of reflective immanence (RP: 113). It is not enough to point out that existence is already political in a fashion that is irreducible to "politics" and furtively resistant to its efforts to bestow a political meaning upon it.

Nancy queries whether it would be sufficient to argue that communities or individuals constitute a political domain that would provide richer resistances to the activities of politics. In other words, it is conceivable that every resistance to politics by communal or individual activities could be swept up into political projects and given a meaning as such. When "the people" (consisting of "individuals") in their sovereignty are given a vocation as agents resisting the political, immanence has merely been sealed again despite this resistance. Such resistances would serve merely to give symbolic meaning to the "individuality" of closed immanence. The task, then, would be to conceive of this disruptive order of political resistance as something irreducible to the order of domination. In other words, "everything is political" means neither that politics dominates the spacing of "the political", nor that resistance on the part of political spacing saturates all social reality with an overweening political value. Nancy suggests that we strive to discover a condition of the "refusal of domination" in the very spacing of community itself. One might say, then, that sovereignty is not a domination of any kind in the relation between politics and the spacing of community, but the very resistance to such domination. Unfortunately, this poses the task of articulating a "symbolization of a non-figuring" of such resistances to the order of symbolization itself. The finite thinking of the crisis of sense, of the question of a politics of non-domination, must concern itself with the circulation of sense in the "with" or "between" of social relations themselves. That is, it addresses "sovereign" groundless finitudes and their vectoral relations, especially where sharing and the plurality of voices are expressive of sense (P: 20–21; RP: 132–4).

"Replaying the thirties": rethinking the democracy–totalitarianism dichotomy

Thinking co-appearingly with Lacoue-Labarthe, Nancy confronts a number of the presumptions of the democracy–totalitarianism dichotomy: both democratic presumptions about precisely what there is to fear in totalitarianism and totalitarian presumptions about the inevitable crisis of democracy. His proposals are as follows: (a) totalitarianism is not merely a historical phenomenon that might experience a renaissance in its old forms, but could assume new figures latent in market democracy itself; (b) new totalitarian forms might be "softer", that is, suggested by consistency of election, the reincarnation of the body politic, and the irrefragability of political ideologies by which everything is already saturated by political values; and (c) the very distinction between totalitarianism and market democracy could obfuscate the originary sources of future totalitarianism (RP: 128–9).

A political discourse constrained by the politics of "the left" and "the right" troubles Nancy. It is very plausible that the dichotomy between democracy and totalitarianism on which it revolves might effectively disguise commonalities between contemporary democracy and future emergent totalitarianisms. The "politics of crisis" might conceal these commonalities as the result of "replaying the thirties": the myth in which democracy fragmented to ruination and fell prey to totalitarianism. Such a myth provides a reflective immanence within which political discourse would vacillate between options deployed to the left and to the right. At its inextirpable root is fear that such events could recur, that democracy is destined to repeat the 1930s it replays to itself. Nancy insists that we must rethink political discourse in a fashion that does not presume the tenacity of this immanence and does not swing back and forth between the antipodes of democracy and totalitarianism. Instead, it is necessary to examine whether the "metaphysics of our age", discretely traced in modern lifestyles and untainted by the nefarious tendency to "replay the thirties", would be the "metaphysics of the deconstruction of the essence, and of existence qua sense" (SW: 92). In other words, we should look closely at the various aspects of singular events that compose modern life and enquire into the conditions that make new forms of totalitarianism possible.

Nancy is adamant that political discourse should be troubled by the potential emergence of characteristics of totalitarianism from banal aspects of market economy.[2] In so far as totalitarianism is the "total completion of the political" and the "undivided reign of the political", which completes the philosophy of the subject, we should examine where its banal aspects reveal such potential immanentization. Although the originary situation of "the political" is the "bare exposition of singular origins", under totalitarianism specificities disappear and political questions are not even asked, since every enquiry is already politicized and merits no further scrutiny. Politics of this order is active without negativity, as if every resistance to its reflective immanence is ground under foot in the name of the subsumptions of its symbolic–ideological order. In another sense, totalitarianism is "the attempt at a frenzied re-substantialization" or "re-organization" of the "social body". However, the possible dormancy of totalitarian aspirations in contemporary democracy should undermine any confidence that democracy is too strong to lapse into the dissolute conditions that serve as the seed-bed of 1930s-style fascism and Nazism. Totalitarianism exhibits a "mimetic will-to-identity" and an anticipated fulfilment of its own form, each of which is definitive of the essence of the West's sense of destiny. Neither an aberration of the West nor merely a political abomination safely ensconced in the past, it has a seductive vitality that not even the "certitudes of morality and democracy" could surmount, certitudes that, in truth, might disguise its very emergence (BSP: 25; RP: 126–7; NM: 312). Nancy offers a dichotomy between, on the one hand, totalitarian desire that is "full of its lack" of truth and, on the other, democratic truth that is "empty of its fullness" of sense. Together, they serve as "postulations of self-sufficiency", each of which provides a version of reflective immanence that "replays the thirties". "The left" and "the right" are forced to think these postulations in terms of possible concatenations of the axiology of subjectivity/citizenship and sovereignty/community. Each postulation glories in discrete humanistic presuppositions about "man" as the ultimate figure of self-sufficiency. But this does not enable any resolutions of their aporetic tension. Even to Christianize or socialize the notion of man offers no possible relief of this tension, since each merely provides motifs by which reflective immanence is reinforced (as with the intense sacralization of politics in the US).

Totalitarianism in particular forces us to evaluate the question of "sacrificial politics", or a politics of sacrifice to a cause. The totalitarian leader, perhaps in a fashion similar to the Hegelian monarch, has no symbolic role in the sense that he is the sovereign figure of power symbolic of substantial relations from which power flourishes (BP: 120). Such a leader is, in a sense, the impotent figure by whose significations all symbols gain potency. In this respect, totalitarianism is a total demonstration of the sense of myth as the truth of the pure immanence of politics. This is what Nancy refers to in association with the political philosophy of Carl Schmitt as a "theologicopolitics", that is, one in which the symbolic politics of sacrifice would provide access to a truth already anticipated by political discourse. Totalitarianism, then, is a rejection of the world, a turn away from it in the name of a cause that, immanently, provides a rich meaning that can be taken for the sense of truth. It thrives on myths that are productive of power and that set people to work under common symbolic ideals whose etiology is an original moment of mythation that need not be archaic. Not only does totalitarianism thrive on myths, but all myth itself resonates in a totalitarian fashion because it aims for the reflective and mediated "absolute community" devoid of the ties of sharing in actual communal life (SW: 89; IC: 46, 56–7). And it is precisely this inversion that opens any market democratic myth ("the individual" or "capital") to totalitarian encroachment.

Totalitarianism obviously includes "communism", which Nancy under-stands to be:

> an emblem of the desire to discover or rediscover a place of community at once beyond social divisions and beyond subordina-tion to technopolitical dominion, and thereby beyond such wast-ing away of liberty, of speech, or of simple happiness as comes about whenever these become subjugated to the exclusive order of privatization; and finally, more simply and more decisively, a place from which to surmount the unraveling that occurs with the death of each one of us – that death that, when no longer anything more than the death of the individual, carries an unbearable burden and collapses into insignificance. (IC: 1)

Communism is capable of reducing singular events and beings to an interpersonal immanence in which the goal of immanence is the actualiza-tion of the essence of humanity by economic, technological and political means. The existence of human beings is put to work to reveal this essence, as if the essence of human beings is to accomplish the pure closure of immanence in the realization of essence. However, Nancy insists vehe-mently that this immanence is synonymous with the "general horizon of our time, encompassing both democracies and their fragile juridical para-pets". It can assume many forms, such as individualism and communism, which, whatever faults one might deem them to have, at least acknowledge that being is "in common" or that "we are commonly" beyond the imma-nence of market democracy (IC: 3; BSP: 42; C: 378). In so far as it does not recognize this, market democracy itself might be the condition of possibility of the emergence of new forms of totalitarianism.

Therefore democracy, which offers merely general or "flat" appropria-tions and "lacks being", is a deceptively dangerous antipode because there is no definitive intrinsic limit or region precluding a resurgence of totali-tarianism. Indeed, totalitarianism is often understood to be synonymous with certain characteristics that market democracy might reveal discretely, as when authority and tradition disappear, power is disembodied, critical distance is obviated, hierarchies are disrupted, the political is de-localized and politics is given over to vested interests (BC: 11; RP: 127). If for totali-tarianism there is a pristine transparency reflective of an immanence of truth, for democracy there is nothing but indeterminate (or even straight-forwardly empty) truths of the kind fostered in the money markets and shopping complexes. Strictly speaking, for contemporary democracy, there is no sacrifice *to* the cause and its truth, but on the contrary a sacrifice *of* this truth. It thereby divests itself of the means by which the seductions of the cause can be combated. In fear of giving way to the immanence of the cause and its rhetoric, democracy offers nothing in compensation: "Truth without figure of sense, truth of the absence of sense: law in its absence of foundation, ecotechnics in the guise of Cause ..." Liberalism, the very value of market democratic life, is exhausted by its "eager repression of the very question of being-in-common" after the collapse of socialism. It offers only the "pale, derisory, fleeting evasion of the 'civilization of the individual' (or of the 'person'), liberal without liberation". Moreover, it can be defended that the "man" of liberalism is not so much alienated as simply devoid of identity, propriety, purpose and proportion (SW: 90; BSP: 43; C: 377; P: 18). Thus democracy has sacrificed the very politics of sacrifice itself, thereby weakening itself in the face of the possible emergence of political totalitarianism. But the other horn of democracy's difficulty is that it cannot appropriate the rhetoric of sacrifice without actively setting the condition of this emergence.

Nancy wonders whether we might not gain insights into emergent totalitarianisms by re-examining the mythic figure of the democratic individual, the figure of the symbolic order of market democratic immanence (the good middle class family-orientated business man). What complicates this purview is that, under the immanentist lights of communitarian and libertarian thought, the individual is merely the "residue of the experience of the dissolution of community". In a sense, one is entitled to think of the individual as the constitutive unit of political community if only because of the myth of the dissolution of community. However, in so far as the individual is a fabrication of a politics that subscribes to such a myth, market democracy's confidence that "the individual" would resist the emergence of totalitarianism is one that sets "the individual" on a potentially totalitarian plinth. (The good, wholesome market democrat would never permit totalitarianism to raise its hoary head, even if that resistance required novel expressions of totalitarianism.) Different as they otherwise are, individualism and communism equally deny the "ecstasy" of vulnerability and sharing in open community (IC: 3–6). In that sense, both already provide the immanential space from which totalitarianism might irresistibly spring.

If totalitarianism is a symbolic politics of sacrifice to the point of the suicidal, and democracy lacks determinate content and purpose (that is, is devoid of both *demos* and *kratein*), then a finite thinking of the sense of "the political" requires a divorce from the "theologicopolitical" myth of the 1930s. According to that myth, democracy's "truth without figure or sense" rests on the unnameable, ungrounded institutions of justice and law, yet it is precisely such institutions that have not been able to offer resistance to the nationalisms arising in the post-Soviet world. Instead, the subject of that fear should be a market democracy that apperceives itself in libertarian (and occasionally communitarian) terms and increasingly exhibits totalitarian figures. In the main, market democracy as contractarian immanence lacks both the spacing of singular beings that enables the free circulation of sense and the ties that enable the sharing of community. One might say that democracy labours in its struggle to be stateless in such a fashion that it is easily exhausted and prone to totalitarian or religious interpretations. Ultimately, it becomes the absolute subject whose figure would be capital itself, not the subject, citizen, sovereign or community. Market democracy itself seems to tie individuals together, but capitalist commitment renders it ignorant of the question of how the knots of singularity are tied. Only political writing, or writing as a resistance to politics, can do more than expose the empty truths of democracy and the "grey tones" of Weimar in the 1930s. It must offer alternatives to the postulates of self-sufficiency at "the left" and at "the right", not by valorizing capital, nor even by glorifying the religious determination of "man" or the secular alternative of the citizen. On the contrary, it must enable singular identities to write themselves expressively, which is to "know and practice themselves as (k)nots of sense" (SW: 91, 108, 121–2). Political writing is resistant to politics itself because it "writes" the resistance of such ties to the very market democracy that serves to shape them. Although this is not an especially resounding conclusion from the vantage point of politics, it might very well be that writing is the subversion of politics that opens the essence of the political itself to discourse without permitting its complete exposition.

Untying the knots of the social contract

Nancy offers several appreciative perspectives on the role of the bonds among singularities in contractarian thought, especially that of Rousseau. Poorly named as it is, Rousseau's "contract" exalts mankind and does not merely create social arrangements; it also provides insights into the essence of "the political" and of insubstantial community (BSP: 34). Nevertheless, Nancy objects to the subordination and subsequent dissolution of these bonds into a tacit agreement that then serves as the sole relation between singularities. Nancy utilizes the very awkward rhetoric of "tying" and "knotting" to elucidate the difficulty of addressing such relations in a fashion that does not merely fall prey to the reflective immanence of political discourse.

According to the contractarian notion of sociality, communities are groups of pre-existing individuals whose bonds politics strives to tie or untie. In other words, politics is always threatening to reduce the bonds of community that compose "the political" to a closed immanence. The question of "the political" is how such ties can be kept completely untied, that is, to change the figure, "to configure a space of sense that would not be reabsorbed into its own truth". Such a configuration would "trace the form of being-toward in being-together without identifying the traits of the toward-what or toward-whom, without identifying or verifying the 'to what end' of the sense of being-in-common". In the absence of such a configurative sense, there is merely totalitarian truth (SW: 90). In other words, there is a threat of totalitarian immanence wherever one demands that such togetherness in community should identify itself in terms of a resolute social striving for a determinate goal.

Nancy is fascinated by the possibility that "the political" and the sharing of ties within a community could produce figures and practices that are irreducible to political paradigms of immanential truth. Such bonds must be conceived as if they were not self-sufficient ties of "love or hate, force or law", he maintains, because they are always supposed to be tied already. In other words, we should not presume that communities consist of determinate knots that could (or could not) be untied. What is needed is a "politics of nonselfsufficiency", in which the sharing of vulnerability among singular beings is not taken to consist of determinate ties among determinate entities whose total hypostasization would be accessible to resorption into political truth (SW: 303, 111). In yet other words, there are communal knots produced politically that not even politics can tie or untie. Nancy describes this conceptual scenario:

> The political, if this word may serve to designate not the organization of society but the disposition of community as such, the destination of its sharing, must not be the assumption or the work of love and death. It need neither find, nor effect, a communion taken to be lost or still to come. If the political is not dissolved in the sociotechnical element of forces and needs (in which, in effect, it seems to be dissolving under our eyes), it must inscribe the sharing of community. The outline of singularity would be "political" – as would be the outline of is communication and its ecstasy. "Political" would mean a community ordering itself to the unworking of its communication, or destined to this unworking: a community consciously undergoing the experience of its sharing.   (IC: 40)

One might say, then, that the political inscribes the sharing of community by untying the knots of communication that are accessible to political appropriation. What Nancy demands is a new thinking of the knots whose ties compose the singular relationships of and within a community. The end of a "politics of nonselfsufficiency" would be the incessant tying or enchainments of social relations themselves, not any politically structured immanence of untying such knots in order to retie them for political ends. Therefore, although politics lacks form and substance, it consists in the infinite (or at least indefinite) gesture of tying such necessarily ineradicable knots. They are neither already tied by democracy's contractarian implication, nor potentially tied by the totalitarian mission.

The rhetoric of "tying" and "knots" is cumbersome at best, but political discourse has it own ways of rendering it intelligible. Most succinctly, the contractarian thought of Jean-Jacques Rousseau intrigues Nancy in so far as it offers deconstructive possibilities of sovereignty, community, subjectivity and citizenship. Nevertheless, Rousseau elicits a certain ambivalence in Nancy: on the one hand, Rousseau's contribution to "rethinking the political" is positive in so far as he ponders the sharing in co-appearance of community; yet, on the other hand, he is also the thinker of the dissolution of community into a political general will. Nancy regards Rousseau as a thinker who substantializes community and subordinates it to a "public" will, passing over the openness of insubstantial community and the sharing that composes it in order to establish the reflective immanence of political ideology as the mode whereby community is determined. In this sense, Rousseau represents the substantialist and immanentist thinking of the political that facilitates the constitution of the "political animal" by means of the tying of a social knot tied by and available to politics. However, if the model of the social contract is impoverished by its presumption of "the political" in terms of contractually constituted and tacitly bound subjectivity, then it is as if there were no ties at all among singular beings *prior* to this tacit agreement. Rousseau thinks "the sense of the in-common neither as the truth of a common subject nor as a 'general' sense superimposed on 'particular' senses, but, to the contrary, as the absence of any 'general' sense outside of the internally numerous singularity of each of the 'subjects of sense'". Strictly speaking, contractarian thought disavows the persistence of the bonds of community in the process of the establishment of the public good by tacit consent. For Rousseau, the contract establishes a bond that links and separates individuals who are themselves neither linked nor separated in the state of nature. If the contract exposes the essence of "man" to judgement, then it provides originary linkages that are not shared by singular beings and that dissolve singularity into the condition of group individuality. In so far as he unveiled the tenuous links of community prior to subordinating them to and annulling them by political ideology, Rousseau is "the thinker par excellence of compearance", of the fragmented, indeterminate sharings of community (RP: 93; IC: 29–30).

As noted above, Nancy explores the various aspects of the contract, especially the quadratic axiology of subjectivity, citizenship, sovereignty and community. Sovereignty and community are formal notions that enable sense to emerge absolutely in a manner that enables the subject and the citizen to become definitive figures of political discourse from whose perspective sense is postulated. Interestingly, Nancy remarks that there has never been a pure example of either a politics of the subject or a politics of the citizen. For example, a citizen is always one among many "someones" within the "everyone", whereas the subject is the one raised to the power implied in a unity of subjects. "The citizenship comprises numerous unicities, subjecthood comprises an identificatory unity", he writes. In other words, the citizen and the subject are figures of contractarian imma-nence, yet their difference is determined by the substantialist criteria. The citizen is an individual in a group that attains its measure of individuality within the group itself, whereas the subject attains an ontological status by means of subordination to and dissolution within a realm of anonymous sovereignty. The citizen assumes its place in a created public space, within which there is a circulation of sense. Occupying, traversing and being defined by sharing in this exterior space, the citizen is a complex unity of formal "rights, obligations, dignities and virtues" that are reified as defini-tive of the autonomous person. The "contract" of Rousseau, then, presup-poses a dimension of sharing that is eradicated in the very formation of the figure of the citizen to which the contract invariably lends coherent shape. The sharing within and of a community of citizens just consists in partici-pation in the collection of roles and signification that constitute "citizen-ship", not in any preceding sharing that might anticipate the sense of the community.

However, Nancy insists that Rousseau shifts emphasis in this axiology towards the notion of the "people". Roughly speaking, the citizen is no longer conceived merely as a participant in a created political space, but rather as a citizen subject to the ends of a particular people whose history is a history of the citizen's own status within "the people". If so, then there is a complex interplay between citizenship and subjecthood:

> The citizen becomes subject at the point where the community gives itself (as) an interiority, and at the point where sovereignty no longer contents itself with residing in the formal autoteleology of a "contract", or in its autojurisdiction, but expresses also an essence (and it is indeed thus that, in the context of theologico-political essentiality, history has produced the concept of sover-eignty). Reciprocally, the subject makes itself into a citizen at the point where the expressed essence tends to express itself in and as

a civic space and, if one can put it like this, to "display" subjective
essentiality.   (SW: 106)

"Imperial" politics arises when the heterogeneity of citizenship and
subjectivity buttress one another in a play of reflective immanence: subjectivity is delineated historically by virtue of the activities of citizens, and
citizens' activities are informed by this history. When this occurs, political
immanence appropriates them in the form of the thoughts of a leader,
country or peoples whose self-purposiveness serves as definitive of self-
identity. All negativities, all foreign elements including other peoples and
their ideologies, are appropriable by a self-purposive entity that mirrors
and enlarges the autonomies of the citizen–subjects that compose it.
Reflective immanence has a way of expanding subjectivity in order to
express the autonomies of all, such that the individual citizen–subject's
interiority is realized in the operations of an expansive market democratic
"imperialism". Nevertheless, such a tension among the figures of citizens
and subjects, political sovereignty and the community of "the people" is
resolved in a dissolution of subjects and citizens into reflective immanence.
This dissolution forbids both any infinite return of the singular being to its
own existence and any sharing in the finitude of existence with other
singular beings. In other words, immanentism, whether in totalitarianism
or market democracy, plays politics back to "the people" in the form of the
symbolic order of the general will, thereby reducing to silence any alternative discourses, speaking only within the prevailing paradigm, refusing the
recognition of dependences upon any open community, and ultimately,
eradicating the singularities of the entities that compose it. It is precisely
this tension that is present in all contracts and revolutions. The tension
between the immanence of the circulation of sense among singular events
and the immanence of the symbolic order of politics are entwined in such a
way that the question of political discourse is one that political discourse
itself cannot address.

Ultimately, contractarianism dissimulates the entanglements of political
discourse. It offers a political interpretation of political ties, thereby subordinating the open, circulating immanence of the sense of "the political" to
reductive and appropriative political discourses. Entanglements, Nancy
writes, presuppose a "heterogeneous *realitas*" consisting of "proximity and
distance, attachment and detachment, intricacy, intrigue, and ambivalence".
However, the question is whether contemporary theory can conceive the
knot without immediately utilizing the "juridicocommercial model" of
market democracy (which merely presumes a bond among people, as if that
would legitimate the appropriation of communities of singular beings under
the rubric of a political sovereignty they did not initially possess). It is

138

precisely this presumption that is "the founding abyss or decisive aporia of the *Social Contract*". Unfortunately, what Rousseau cannot acknowledge is the notion of related singularities and their sharing in community as the original state of the human condition because they are knotted with other singularities in a tying that has no end in the will of the people or the establishment of pure immanential sovereignty.

In conclusion, Nancy finds that Rousseau has indeed noticed the entanglements of sharings among individual persons as singularities. Unfortunately this is intelligible solely in terms of the substantialist presupposition of tacit consent among atomic individuals that offers cohesion to community. Presumably, what Nancy finds so fascinating about Rousseau is his effort to think the very bonds of community, even if he regards them as dissolved into the general will that offers new modes of mutual implication within the closed immanence of politics. Rousseau has conceived of a space of sense constitutive of community, but he has not guarded against the resorption of that space into the political sense of truth.

Conclusion

- Nancy's fixation with politics is informed by a desire to address the question of politics itself: is everything political? Drawing a distinction between the empirical practices of politics and the essential nature of "the political", he suggests that we should not merely invert priorities of domination and self-sufficiency but strive to find a way of disrupting its spacing in order to secure it from such domination. The question of "the political", in other words, can only be approached if sovereignty is understood to be completely divorced from and inappropriable by any form of political domination.
- Totalitarianism is a threat to contemporary democracy, Nancy proposes, but not because it might return in the form of 1930s-style fascism. On the contrary, the most banal aspects of contemporary market democracy could yield novel totalitarian forms of politics without massive social change. Wherever there is closed immanence, in particular wherever there is mediation and routinization that reduces singularity and anticipates resolution of discourse, there is the potential of an emergence of a new form of totalitarianism.
- Contractarian thought attempts to demonstrate the manner in which the linkages between individuals constitute social reality. Yet such linkages come in the form of agreement among pre-existing individuals, which are figures of substantialist and immanentist thought. Thus,

even though Rousseau exposed the condition of sharing among singular beings, he immediately superimposed "political" criteria upon it, thereby appropriating it to political discourse. Contractarianism is based on presuppositions about the pre-originary circulation of sense and the sharings that constitute community, but it eradicates their vitality in the name of political standards of appropriation.

CHAPTER 8
Ecotechnics

With considerable sensitivity, Nancy addresses the contemporary question of the deleterious effects of the circulation of capital on the circulation of sense, and thereby, on open community itself. He insists that we are too hasty, too undiscerning, when we lament the demise of community in the face of capital's relentless expansion. For example, Nancy concurs with Hardt and Negri in their view that the circulation of capital "manages hybrid identities, flexible hierarchies, and plural exchanges through modulating networks of control".[1] Yet, he argues, although it is surely the case that capital does threaten to produce reflective immanence and substantial community, it depends for its sustenance on the circulation of sense through social reality. And, he concludes, capital can actually enhance and expand the linkages that constitute open community.

In order to address this point in greater detail, Nancy introduces the concept of "ecotechnics", the calculative operations by quantifiable means that inform the reflective immanence technological deployment engenders. It is omnipresent in market democratic life and pervades its values. It is also a global phenomenon that provides a simulation of sovereignty in the exercise of military means to peace. "Capital", which encompasses many ecotechnical equipollences, is often thought to establish the "cohumanity of an antihumanity", a "community of operations, not of existences". It also offers up the sharing "in" and "with" that composes open and insubstantial community (BC: 10). No matter how exhaustive of human life technology might appear to be, it can (and often does) enhance the communal sharing constitutive of human being. In other words, the justice (and indeed even morality) already embedded in the circulation of sense is irreducible to the paradigms of ecotechnical sovereignty now effaced in the withdrawal of sense; yet capital and its equivalent quantities can provide new links among singularities and strengthen the old. Nancy insists that since there is a measure of sovereignty in this social reality that

141

cannot be eradicated by ecotechnical modalities, a mode of *technē* in which sharings among singularities offer the potential of civil community. Nancy always encourages us to look forward to the futural question of whether such a measure of technically enhanced sovereignty could serve as a potential resistance to the demand for (and fascination with) the immanential figures of sovereignty promulgated by ecotechnical war-making. One might say, then, that technologies create problems of community, yet also provide the means for addressing them.

Although technology could be regarded as "colossal", it facilitates diversification, variation and brilliant ephemerality, which are precisely the singular conditions of open community. That is, it may be a "common ground" or habituation in the production, invention and incessant transformation of ends that are never given; but it also provides the very linkages by which the existence of the open sharing of community is revealed (BSP: 185; P: 19). Although he is critical of global ecotechnics, he regards any cynical denunciations of its "diabolical" or "conspiratorial" tendencies to be misconceived. Despite transforming and even partly destroying nature, technology has not lost the definitive end to which it purportedly strives, which has become merely the pure exercise of its means, as with trivial innovations for the purpose of "convenience" (MMT: 97). We should speak of technologies in the *plural*, he insists, and avoid the presumption that technology (singular) represents a ubiquitous conspiracy against humanity and its communities. An overdetermined concept, "technology" is often used as if it referred to a "vast machinic or combinatorial apparatus embracing technologies" whose "absolute nexus" admits of no location. However, he concedes, there is no end to the proliferation of interdependencies among technologies, but these do not indicate any common property that might suggest such a nexus. We must ask what a given technology is "for" and what manner of enhancement of immanence it provides when it strives to appropriate whatever is non-immanential in nature and society, and especially when success is measured in terms of the essential technification of existence itself. Generally speaking, the very term "technology" conceals our inability to grapple with finitude, which is reflected in both our terror in the face of untamed nature and our fear of the consequences of our potential mastery over it. In other words, mindful of the potential destruction of humanity that the unfettering of technologies might facilitate, Nancy insists that it is better to consider precisely how the "finitude of sense" is exhibited to us by means of our devolution of a global ecotechnics.

Destruction, purity, sovereignty

Contemporary global culture is no exception to the inherent destructiveness of all culture, Nancy soberingly suggests, a potential devastation that might very well be the referential index for contemporary values. Implausible as this might sound, one might consider that even the value of "reconstruction" (e.g. in Afghanistan and Iraq) testifies to the "power of ruination" in the symbolic orders of contemporary thought. Destruction "haunts our manner of existence and thinking" even as it is a significant topic of political and social discourse. A deconstruction of the structural intersections of sense among finite beings and singular events, it is a renunciation of sense in a spirit of hatred or despair of existence itself (not merely random acts of atrocity against singularities). In other words, when there is an attempt to undermine an enemy's way of life, culture destroyers express their despair about sense and struggle to dismantle the very structures composing its circulation. In the effort to impose reflective immanence, their actions shatter the meaningful structures of cultural formations by removing them from the "crucible of sense, from the points at which a sense is either emitted or concentrated" (FT: 78–80). Destruction, then, is reflected in the consolidated effort to render any excluded "other", any enemy beyond the substantial community, as an inoperative historical reference point.

Genocide at Sarajevo and the subsequent attacks by UN forces upon it, Nancy argues passionately, illustrate this destruction very well. "Sarajevo" is a "dimension-less point of a diagram of sovereignty, an ortho-normative gauge on a ballistic and political computer, a target frozen in a telescopic sight, and it is the very figure of the exactitude of taking aim, the pure taking aim of an essence" (BSP: 145). Generally speaking, the meaningful structures of Sarajevo were disrupted by genocide, and then further fragmented by the usage of precision weaponry in the name of the sovereignty of humanitarian aims. In the intercommunal struggle for immanential purity (of race, of nationhood, etc.) sovereignty became associated with destruction. Nancy's captivating exploration of the existential conditions of destruction shares affinities with his discourse on wickedness (see above). The destroyer resents finite "connections, interplay, assembly and its complexity" and in so doing "releases an infinite sense or nonsensical infinity" in which even self-destruction is the nonsensical norm. The culture of destruction dismembers culture itself by rendering all cultural arrangements opaque to the finite thinking of sense. Of course, the assumption here is that a culture of destruction strives to establish a simulacrum of reflective immanence. That is, it merely plays back to itself whatever its capacity for cultural iconoclasm necessitates, and that would be only the nonsensical affirmation of the sense of destruction. The opacity resulting from destruction's affirmation of its own sense poses myriad singular destructions, potentially severing the links required for the circulation of sense. By means of operations of reflective immanence, Sarajevo witnessed the association of "Sarajevo" itself with the figure of the destruction of sense itself. For example, the rape of Bosnian women represented a hatred for the complexities and impurities of mixed communal life and a desire to remove the potential of sovereign expression by the Bosnian people and their culture. The rapes were intended to produce "impure" offspring, unacceptable "bastards" whose very existence would "defile" the "purity" of the Bosnian people and annul the possibility of any mixing of community. If the temporal persistence of singularities is suspended by the time of destruction itself, then this interruption of the future makes the present potential of the future "stillborn". It is worthwhile to recall that the evil of wickedness consists in the surprise of the good, interrupting and permanently suspending its goodness in a fashion that renders it, too, "stillborn" (FT: 80–82; BSP: 146, 155; EF: 126). Again, a culture of destruction that strives to affirm its own sense affirms only the sense of destruction, interrupting but not nullifying the potential of goodness erupting in future communal relations.

The destroyer asserts its own finitude and affirms its infinite power as such, Nancy proposes. Every instance of destruction is a kind of self-destruction; the destroyer's affirmation of its own existence as an infinitely powerful finite being is as much a destruction of the destroyer's self as of the self of the destroyed. This is especially true in the "politics of sacrifice", in which the "final figure of self-sufficiency" turns away from the world towards an affirmation of its own sovereignty (SW: 89, 110). This turn amounts to a movement of affirmation of one's own reflective immanence and substantial community, which may encompass any resisting singularities. What the self-affirming destroyer desires is the focus of a sovereignty that eradicates finite transcendences and establishes the terms of its own immanence and substantiality in order to do so. Perhaps more profoundly, the destroyer typifies a certain wickedness in which there is "hatred of existence as such", a refusal to acknowledge the singularity of the destroyed and a desire to affirm that one is more than merely a participant in existence in general. However, this desire is limited by the seemingly indestructible sovereignty of the world itself. In a captivating manner, existence itself resists and nullifies the potential success of the destroyer's unfulfillable desire for sovereignty. Both of these destructions lack reality, which is possessed only in the moment of touch between singularities in the sharing of being that poses the primary resistance to destruction (FT: 84–6; EF: 128). Yet Nancy is adamant that this mode of mundane resistance is refracted into the resistance offered by the multiplicity of singular events and the finite beings that share in them communally. For example, Nancy writes poignantly that the "purity" of unified community and its unchallenged sovereignty is impossible, since mixture is constitutive of all communities in so far as the limits of all such communities are intersections at which being is shared in and sense is circulated. Communities are not identified negatively against one another; they serve as venues of sharing in which singularity finds sense accessible according to practices that require connections and intersections. The destroyer striving for this purity and sovereignty has an impossible task, since any achievement of purity would result in nothing at all if being singular requires the mixtures the destroyer strives to eradicate (BSP: 156). In alternative terms, one might say that cultures pose a form of essential resistance to the imposition of sovereignty precisely because of the plurality of singularities that compose them. Ultimately, cultures do not mix, he avers, because they are mixtures already, mixtures without the requisite horizons presupposed by "mixing" that would facilitate the eradication of "mixing" with others (BSP: 151; MMT: 91–2). This question of the destructive potential latent in the political striving for sovereignty is essential to any examination of contemporary warfare and the role of technology within it.

Sovereignty and the ecotechnics of war

Nancy examines contemporary warfare in a stirringly insightful manner. As a "figure" in our symbolic space, war, despite its seemingly interminable history, serves as an indicator of a singularly new form of the deployment of technology. Of course, much of the world practises warfare as it has always been practised, but the Balkan wars, Iraq I and Iraq II suggest its contemporary global nature. Contemporary warfare is an exercise of sovereignty on a global scale, which may be the conceptual basis for the obfuscation between, on the one hand, "police actions" against warlords whose sovereignty is precarious or unrecognized and, on the other, interventions in unstable conflicts in which sovereignty is completely lacking. Contemporary representatives and figures of sovereignty, such as the US and the UN, exert and establish their sovereignty through a variety of global stratagems. What is surprising, according to Nancy, is that the paradigm of "legitimate state–national violence" has resurfaced and gained credence. During a period when "the State" and its sovereignty were held in considerable suspicion, nationalisms committed to warfare arose, often under the newly fashionable rubric of the humanitarian defence of human rights. "Spontaneously modelled from within a wholly available, general legitimacy", nationalisms and their figures (whether they be American presidents or Iraqi dictators) are often as ridiculous as they are heroic in their acknowledgement of few limitations to their willingness to extend the sovereignty of the nation they represent. Nationalism and its figures are already latent in the commitment to sovereignty that the destructive potential of technology offers.

In the name of "freedom" and "democracy", international law (which is uncertainly founded on "universal" principles, yet possesses no sovereignty of its own) provides a simulation of legitimacy for humanitarian warfare. Even so, Nancy maintains, it lacks universality and sovereignty even if it is "structured by the techno-economic network and the supervision of Sovereigns". Resistance to this sovereign power of war becomes dissipated when public opinion is favourable to the notion that warfare, when fully justified by international law, is a legitimate and legitimizing exercise of sovereignty. Resistance to this immanence of humanitarian principles is marginalized or effaced from the symbolicity of politics. From its points of reference, pacifism, for example, is an unglamorous, impotent and somewhat disreputable "*habitus* without substance" which pales in comparison with the grandeur of the "tragedy of the warrior". The result of an exclusionary political ideology is a sovereignty in which the *ethos* of war and the justification of the exercise of sovereignty are simply two aspects of the same process. In the name of a commitment to "policing" the world according to the highest democratic ideals, there is no internal resistance or intrinsic delimitation that might facilitate opposition; indeed, even partisan opposition is merely another aspect of this immanence. Interestingly, if war waged in such terms is legitimized by no initial sovereignty, and yet it offers legitimization to such sovereignty, then it exercises a sovereignty acquired solely through successful exercise. Law legitimizes war and war legitimizes law in the suspension (or exception) of the process of legitimization. "The right to wage war excepts itself from law at a point replete with sovereign brilliance", a brilliance (lacking in the exercises of law) that dazzles the media's audience (BSP: 105–6). Nothing conjures the figure of humanitarian law better than the deployment of military resources, which are, by modern lights, necessary for the establishment of sovereignty wherever it is lacking.

However, there is enormous tension between this exercise of sovereignty and the universal commitments of international humanitarian law. The very notion of a "just war" is troubling to this law, which nonetheless appears to gain credibility solely through the exercise of precisely such "just" warfare. Nancy's guiding question appears to be: does humanitarian law justify warfare, or is it warfare itself that bestows upon such law the legitimacy requisite for the justification of war? After all, from the world wars through the cold war, the West did not regard war as an entitlement or prerogative for the enforcement of sovereignty, Nancy insinuates. Often disparaged in association with the memory of the "dirty war" of Vietnam, the notion of a just war receives popular credence when ecotechnical deployments and humanitarian law combine and promise to establish the sovereignty of the West in the name of what is best for the world itself. In other words, the West will deploy militarily for the establishment of peace if its own sovereignty and prosperity are enhanced (although that is not to maintain that hegemony is always the dominant paradigmatic goal of peace-keeping).

There is a conventional assumption that only democracy and its ideals can possibly offer peace in an age of precariously balanced, or absent, sovereignty. Yet democracy has become the art of endowing the public of a given republic with the power of sovereignty by enabling it to declare war in the name of "humanity", "justice" and "morality". Today, it is commonly acknowledged that the public cannot declare war on sovereigns *per se*, although it can wage war on rogue leaders whose policies and practices are contrary to the principles of humanitarian rights illuminated under democratic ideals. Captivatingly, the public can take onto itself a degree of sovereignty that no prince could impose upon himself (if only because a prince is merely exerting his own sovereignty, while the public act on behalf of moral–juridical principles of humanity). On more than one occasion, the US and the UN have found themselves locked into a seemingly irresolvable tension because the former has the sovereign *technē* but lacks the sovereign legitimacy the latter possesses (BSP: 123–4). The divorce between the promise of an ideal of legitimacy and the capacity to enforce that ideal is all too apparent, in Nancy's view. Whether a police action or not, Western warfare admits its own sovereignty by denying that it is war that establishes sovereignty; or in other words, in denying that warfare is its own end, but rather serves humanitarian goals, it affirms itself as the most viable and legitimate means to that goal. One might suggest, then, that the humanitarian ideal of peace, assisted by the latent pacifism that champions it, lacks grandeur and enervates war. By contemporary standards, if peace is to be established, it must be so according to the sovereign *technē* of police action–warfare motivated by the reified ideals of international law. War gives legitimacy to technology even as it produces sovereignty from humanitarian efforts. That is, when technology is deployed in the service of peace, it cannot resist being reduced to the immanence of sovereignty's affirmation of its own technicity. It would be very strange if the sovereign exception of war in democracy, impelled by the ideal of peace, were to efface itself in the accomplished end of peace. In other words, if war is the technical means of affirming sovereignty, then to establish peace in the name of humanitarian principles would be to affirm such principles, not sovereignty. Perhaps it is in this sense that the US now identifies itself immanentially as the guardian of such principles, such that its own affirmation of sovereignty is equipollent to the establishment of peace under humanitarian ideals. Hence every war it wages is a war for both the "good" of the world and its own sovereignty within it. This, Nancy insists, is not to denounce a cynical stratagem of politics, but merely to suggest the co-implication of national interest and humanitarian aims in the paradigms of politics and their reflective immanence.

Nancy queries whether sovereignty demands war by carrying exceptions to law within itself, that is, whether sovereignty itself implies transgressions of law. Indeed, even the prevailing humanism, impotently non-militant as it is, promises to moralize politics; and yet it also arms the law with a not-yet-moralized politics, namely, that of the "just war" paradigm. There is merely a gaping disjuncture between "the always weak and troubled schema of the 'war of law (police action)' and a reactivated (warmed over?) schema of 'sovereign war'". In contemporary warfare, it is not clear whether anything distinguishes police action and sovereign warfare (both are exercises of the legitimacy of humanitarian law). Nevertheless, again, Nancy does not commit the potential error of assuming that the West manipulates humanitarian law for its own military ends. Rather, if war has returned as a viable figure of public discourse, this is an expression of a public frustration with the process of legitimatization in global politics in an epoch when economics is denied its own "universally legitimated finality". War, the "ambiguous sovereign-slave of economics", is the gilding on the shield of sovereignty that provides protection in the effort to rescue the politics of impotent "juridical-moralism that is without sovereignty" (BSP: 109–11). Generally speaking, the impotence of humanitarian law is apparent when it is warfare that establishes its principles.

For Nancy, the secret of the unnatural alliance between warfare and humanitarianism might reside in the fact that reflective global immanence includes the representation of the lack of sovereignty, and a desire for it. When "the media" celebrates the "brilliant, incandescent, fascinating sovereignty" that traditional warfare exhibits, it serves as both the catalyst for and the framework within which the sovereignty of reflective immanence can be established. War, depicted moment by moment in the media, portrays an epic spectacle replete with traditional heroisms, as if there were no difference between contemporary warfare and traditional war films. Images of war are a part of the war itself, for they play a nation's desire for sovereignty back to itself, monitor its successes and call for greater sacrifice when misfortune is experienced. Since the imagery and the reality are intertwined in such a specular fashion that the simulation/ reality distinction has fragmented, it is simply not possible to dismiss this media figuration of warfare as a merely ignorable simulation of reality possessing only symbolic value. Although the media portrays warfare as an epic phenomenon, precision technology and road-side bombing alike have no tinge of epic value. The figures of the simulated epic serve to reinforce the immanence within which war is played back as an exercise and fulfilment of sovereignty (the fireman coming from the ashes of the twin towers of the World Trade Center, the US soldier playing with the Afghan boy, the bearded terrorist glowering at the camera). Contemporary conflicts as depicted by the media do not presuppose the simulation/reality dichotomy crucial for the determination of the epic.

Vital to media-inspired reflective immanence is the portrayal of techno-logical and psychological aspects of warfare. All of the figures of ecotechnical sovereignty are in place in the media itself, although objects such as uniforms, flags and missiles "lose their symbolic character to the extent that their technicity grows". However, such objects can be symboli-cally reinvested into the immanential portrayal of warfare. Since precision weaponry is both humanitarian in nature and indicative of the stellar legitimacy of the humanitarian cause it represents, media images of weap-onry and its destructive potential affirm "the sovereign right of the sover-eign power to execute sovereign destruction". The figures of the symbolic order, such as precision weaponry, Nancy remarks, produce effects upon the reality of the "space of the presentation of Sovereignty", which is political immanence *par excellence* (BSP: 121, 128). There is, however, a certain polarity within the immanential portrayal of warfare. On the one hand, the technology of Western powers is celebrated with a kind of fascination for both the enormous potential of destruction and the precision of missile technology. In a self-congratulatory manner, it is always portrayed as a result of the "cleaner" manner in which warfare could be well executed and even "surgical", with "collateral damage" kept to a tolerable minimum. On the other hand, the depictions of the dangerous "weapons of mass destruction" possessed by the nefarious rogue nations are crucial to the economy of ideo-logical immanence. Ultimately, the surgical weaponry of the heroes and the massive destruction promised by the weaponry of the villains polarizes within the representations of reflective immanence. One might add that there is a significant humanitarian dimension to this polarization: on one side, there are weapons that minimize "collateral damage" and on the other, there are "human shields" against precisely such a threat.

The representation of technology is as important for the ends of contemporary warfare as the usage of high-tech weaponry can be. As *physis*, war is natural and expressed through the most "brutal instincts", and as *technē* (in the sense that the "coldest calculations" are at work), it is representative of the total consolidation of sovereignty and its focus on a single point of resistance. Nevertheless, technology is not responsible for warfare, although it is often insisted that technology itself drives war efforts and its very usage is an end in itself. Nancy suggests that "war is sovereignty's technology *par excellence*" in the sense that war puts this technology to work as a "mode of execution, manifestation and effectuation". War, then, is the means of realizing the ends of politics, and technology provides the modes whereby such ends are achievable. The question, Nancy states, is whether the technological modes of such military means are themselves finite or infinite. Technology has not merely furnished the finite means of destruction, but rather the infinite mastery of destructive ends. The "end" of technology is always in process of "resolute infinitization, the incessant displacement of ends" in the sense of being focused through an infinity of means upon the finite end which only technological destruction could promise – the apocalypse of nuclear destruction. In a movement in which "infinite nuclear finitization" finishes humanity itself, technology, then, could destroy the capacity to destroy completely (BSP: 117, 120; FT: 84–5). A "question of technology" can only be addressed if technology itself is regarded as an end in itself, a "finish of Being" or capacity for final destruction. Although there is a significant tradition of denying that technology could determine its own ends, or indeed, even be the completion of itself, we must hesitate, Nancy remarks, before we conclude that the principles regulating technology are extrinsic to technology itself (BSP: 118–19; MMT: 97). In other words, we must beware of depicting the problem as if it consisted of a singular technology that, on the one hand, in its very essence determines its own end, and, on the other, must always be adapted to ends that are not themselves technological in nature. This presupposes the inside–outside distinction of reflective immanence, in which truth is created and resorbed intrinsically, or is imposed and absorbed extrinsically.

Although technological war is an execution of sovereign ends, it can serve as a sovereign end to all sovereign ends themselves in a manner that cannot be subordinated to any other principle. As we have seen, Nancy offers the remarkable thought that war is both the natural *physis* and the political *technē* of sovereignty itself. One might suggest, then, that war is a kind of art in which a "mode of execution of Being, as its mode of finishing in the explosive brilliance of the beautiful and sublime, that doubled rivalry for sovereignty that occurs within the blossoming of *physis*", obtains (BSP: 122–3). Technologies are all attuned to some engagement with nature, and they strive impossibly to gain sovereignty over the absolute sense of the world, whether that be represented by the natural resistance of a mountain range to irrigation practices or the political resistance of criminalized "rogue nations". Technologies' "sovereign" transcendence over nature erases itself when it puts into play the exteriority of nature itself, thereby revealing only that there are technologies, not any global technology, that interact with nature in a multiplicity of ways (FT: 25). In other words, warfare enables the artistry of the clash between nature and technology to be brought together in an explosive and incandescent affirmation of sovereignty. This military artistry has effects not only on nature, but also on the very societies striving to affirm their own sovereignty by destructive means.

Nancy proposes what he refers to as "ecotechnics" in order to examine the logic of technologies in terms of both *physis* and *technē*. Generally speaking, in an age in which it is not certain that the absolute subject of the world is not the "logic and global figure" of capital, and that the "disappearance" of the West plausibly results from the expansion of the "generalized" uniformity of capital, Nancy postulates that the operations by which market democracy circulates quantities deserve to be conceived in terms of "ecotechnics". This multifarious concept denotes the circulation of the figure of capital in myriad forms (statistics, ticket sales, dollars, kilowatts, volts, megabytes, optical fibres, calories, body bags, "collateral damage", weapons, etc.). Against the backdrop of the capitalistic paradigm of the equivalences of singularities and the plurality of forms of circulation, everything is of "market value and can be exchanged, even 'humanity'" itself (SW: 109; BSP: 22, 73–4). Every event can be translated into an ecotechnical equivalent: the outbreak of war represents an increase in defence contracts; a plane crash represents not only death but a decrease of airline ticket sales and an increase in the relevant insurance premiums; or if a less-than-dynamic sports team makes it to the finals, that might represent less media coverage and advertising revenue. The political and social news matters in as much as it affects one's bank account (e.g. the capture of Saddam Hussein); even "human interest" fluff is translatable into preferences and aversions that possess ecotechnical value.

Ecotechnics falls under the criteria of both affirmative and reflective immanence: it is reflective when the essence of man and nature is determined solely by the circulations of capital and its equivalent commodities (in which case there is merely production and consumption that is closed to the sharing of community); however, it is affirmative in the sense that it provides modes whereby the various relations of sharing that compose community can be intensely enhanced. In brief, ecotechnics provides both the means for the dissolution of substantial community and the resources for the improvements of communicability that keep communities open.

In our "planetary technology", a coherent network of ends and means that purportedly provides no end to the means of its own deployment, ecotechnics is nothing other than the expression of sovereignty by technical means. Ecotechnics facilitates the inordinate pursuit of technological application as an end in itself, but since the resources of technologies are seemingly infinite, there can be no end to this process. Post-Neolithic technology has distorted and even devastated *physis* and thereby reduced itself to being an "operation of means" towards a non-given end. As we have seen, international law, despite its ideal of being above the fray, is nonetheless the "guarantor" of ecotechnics because it provides legitimacy for its infinite application even in its depredations against nature. Ecotechnics consists not only in the massive logistics of destruction but also in the cultural figures by which the war itself is represented. Unlike traditional warfare, or the false "epic" of the media presentation of warfare, ecotechnical warfare presents a "destructive and appropriative maneuvering without sovereign brilliance" (MMT: 97; BSP: 133–4). Although traditional warfare presents an incandescent burst of spontaneous sovereignty, the ecotechnics of warfare, being of purportedly infinite potentiality, lacks this spontaneity and thus becomes coextensive with humanitarian law. It is a slow, low-intensity deployment of resources in a systematic fashion, such that one could speak of warfare solely within the terms of systems in conflict (e.g. sanctions, no-fly zones, counter-terrorism). Understood as global, as high- or low-intensity conflict, or as police action, contemporary warfare has operational means of conflict that deploy ecotechnical commodities.

In other words, Nancy is arguing that contemporary ecotechnics has transformed war almost beyond recognition. It is no longer merely the occasion of declared hostility in which sovereign faces off against sovereign. It is often not even a matter of combat at all, and indeed, appears to strive for a reduction (or even eradication) of hand-to-hand combat altogether. It spreads everywhere, seemingly without limitations, infecting the whole civil space in an all-encompassing "total" warfare without struggle between singularities. One might say that war is everywhere in the circulation of capital and its equivalents, yet it is nothing and nowhere in the intersections of singularities. If ecotechnics is "the pure *technē* of non-sovereignty" in which the lacuna of sovereignty is filled by the systematic behaviour of capital, then sovereignty is simulated through the devastating attack dealt by technologies themselves wherever military blows are struck. Indeed, sovereignties function ecotechnically wherever there is coincidence of means and ends, yet ecotechnics can also subvert sovereignty wherever they do not. In fact, Nancy notes, many of the traditional military paradigms have been fragmented by ecotechnics: "ecotechnics gives value to a primacy of the combinatory over the discriminatory, of the contractual over the hierarchical, of the network over the organism, and more generally, of the spatial over the historical" (BSP: 135–6). And within the spatial, it gives priority to delocalized spatiality over unitary, concentrated spatiality. Nancy asks, then, whether we can distinguish the very space within which sense circulates (or rather, the spaces composed by the circulations of sense) from the fragmented spacing of the world of ecotechnics. Either sense is diluted in the moral–juridical discourse of consensus, dialogue, communication or values, or it is transformed into gaping sutures of undecidability held open despite this discourse.

In its reflective immanential capacity to subvert the need for social conditions of justice, the danger of ecotechnics does not repose in its inability to grapple with such basic problems as the establishment of justice and peace. On the contrary, what threatens ecotechnics from within itself is that although there is a "combinatory" aspect of technology, it always disintegrates into a plurality of technologies interacting with a "nature" that is either deemed a surmountable obstacle or an instrument of technological appropriation (FT: 24). In brief, in so far as it always defines its own terms and predetermines its successes, ecotechnics offers combinations of singularities it has itself chosen in the light of the necessity of applying itself.

Nancy insists that this line of questioning leads us to think within the space of the absence of sovereignty, in which the ends of goodness, justice and presumably perennial peace are empty or inaccessible. We must simply accept that the play of ecotechnical warfare has emptied the sovereign State of its legitimacy. The matter is obfuscated by the fact that media ecotechnics can forcefully jam the *figure* of sovereignty into the empty place of sovereignty, resulting in the occasionally brilliant display of sovereignty in contemporary warfare. Nevertheless, there is nothing but a facsimile of sovereignty in a sovereignty that has no power in itself but must police the world with humanitarian justification, guard natural resources in the name of legitimacy, and rely on credit in order to do so. Strictly speaking, ecotechnics has the capacity to provide a simulation of legitimacy in the name of humanitarian principles. Under these circumstances, the danger is that we will permit the immanential figures of the media's portrayal of ecotechnics to create widespread cynicism about humanitarianism and its humanistic ideals. Again, there is risk in the propensity to frame in ecotechnical terms the sense of a global humanity and its world that is replete with a sovereignty irreducible to the exalted power of politics. In other words, he is warning us to distinguish the discrete spacings and sharings that compose the circulation of sense from the dramatically different ecotechnical spacings of the circulations of capital. All that ecotechnics can provide in its assertion of sovereignty are "non-sovereign meanings" that circulate in a fashion that is irreducible to ecotechnical immanentist practices. Alternatively put, ecotechnics can offer an absence of sense that it cannot itself appropriate by immanential thinking.

"The very spacing of the world, the opening of the discontinuous, polymor-phous, dispersed, dislocated spatio-temporality presents something of itself in Sovereignty: just this side of its figures and their urgent, eager presences" (BSP: 137–8, 150). The space of open community is the openness of singu-lar ones to other ones despite the superimposition of the numerical terms of calculative reasoning (crowds, multitudes, populations, etc.) (C: 373). There is a form of inaccessible sovereignty in the community of sharing among singularities that precedes the instrumental utilization of figures of sover-eignty. The circulation of sense in community lacks the brilliant intensity of the "epic" of media coverage of warfare and other "tragedies". Yet there is a certain grandeur in the "inoperability" of community that enables it to resist immanential (that is, political and media) domination. The inexpressible communicability of sharing composes a sovereignty that will never reach a limit, never achieve the immanential end of sovereignty for which ecotechnics purportedly strives. Indeed, Nancy suggests, in the community of sharing that has some measure of irreducible sovereignty prior to its figuration there is a lightning-like peace that presents its own violent resist-ance to warfare. This community is not disclosed to or by ecotechnical asser-tions of sovereignty nor by the multiple reticulations of its application through industrial production, commercial distribution, warfare or media entertainment. Buried beneath the ecotechnical circulation of capital and the "sovereign logic of war" is the technology that assists in the circulation of meaning as an end in itself. If communication systems expose the "bare web of the com", then the network of communication exposes us to the inter-leaved reticulations of existence. Putting the same point more vividly, Nancy notes that the global condition of the world is one in which there is spacing, not finishing; the intersection of singularities, not the identification of figures; and the exhaustion of the very ideal of sovereignty that, in reality, is lacking in itself (BSP: 28, 139–40). Irreducible to ecotechnical reflective immanence, these are the indicators of insubstantial community and the reflective immanence that appears to sustain it.

In conclusion, Nancy recognizes the duality of ecotechnics as a manipu-lation of sovereignty and as an expression of the underlying community of sharing that cannot be manipulated. If ecotechnics, despite the opacity of its closed immanential reduction of pluralities to equivalences of capital, also lays bare the intersections of sense that compose community, then it is con-ceivable that ecotechnics could be emancipated from the political ends of the establishment of figures of sovereignty. In its opacity, ecotechnics fragments into precisely such singular events and their myriad reticulations. It thus provides some insight into the underlying community it overtly obscures. As inconceivable as this task is according to our prevailing paradigms, the only alternative is low-intensity warfare and the continued global deployment of armies in the name of humanitarian ideals, as well as the persistence of competing ecotechnical figures of sovereignty. It could be said that the curious alliance between humanitarian legitimacy and ecotechnical warfare results in a dichotomy between war and peace which takes place solely within the "closed" immanence of ecotechnics itself. Nevertheless, more pre-originary than even this immanence is the open immanence of the circulation of sense in which it offers a capacity for thinking the finitude of beings and the multiplicity of their relations. A "globalness" consisting of intersecting singularities, however, would require that the models of immanence should be scrapped in the name of a proliferation of identified singularities without end or model. Ecotechnics itself may facilitate such a global, but "open", immanential paradigm. Ultimately, there is no global technology nefariously plotting against (or assisting any global conspiracy against) humanity and human beings, but rather merely an inessential technicity revealing (or at least enabling us to address) the question of the finitude of sense and of our own existence. Whatever ecotechnics may strive to do to our contemporary world, the sense of the world will be reflected glimmeringly in the relational sharing of being that composes community.

Conclusion

- Ecotechnics is the circulation of capital and all its equipollences that appears to inform the values of all contemporary social reality, especially where globalization is at issue. However, it provides linkages, or conditions of communication, through which sense may circulate. Hence, although it appears to enclose all sense in a closed immanence, the enhanced and expanded linkages it provides can serve as intersections of sharing through which sense may circulate. Perhaps this could mean that although community is under threat, we at least share exposure to the threat to community.

- On the one hand, in its "media" presentation, war has become a spectacular event, but on the other, has assumed a slow, grinding form in the ecotechnical expression of "total war" and "police action". Despite this incommensurability, it has become a mode whereby legitimacy is established and sovereignty secured. International law possesses the legitimacy that technological warfare lacks, but war can acquire legitimacy when put to the service of establishing it. Where sovereignty is lacking, its figures can be produced and secured by military means.

The future as openness to uncertainty

Each of these chapters' subjects represents a perspective on a core commitment: Nancy's critique of substantialist, transcendentalist and immanentist metaphysics.

Against substantialism, Nancy argues persuasively that singular beings are not predetermined by reference to a general ground of Being. Rather, the Being of the singular being is bound to its own singularity, a groundless and uncertain state through which a multiplicity of meanings circulates whenever singular beings are "with" one another. Properly speaking, Being is in some sense the "between" of relations of singularity and not some antecedent condition in which singularities take a position and relate with one another. Challenging transcendentalism, he insists that there is no reserve "outside" the world that could serve as a source of meaning or value in the determination of singularity. There is *only* the "inside", devoid of transcendental reference to an "outside", he proposes, which is tantamount to a rejection of the thought that the world is merely an "inside". The sense of the world itself is coextensive with beings, such that the inside–outside dichotomy is disrupted and suspended by the finite thinking of singular beings and their reticulations. Again, contrary to the terms of immanentism, he holds that there is no such reserve "inside" the world by which singular beings' identities could be mimetically determined and reflected. Immanentism merely subrogates external and internal sources of meaning and value, and thus, generally speaking, commits the same debilitating mistake of assuming that the world itself could not possibly be (or provide) its own sense. There is nothing but the world, a non-place and lack of sense, without an "outside" but also without an "inside". Hence being is never predetermined by the identification of singular beings through the reflective operations of immanence, since this would close singularities within circumscribed perimeters, reduce their being to the common ground of the symbols and concepts of reflection, as well as subsume their relations to the concept of relation among pre-existing beings.

One might hazard to say, then, that irreducible and inappropriable singularities (and their multifaceted relations) are the locus of being and the primary datum (even the essential precondition) of philosophy. "Sense" is neither a pre-existing condition into which singularities are introduced nor the result of reflection by means of reserves of signification figuring either "outside" or "inside" the world. Sense just is the world composed of the relations of singularities; only a philosophy dedicated to the daunting task of a finite thinking that resists the generalizations and symbolizations encouraged by metaphysics could gain even a glimmering of sense. Perhaps Nancy's hybrid empiricism comes into play where the order of experience consists of (and has access to) the kaleidoscope of circulating sense swirling through the relations of singularities, and the order of sense itself is the singular sense exposed each time that experience enables the finite thinking of singularity.

Contrary to libertarian requirements, freedom is not merely a condition of philosophy and politics. Theories of freedom that substantialize and immanentize human being forbid the finite thinking that freedom genuinely demands. A finite thought of freedom would be a free thought, a thought free of the conceptual constraints of libertarian "rights" and Kantian "facts of reason". Neither a generalization about singularities nor a general term of thought, a finite thought would be one that was always surprised by what it took freedom to be. That is, freedom itself is the incessant surprise of existence in multiplicity and the community of being. To understand that "surprise" it would be necessary for the thought of that surprise itself to be surprised. Hence, what one can best say about freedom is that it is a surprising thought about a surprising condition of existence, surprising at each instant, surprised in each singular "one" in the circulation of sense. The future, then, is not decidable and calculable in terms of the assertions of a predetermined freedom. On the contrary, if this surprise is absolute and ineradicable on each occasion, incommensurate with any thought of freedom, then the future is wholly beyond the reach of free agency. The future is an open space of existence resulting from incessant surprisings of experience. The thought of freedom itself is open to this future: since freedom itself is never certain and decidable, the openness of the "to-come" is uncertain and undecidable. Generally speaking, the thought of freedom is a finite thought surprised by its own incommensurability with the surprise of freedom itself, a thought that is always uncertain and undecided about the exigencies of existence. One might conjecture, then, that for finite thinking, the future is not a predetermined space into which free initiative is thrust, but the space that uncertainty carves in the heart of human existence itself.

The deconstruction of Christianity and the suspension of religious values are necessary operations of such finite thinking. Although deconstructive strategies are indebted to Christianity itself, ultimately Christianity also provides the kinds of generalities and symbols that obstruct finite thinking. Perhaps any institutional religion exhibits substantialist, transcendentalist and even immanentist practices, but Christianity has philosophized itself into the condition of being representative of precisely such tendencies in a "globalizing" world. In implying the imperative of the question "What does this (the incarnation, the resurrection, the trinity, grace, etc.) mean?", Christianity created the demand for solutions that were optimally provided through the production of a certain atheism, secularism and, of course, technology and science generally. Hence, even the alternatives to Christianity that this religion inadvertently produces are themselves inheritors of the substantialist, transcendentalist and immanentist currents of Christian thought. In a paradoxical fashion, Christianity has emptied itself of its value, and therefore lacks the ability to provide the kinds of worldview to which it had become accustomed to mimetically producing; yet, in addition, secular thoughts and practices have inherited too many of these Christian conceptual tendencies, and thus are not genuine alternatives for finite thinking. Roughly speaking, Christianity must deconstruct itself or be deconstructed, that is, efface itself and learn from the trajectories of its traditional proclivities. This does not rule out that there might be a "future" Christianity or a Christian "future", but only that, whatever Christianity will be, it must be a presently undecidable "to-come" facilitated by present deconstructive practices. That is why I have proposed to refer to Nancy's approach to religion as "critical atheism", since it is neither friendly to a renaissance of Christian thought and purview, nor churlishly critical of theism by means bequeathed from religion itself. Nancy wishes to clear out a space in which the futural "to-come" could be received and addressed by finite thinking, which implies a certain philosophical tolerance of even the incertitude and undecidability of salvation that contemporary Christianity cannot actively appreciate.

The issue of community and, by extension, of the social contract is of prime value for Nancy, not only because of his political enquiries, but also perhaps because it is in a prevailing misconception of community that substantialist thinking is most obviously discernible. A community is not an entity that consists of isolated atomic individuals into which other individuals might be introduced. It is neither a pre-existing substantial entity ("our town") nor an entity that gains a substantial identity through mimetic reflection and playing back (ideology laden with platitudinal wisdoms and traditional symbols) or through reference to transcendental values ("the Chosen People", "His Most Christian Majesty", "God Bless America and to Hell with All the Rest"). In some respects, it is not merely academic communitarianism, but also our very common-sense intuitions about community, that imply the nostalgia for a lost ideal of community which could be regained through mastery of our communal future. On the contrary, although it is less precisely intelligible, community is insubstantial and open to uncertain exigencies, which is to say that it consists of irreducible relationships among singular beings, trajectories of banal exposures among singularities and experiences in which we share and whose sharings are themselves subject to experience. The social contract implies a tacit consent that supervenes and transforms this insubstantiality, thereby providing an immanential ground by which to lend closure and determination to an entity that is little more than a name ("community") for such sharings. To understand community in even the vaguest communitarian and contractarian fashion is already to utilize substantialist criteria; but it is also to move resolutely to a future that could be appropriated by a politics that draws totalitarian inspiration from communitarian nostalgia and contractarian conceptual figures (the political "subject" or "citizen"). Yet the myths by which totalitarianism is necessarily promulgated are ideally interrupted by such sharings that suggest the circulation of sense. Moreover, although the suspension of history in this much-discussed "crisis of sense" might enable a re-emergence of a palimpsest totalitarianism, the question of the undecidability of the future, the possibility of an openness "to-come", severely restricts the means by which its motivational ideals might hypostasize in community.

The question of globalization figures in Nancy's philosophy on several registers of thought. In no way unique, a global culture would simply be a substantial community writ large and identified reflectively in immanence. Yet, just as every community is disrupted from within by the circulation of sense that betrays its substantialization, so do the technological links of globalization serve the possible role of throwing us back onto an awareness of the sharings in which even a global community must consist. Eco-technics might strive to superimpose the circulation of capital onto the circulating sense of community, but even the operations and linkages by which this quantification would occur are themselves refinements and expansions of the means of sharing within community. Intriguingly, globalization calls for deconstruction, and provides the very terms by which it can be deconstructed.

In each case, institutional religion, community, the political accessibility of the social contract, market democracy, globalization and even the vaunted ideal of freedom are notions that deserve a finite thinking of their future. Instead of appropriating their senses in order to make predictions of their future behaviours; instead of reflecting a consoling vision of the futures of such things; indeed, instead of empowering ourselves by treating such notions as significations of a controllable future, it is imperative to deconstruct their terms and contexts in order to free them from corrosive presumptions that anticipate the form the future will take. The open immanence of sense, the fragmentedness of bodies, the surprise of freedom, the openness of insubstantial community, the destitution of religion and its practices: these are spaces (or spacings) that expose an open future, an uncertain and undecidable future, unanticipated and unpredictable. Such spaces not only expose the possibility of a future "to-come", but offer a poignant exposition of ourselves as we are exposed in this spacing to a future that is always already "to-come" and only contingently what we conceive it to be.

One might conclude, then, that Nancy has offered a fascinating depiction of humanity as many finitudes that are, singularity by singularity, relation by relation, vulnerably exposed to a future. This is an exposure subject to finite thinking, and indeed one that even demands such subjection. "We" are futural, surely, but not in the sense that we project ourselves into the future; rather, the "we" just is this ability to open ourselves to the spacing of a world, a world that is always "to-come". Perhaps Nancy is summoning us to an openness without anticipation, a preparedness for surprise that could never eradicate surprise, a world in which incertitude and undecidability are understood to be definitive of the human condition.

The future of philosophy[1]

BCH: Professor Nancy, I would like to ask you a number of questions about the future of philosophy. Initially, what is the "crisis of sense" and how do you approach it?

JLN: The "crisis of sense" signifies that we are coming out of an age in which meaning is guaranteed by certain principles (e.g. God, Man, History, Science, Law, Value) that support (or at least initially outline) the possibility of an accomplishment of sense.

What puts this crisis in perspective is the dissolution of such points of view posed as if they were outside and higher than the given world. The history of the modern world is like Nietzsche's "end of the worlds behind". Sense can no longer be referred from beyond: that is certain. However, this is not merely a crisis to be overcome. It is a mutation: we are changing our world. There has been a world of myth and ritual; then there has been a world of citizens and cities; and then there has been a world of infinite knowledge and desire. Today, there is another world on display, one for which it is no longer possible to give the formula: it will forge its own history.

"Sense" itself is a concept whose sense remains to be reconsidered. If sense is always a "reference to . . ." (the sense of X is in reference to Y, the sense of my life is beyond my life, the sense of the world is beyond the world, according to Wittgenstein), then how is the reference of sense operative if there is no term or instance that is beyond the world – or better yet, if the "outside" is understood to be the same as the "inside"? Or in other terms: if truth is destitute, if it is not finished but merely suspended or cancelled, then what can one say of the reference to this truth? This is not merely a problem of nihilistic position; it is a question of that about which "nothing" can be said. "Nothing", it is something, it is the same as something: nothing is not nothing, no-thing means no one of the many things in the world, and no one imaginary thing out of the world, but the no-thing as such, the "thing" of nothingness. "Sense" means precisely no-thing, means something which doesn't fit with any thing.

BCH: What are the most basic contemporary philosophical issues?

JLN: I propose readily that that would be the question of fundamental philosophy: the question of philosophy itself (which, moreover, has never ceased to accompany all philosophical questions since Plato). What is philosophy? – this question is constitutive of philosophy itself. It is regularly addressed with certain answers: for example, philosophy is knowledge, or the good, or rationality, or it is argumentation or clarification of notions, or it is a suggestion of values, of "visions". But none of these answers address the question of basic philosophy: what is "reason", "value", etcetera? After all, doesn't philosophy always raise the indeterminability of the proper notions "philo", "philein", that which it is about? Of which love or which friendship? What is worthy of love or delectation? Of which affect? And "sophia", what is that, then: wisdom, knowledge, science? Are such words adequate?

Today we must understand that this infinity of the question constitutes a means of surpassing such questions themselves: philosophy does not need to await an answer to substantial questions (a "true knowledge", a "just value"); rather, it questions the questioner himself: what does he want? What does he require? He asks himself, he himself asks: he seeks a place, for himself and for his world, but not merely another world that is an "otherworld" to which it can be bound (divine, superhuman, scientific or ideal). Philosophy is man in isolation. That was already the case with Plato; but today this solitude has been laid bare, enlivened, made a given concern. Perhaps all of the received meanings of "philosophy" have become impracticable ... Yet philosophy owes a debt of justice to the isolated person in the world alone. And this justice is without measure, without law, infinite.

BCH: Can one philosophize about the future of philosophy?

JLN: Of course: philosophizing always turns itself towards the "to-come" (*avenir*) of philosophy. But this coming is not exactly a future. A future is predictable, calculable, appreciable or imaginable. A "coming" is incalculable and inappreciable. In a sense, philosophy is always, in essence, "to-come". It is not ever given, never already done or befallen. It always begins, as the essential beginning of an inchoate thinking that knows itself as such. Thinking is not merely another object of thought (for such an object is the cessation of philosophizing). The coming philosophy will be without a doubt as different from the thoughts of Descartes as they were from those of Aristotle, or those of Husserl from those of Hegel: they are as rigorously heterogeneous among themselves as they are very profound and almost secretive. It is that which, it seems to me, is a way of coming, without a doubt thinking as an exercise and a test of the inconceivable, the suspended sense.

BCH: What are your unique contributions to the humanism/antihumanism debate?

JLN: I do not comprehend the meaning of "unique" in this context. But if I overlook that point, I shall try to respond: for as much as "humanism" designates a representation of man as subjectivity and definite substance, qualifiable, whose destination and whose excellence are clearly determined and present, "humanism" lacks man, it lacks that which in man does not exceed any qualification of the human or of humanity. It fails therefore to purge man of a complex relation with the living and moreover with the non-living, with the divine, or even with the totality of the world. In a sense, "humanism" knew its limits as soon as Pascal wrote: "man infinitely surpasses man". But on the other hand, man is nothing other than a power of estrangement: of the denaturation of nature, of the dissolution of gods, of the transformation of man himself. Man is the strangeness in and of the world.

BCH: It is often stated that philosophy is experiencing a crisis. Which philosophers and philosophical concepts remain virtually unexplored and might provide resources for the rejuvenation of philosophical discourse?

JLN: I think I have already responded on the subject of the essentials of the crisis. It is not a pathological episode but a permanent state of philosophy: in Plato, in Aristotle, and in the Stoics, in the Aristotelian scholastics as well as the nominalists, in Bacon, Descartes, Kant and Hegel. Do we not see that they merely deferred the crisis? The crisis is a state of philosophy, not an episode. Or rather, it is a state that is impossible to eradicate. Cartesian evidence, Hegelian absolute knowledge or Husserlian intentionality are aspects of the crisis: that is to say, they do not provide normality, the constancy of health, only the leap, disequilibrium, hazards and risks. There is no need for a "rejuvenation" of a philosophy that is always young and always in a state critical of youth or in the non-state of invention, initiative or inauguration. In a sense, all the philosophers and all their concepts are always there, all together, as readily available as they are obsolete. If you consider Plato's "friend" from a certain point of view, it is a completely inoperable concept today. But from another point of view, it introduces something fresh: sense, truth and "the body" itself, which appear in opposition and in negation. Plato's "friend" offers a questioning of the body as sense.

BCH: In what sense is "the future" a philosophical concept today?

JLN: In the sense that I have already indicated. That is to say that the "future" is not merely the concept of the "present-future", the representation of a coming present that nowadays exposes the access to the scheme and the qualifier of presence. The word "future" is a relative of the Greek *phusis* which speaks to the idea of increasing self-determination.

That is why it is sometimes said, without paradox, that the world of *phusis* cannot be without future, because the "future" arrives when *phusis* gives way to *technē*. In such a case, the future requires a representation of the *phusis* of the *technē* as a peculiar self-determining (*autonome*) and quasi-mechanical (*quasi-automatique*) growth. A history capable of projecting its own end as if it were the end of the tree is projectable as its fruit as well. But in so far as we can grasp the point that *technē* is not *phusis*, the point at which the technical is not in this sense physical, then we can comprehend despair about the "future" ("no future", if we may recall a standard statement of punk); or else it becomes technical: that is to say it opens and exposes itself to the indefinite in-finition of the technical itself. Thus I would prefer to replace "future" with "morrow" (*lendemain*): "tomorrow" (*demain*), the day after, the morning after (*mane*, Latin for tomorrow, the morning after, and *Morgen* in German, *mañana* in Spanish) – that is to say, to start a new day: to be always uncertain (a little thought from Hume). The chance and the danger of the new beginning: how each evening we are unaware of "what tomorrow will bring", as one might say, and how each morning then starts again from zero. The morrow, that is the "place" of "expectation" (*l'espérance*), and "expectation" – according to the concept of the theological virtue – is not "hope" (*l'espoir*), not anticipation of a more or less certain future, but a way of abandoning oneself to the possibility that there is precisely not any future at all.

BCH: You propose that "the future" is a transgression of universality through repetition of singular events, a "to-come" from the past. What resources does "finite thinking" have to address this future?

JLN: The morrow indeed comes like a repetition of the last day, but as a repetition of the passing of the very past, the very ancient, if the ancient is not presented through any memory. It is the absolute last past of the beginning itself, of the beginning of all the beginnings, if you will; but more precisely, there is no beginning of the beginnings, because the beginning is always only itself the collapse of the past into the immemorial, into the non-presence which opens at the same time another non-presence, that of the morrow. And between the two there is no intermediate space: there is the present that is always succeeded and always preceded, which is not nowhere but makes our situation always singular,

163

according to which one oscillates between the immemorial and the unforeseeable, and according to which one happens to exist here and now, so to speak, totally without place or present moment, but precisely in existence (*ek-sistence*).

BCH: You suggest that the very spacing that makes history and community possible comes from a future that is not merely a "future present". This future is the very difference of time itself, the space by which time differs, and the space of community in its existence. How is the "openness" or "insubstantiality" of community futural?

JLN: Precisely, though perhaps one should not say "futural", but the "spacing" of the assemblage of being and of the being-of-the-world (it is the same thing: we are not merely an ensemble of individual persons, but of beings, living and non-living) consisting also of the spacing that separates "today", "yesterday" and "tomorrow", the spacing that provides incessant re-creation and dissimilarity. The space by which time differs from itself is the space by means of which it divagates towards the non-presence of the two dimensions or the two tensions, yesterday and tomorrow. As it turns in this manner, it knows itself to be essentially proportioned, or situated, by the certitude of the past without origin (the past that is identifiable and memorable) and by the incertitude of the morrow without future. That is the tearing of time by time: that exposes the instant present like an opening of our speech that is nothing other than an opening, that is to say the place of sense, itself thus opened. Ultimately, it is the question of the sense of the present moment: nothing else.

BCH: What is the "surprise" of freedom? Is libertarianism an obstacle to thinking of freedom?

JLN: The "surprise" of freedom means that freedom is never "my" freedom but comes to me from elsewhere, from the outside of everything that is supposed to be "mine". Freedom is the power that exposes me to myself as transgressing "my" self, a going out. Freedom is not a property; it is a being, an existentiality. Therefore, when I am acting, doing something, there is always something new, unexpected, in what I do and/or in myself as the agent: the text I write, the words I say, the face I show to my partners, etcetera are always surprising to myself. I cannot say "I did not intend to do this or that"; I must take it as "mine" because it did occur to "me" and "I" am made only by such occurrences. Then, this "surprising" freedom is not libertarian freedom, which presupposes a free subject before any acting. One could say: to be free is first of all to be free of the self.

BCH: Is the deconstruction of Christianity necessary for the future of philosophy?

JLN: Yes, I believe so. I believe that modern philosophy has very steadily and vigorously both driven back and reinvested the great Christian motifs – love, the hidden god, faith, hope, equality, salvation. Christianity itself is attempting a philosophical re-elaboration of previous motifs: the "religion" in it became philosophical, and its philosophy became exposure to the unthinkable. Deconstructed Christianity would like to say: replay the philosophical stakes that subjected philosophy to enormous difficulties concerning the notion of a complete, consistent and substantial presence. At least since Hegel there has been no question of anything else. And that does not mean any form of "return to the religious" at all. Religion is finished as a system of assurance about another world. The end of religion is identical with a transformation of philosophy. But there remains, precisely, the incommensurable non-present, the exposition of an "outside" that opens even here. There remains the "watch and pray

164

because you know neither the day nor the hour": you know nothing and there is nothing known through calculations of time; the question, on the contrary, is not about calculations and being ceaselessly in prayer – which is to speak, in a private sense, not of the demand for security, but of the adoration, or in other words, the address, the exclamation, the turn towards the outside itself. Perhaps this does not mean the same as "deconstruction", if this word supposes an edifice composed of demonstrations and analysis. Perhaps one should speak rather of disclosure: to undo the closure of the religious, to release it from its limits (God is the supreme being, etc.). The opening question might be this one: what made Christianity (or the three monotheisms, in conjunction with Greek philosophy) able to structure an entire civilization, until what goes by the name "secularization" drove it back, drew it aside and subordinated it to all of the major traditions of modern, humanistic and rationalistic thought? What does this repression mean, if not something that suggests a process much more subterranean and decisive?

BCH: In what sense do "ecotechnics" and market democracy provide problems that the philosophy of the future must address?

JLN: "Ecotechnics" is a word (or rather, a simple label) that I employ in order to suggest this: our ecosystem (that is to say, our ecology, our economy in every sense of the term) is technical through and through, and it has become necessary to quantify everything. This means that we do not possess given and stable reference for an "ecology" that would be assured by laws, principles and the constants of "nature". It neither "preserves nature" (because for millennia we have been carried along by ecotechnics) nor regulates modes of production that are natural and balanced (because capitalism, that is to say the self-production of value, is an ecotechnics sustained by money and its functional systems), nor does it define a city, an ethics and an aesthetics which would be referred to a natural (or supernatural!) order. All things considered, the challenge presented to us is nothing less than the Kantian challenge: can one desire a universal covering law of nature when nature itself is withdrawn, supplanted and carried away by indefinitely technical transformations? Is the moral law of Kant indeed regulated by the idea of "nature" to such a degree as to be an idea that is not given by contents, but only in the form of universal legality that supposes the motif of "nature" itself? There is no nature with a moral "design", said Kant, but only with a "type", that is to say an "analogy of a design". But then what is this "analogy" intended to say? What does it mean to speak of what the moral world (rational, juridical, ethical, aesthetic) is "like" on an analogy with "nature", without it being as if humanity were becoming natural and nature were becoming human, as Marx desired? Why assume the absolute invention of man (of being inventors of man, and of all of nature) according to precisely the onto-theo-logic of a ruined self-constitution? Can one think of the paradoxical autonomy of that which is not the "in itself"? Can one think of the freedom of the God of Spinoza (*sive natura*) as the truth of the non-freedom of human existences? Which exercise of thought, of culture, requires this? These questions, these anxieties, are meaningful in the same way: how to return the world to the world and not to God, neither by calculations nor even by the self-determinations of the "man" of humanism.

BCH: Is the market democratic world exhibiting signs of an emerging totalitarianism?

JLN: Yes, certainly it is. All the complexity of the contemporary world composes a huge network of constraints, of needs and means we are obliged to go through (for example, how much we now depend on machines such as computers, 'phones, televisions, DVDs, etc.) We become unable to manage without the help of the technicians, and the technicians manage within the constraints of firms, etcetera. But I have the feeling that, to the same extent, the possibilities of escaping the "system" are growing (we find other means of dealing with all those constraints – we become more sensitive to everything disturbing the system and we are given chances to open it in alternative ways). And most of all we perhaps will reach a situation in which it will be more and more "constraining" as well to disturb the system because suffering in it becomes too great. I mean first of all the suffering of the poor, of those taken as pure means by the system – this has become most visible in what occurs throughout Africa, the Arabic countries, India, South America. We now know something about how a society or culture, a "system", becomes totalitarian, and perhaps this knowledge will be useful.

Glossary

The reader should bear in mind that the definitions that follow are compromises between simplicity and accuracy. These definitions should only be used as a rough guide in the initial stages of reading.

Destruction   Not merely the devastation of beings in their being, but the reduction of sense itself to nonsense. In genocide in particular, destruction is not only the killing of people. It is the effort to dismantle the very structure of the world's sense and to affirm the nonsense of destruction in its place.

Ecotechnics   The circulation of capital and all its equipollences (i.e. whatever is reducible to and possessing the power of capital – megawatts, kilobits, calories, customers, body counts, etc.).

Exscription   If inscription means "to put (sense) in writing", exscription means that writing excludes sense from mere signification (meaning). Roughly, exscription is writing that puts sense beyond writing. Normally associated with finite thinking, exscription does not inscribe the sense of the body. Instead, it takes the body "as" sense, as the irreducible venue wherein sense circulates when bodies come into contact with the bodies of others.

Finite thinking   Thinking that does not avail itself of a transcendent source of meaning or a paradigm of universality. It consists in the labour of thinking singularly about singular beings. It resists the urge to think in terms of generalities or universals that reduce the plurality of singular ones to a common ground.

Immanence, closed   The interior of being determined in relation to an exteriority, a transcendent source of meaning. Beings are presented in their individuality as existing prior to the establishment of community. The essence of each being is determined in general by its being grounded in Being (see substantialist metaphysics). Yet each individual reflects upon the community in which it participates, thereby identifying itself in terms of an available symbolic–ideological order (or roughly, conventional values and meanings). Thus each being is merely an individual identified as a pre-existing being whose participation in community enables it to project and play back its own identity through conventional symbols and figures.

Immanence, open   A totality of infinite relationships without exteriority. The world in its infinitely expressed but singular sense consists of a plurality of singular "ones". Each singular being is not merely an individual together with others in community. It is absolutely different on each occasion in which it is exposed to existence and sharing this exposure.

Insubstantial community The open affirmation of the linkages of sharing that enable communication and social relation to occur. Consisting of a plurality of intersections through which sense circulates, it is the ground of social reality itself, singularizing the sense of each existent's life and enabling the finite thinking of such a life. Death is prominent among the linkages the singular beings of a community share (although only in the sense that each will be exposed to existents in a radically different manner, not in the sense that they all share the common property of dying or being able to die).

Post-secular theology A multifaceted contemporary religious philosophy exhibited in the work of Levinas and Marion, which resists the secularization of discourse by stressing the fragmented "otherness" of a god disseminated throughout the human sciences and traced in its linguistic expressions.

Sense A hugely ambiguous concept in Nancy's work that is strictly singular and incongruous with the traditional immanence/transcendence dichotomy. It is the condition of truth and meaning that circulates through existence and its discourses without being commensurate with the conventional visions of either.

Singularity The radical difference of each existent on each occasion of exposure to existence and contact with others. Discourse fails to appropriate singularity even as it inscribes "singularity as such". Properly speaking, to write of singularity as such would be only to write of individuals participating in being and community whose existence is laid out in advance and whose essence is predetermined accordingly. A singular being is not *some*one (any one of many individuals as such together with and comparable to others) but a some*one* (the specific beings whose sense is incomparably singular).

Sovereignty The "power" of singularity in itself. Sovereignty is singularity in its very specific resistance to political appropriations, not the exalted, superlative power of legitimacy that overrides this resistance.

Strangeness Each singular being is absolutely singular on each occasion of its exposure to existence, which produces a sense of strangeness reflected in art and in social relations. Strangeness is the quality of being incommensurate with generalities concerning the human condition and the universal ideal of humanity.

Substantialist metaphysics The dominant philosophical tendency to conceive of beings as grounded together as such in being, with the essence of each being determined in relation to this ground and with descriptions of its existence possible solely in terms of its relation with a world, including social reality. Nancy opposes to this "being of community" an openly immanential "community of being".

Surprise Freedom is always surprised by the resistance of the world to its own will and by the fact that there is thinking at all. Each event is surprising, even in its very necessity, and perhaps no event is more surprising than the irreducible burst of freedom that thinking itself is.

Transimmanence There is nothing but a world lacking exteriority, a world through which sense circulates in the exposures of singular beings. Sense is neither transcendent (an exterior reserve pregnant with meaning) nor immanent (a pregnant reserve of meaning within the world), but "transimmanent", that is, coextensive with the world in its plural singularities. Roughly speaking, sense passes along being without issuing from within it or from outside it; it slides through social relations without substantializing them. It makes them meaningful without giving them a (reducible) meaning.

Notes

Preface

1. José Saramago, *The Year of the Death of Ricardo Reis*, G. Pontiero (trans.) (New York: Harcourt Brace, 1991), 60.

1. Introduction

1. Christopher Fynsk, "Foreword: Experiences of Finitude", in IC, ix.
2. See Howard Caygill, "The Shared World: Philosophy, Violence, Freedom", in *On Jean-Luc Nancy: The Sense of Philosophy*, D. Sheppard *et al.* (eds), 19–31 (London: Routledge, 1997); Fred Dallmayr, "An 'Inoperative' Global Community? Reflections on Nancy", in *On Jean-Luc Nancy*, Sheppard *et al.* (eds), 174–96; Christopher Fynsk, "Community and the Limits of Theory", in *Community at Loose Ends*, The Miami Theory Collective (eds), 19–29 (Minneapolis, MN: University of Minnesota Press, 1991); Simon Critchley, *The Ethics of Deconstruction: Derrida and Levinas*, 2nd edn (West Lafayette, IN: Purdue University Press, 1999, first published 1992).
3. See Wilhelm Wurzer, "Nancy and the Political Imaginary after Nature", in *On Jean-Luc Nancy*, Sheppard *et al.* (eds), 92–101; and Krzysztof Ziarek, "Is all Technological? Global Power and Aesthetic Forces", *New Centennial Review* 11(3) (Fall 2002), 139–68.
4. See Gary Shapiro, "Jean-Luc Nancy and the Corpus of Philosophy", in *Thinking Bodies*, J. F. MacCannell & L. Zakarin (eds), 52–62 (Stanford, CA: Stanford University Press, 1994); and Anne O'Byrne, "The Politics of Intrusion", *New Centennial Review* 11(3) (Fall 2002), 169–88.
5. Michael Naas, "Practically Not to Be", *Studies in Practical Philosophy* 1(1) (Spring 1999), 68–85, esp. 74.
6. John T. Lysaker, "On What is to be Done with What is Always Already Arriving", *Studies in Practical Philosophy* 1(1) (Spring 1999), 98–9.
7. Peter Fenves, "Foreword: From Empiricism to the Experience of Freedom", in EF.
8. See François Raffoul, "The Logic of the With: On Nancy's *Être Singulier Pluriel*", *Studies in Practical Philosophy* 1(1) (Spring 1999), 36–52, esp. 41.
9. Friedrich Schlegel, *Philosophical Fragments*, P. Firchow (trans.) (Minneapolis, MN: University of Minneapolis Press, 1991), 21 (fragment 24), 79 (fragment 389).
10. See Peggy Kamuf, "On the Limit", in *Community at Loose Ends*, The Miami Theory Collective (eds), 13–18.
11. Naas, "Practically Not to Be", 73–4.
12. Francis Fischer, "Jean-Luc Nancy: The Place of a Thinking", in *On Jean-Luc Nancy*, Sheppard *et al.* (eds), 32–7, esp. 35.

13. Fenves notes of this haunting that "it is a consciousness so driven to drive out the 'fact' of which it is conscious, so ready to gainsay the experience of being implored to act unconditionally that it makes freedom into a mere matter of consciousness, something subjective, fleeting, epiphenomenal, delusive, a necessary deception", "Foreword: From Empiricism to the Experience of Freedom", xxvi.

2. Nancy's influences

1. See Simon Critchley, "With Being-With?: Notes on Jean-Luc Nancy's Rewriting of *Being and Time*", in *Ethics–Politics–Subjectivity: Essays on Derrida, Levinas, and Contemporary French Thought* (London: Verso, 1999); and Raffoul, "The Logic of the With".
2. Michel Surya, *Georges Bataille: An Intellectual Biography*, K. Fijalkowski & M. Richardson (trans.) (London: Verso, 2002), esp. 314; Miguel de Beistegui, "Sacrifice Revisited", in *On Jean-Luc Nancy*, Sheppard *et al.* (eds), 157–73, esp. 157–8.
3. Gerald L. Bruns, *Maurice Blanchot: The Refusal of Philosophy* (Baltimore, MD: Johns Hopkins University Press, 1997), 245–7.
4. Robert Bernasconi, "On Deconstructing Nostalgia for Community within the West: The Debate Between Nancy and Blanchot", *Research in Phenomenology* 23 (1993), 3–21, esp. 7–12.
5. See also Malcolm Bowie's *Lacan* (Cambridge, MA: Harvard University Press, 1991), 155.
6. See also Raffoul, "The Logic of the With", 44.

3. Immanentism

1. Caygill, "The Shared World", 22.
2. Georges van den Abeele, "Communism, the Proper Name", in *Community at Loose Ends*, 37.
3. See also Lysaker, "On What is to be Done", 96.
4. Milan Kundera, *The Unbearable Lightness of Being*, M. H. Heim (trans.) (New York: Harper and Row, 1984), 248–59.
5. See also Fred Dallmayr, "An 'Inoperative' Global Community? Reflections on Nancy", in *On Jean-Luc Nancy*, Sheppard et al. (eds), 174–96, esp. 178–9.
6. Critchley observes that in Nancy's endeavour to lay bare the "real itself of social being", the symbolic is understood to construct the social relation, not merely to reveal it. Social being includes no "dimension of the real outside" of this symbolicity. See "With Being-With?", 244–6.
7. Fischer, "Jean-Luc Nancy", 34.
8. See an especially relevant exploration of Bloch's philosophy of immanence in Wayne Hudson, *The Marxist Philosophy of Ernst Bloch* (New York: St Martin's Press, 1982), 99–104; Peter Uwe Hohendahl, *Prismatic Thought: Theodor W. Adorno* (Lincoln, NE: University of Nebraska Press, 1995), 219–21; and J. M. Bernstein, *Adorno: Disenchantment and Ethics* (Cambridge: Cambridge University Press, 2001), 87–94.
9. Luc Ferry and Alain Renaut, *French Philosophy of the Sixties: An Essay on Antihumanism*, Mary H. S. Cattani (trans.) (Amherst, MA: University of Massachusetts Press, 1990), 4–12, 229.
10. Fischer, "Jean-Luc Nancy: The Place of a Thinking", 36.
11. See Raffoul, "The Logic of the With", 48–50.
12. See Graham Ward, *Theology and Contemporary Critical Theory*, 2nd edn (London: Macmillan, 2000, first published 1996), 115; Shapiro, "Jean-Luc Nancy and the Corpus of Philosophy", 52.
13. Fischer, "Jean-Luc Nancy: The Place of a Thinking", 36.
14. See Fenves, "Foreword: From Empiricism to the Experience of Freedom", xxix–xxxi.
15. Kundera, *The Unbearable Lightness of Being*, 32–5, 195–7.

4. Libertarianism

1. Caygill, "The Shared World", 25.
2. See Fenves, "Foreword: From Empiricism to the Experience of Freedom", xxxi.
3. Immanuel Kant, *Groundwork of the Metaphysics of Morals*, Mary Gregor (trans. and ed.) (Cambridge: Cambridge University Press, 1997), 57 (4: 452).
4. Immanuel Kant, *Critique of Practical Reason*, Mary Gregor (trans. and ed.) (Cambridge: Cambridge University Press, 1997), 28 (5:31).
5. See Slavoy Žižek, *On Belief* (London: Routledge, 2001), 6–9, and "Selfhood as Such in Spirit: F. W. J. Schelling on the Origins of Evil", in *Radical Evil*, Joan Copjec (ed.), 1–29 (London: Verso, 1996). Also François Flahault, *Malice*, L. Heron (trans.) (London: Verso, 2003).
6. Fenves, "Foreword: From Empiricism to the Experience of Freedom", xxix–xxviii.
7. Immanuel Kant, *Religion within the Limits of Reason Alone*, T. M. Greene & H. H. Hudson (trans.) (LaSalle, IL: Open Court and Harper Brothers, 1960), 25.
8. Immanuel Kant, *Lectures on Ethics*, L. Infield (trans.) (New York: Harper and Row, 1963), 210.
9. Fenves, "Foreword: From Empiricism to the Experience of Freedom", xxvii.
10. Andrew Hewitt, "The Bad Seed: 'Auschwitz' and the Physiology of Evil", in *Radical Evil*, Joan Copjec (ed.), 74–104 (London: Verso, 1996).

5. Post-secular theology

1. See de Beistegui, "Sacrifice Revisited", 157–73.
2. For an excellent survey of post-secular thought, see Philip Blond, *Post-Secular Philosophy: Between Philosophy and Theology* (London: Routledge, 1997), which does a fabulous job of surveying the conditions under which a resurgence of interest in religious philosophy arose in contemporary thought.
3. See B. C. Hutchens, *Levinas: A Guide for the Perplexed* (London: Continuum, 2004), 112–21.
4. Ward, *Theology and Contemporary Critical Theory*, 115.
5. *Ibid.*

6. Communitarianism

1. There is no consensus about the precise definitional attributes of "communitarianism". Interestingly, many "communitarians" have not only never professed to being one, but have even questioned the currency of the title. Amitai Etzioni is perhaps the purest of self-professed communitarians, but curiously is less frequently cited in philosophical literature than those philosophers who are reluctant to accept the name. See Amitai Etzioni, *The New Golden Rule: Community and Morality in a Democratic Society* (New York: Basic Books, 1997). For those who are more "philosophical" in nature, it would be most pertinent to consider Alasdair MacIntyre, "Politics, Philosophy and the Common Good", in *The MacIntyre Reader*, K. Knight (ed.), 235–52 (Notre Dame, IN: University of Notre Dame Press, 1998) and "The Spectre of Communitarianism", *Radical Philosophy* 70 (1995), 34–5, esp. 35. For an excellent critical summary of various dimensions of communitarian thought, see Daniel A. Bell, *Communitarianism and its Critics* (Oxford: Clarendon Press, 1993) and Stephen Mulhall and Adam Swift, *Liberals and Communitarians*, 2nd edn (Oxford: Basil Blackwell, 1996).
2. Caygill, "The Shared World", esp. 24.
3. Ignaas Devisch, "A Trembling Voice in the Desert: Jean-Luc Nancy's Rethinking of the Space of the Political", *Cultural Values* 4(2) (April 2000), 239–55, esp. 240.
4. For an excellent exploration of communitarian values, see Robert Bellah *et al.*, *Habits*

of the Heart (Berkeley, CA: University of California Press, 1985).
5. Bruns notes poignantly that, for Nancy and Blanchot, "community must be understood in terms of events and movements", such that "concepts of task and struggle have greater application to community than do concepts of rules, beliefs, ideals, or spirit", *Maurice Blanchot: The Refusal of Philosophy*, 246.
6. Devisch, "A Trembling Voice in the Desert", 243.
7. Fischer, "Jean-Luc Nancy: The Place of a Thinking", 33.
8. See also Bernasconi, "On Deconstructing Nostalgia for Community", 6–10.
9. Of course, the classic text from which the sociological distinction between community and society is drawn would be Ferdinand Tönnies, *Community and Association* (London: Routledge & Kegan Paul, 1955).
10. Bernasconi objects vigorously to Nancy's reading of Rousseau (see "On Deconstructing Nostalgia for Community ", 16).
11. Bernasconi queries whether Nancy is not indebted to the very Western nostalgia he strives to deconstruct (*ibid.*).
12. Ward may be exaggerating to say that Nancy thinks of the modern *polis* as a "Christian parody", for the Christian community is merely one of the symbolic figures ordering our ideal of community: *Theology and Contemporary Critical Theory*, 110.
13. For a fascinating discussion of this Bataillean notion, see Surya, *Georges Bataille: An Intellectual Biography*, esp. 314. Surya notes that Nancy is an excellent student of Bataille's position on death and community.
14. See also Lysaker, "On What is to be Done", 92–3, and Naas, "Practically Not to Be", 80.
15. Caygill, "The Shared World", 26.
16. See also Critchley, "With Being-With?", 239–40.
17. Fynsk, "Foreword: Experiences of Finitude", x.
18. Michael Hardt and Antonio Negri, *Empire* (Cambridge, MA: Harvard University Press, 2000), xi–xiii.
19. See Wurzer, "Nancy and the Political Imaginary after Nature", 92–101, and Ziarek, "Is All Technological?", 139–68.

7. Social contractarianism

1. For excellent surveys of this distinction in Nancy's work, see Fynsk, "Foreword: Experiences of Finitude", x, and Critchley, "With Being-With?", 240–42.
2. Critchley understands Nancy's view of totalitarianism as an "identification of the political and the social" that enables justice to be immanent to the body politic. See "With Being-With?", 101, 149.

8. Ecotechnics

1. Hardt and Negri, *Empire*, xii–xiii.

Interview

1. Translated by B. C. Hutchens.

Bibliography

Works by Jean-Luc Nancy

Nancy, J.-L. 1986. *L'oubli de la philosophie*. Paris: Galilée.

Nancy, J.-L. & P. Lacoue-Labarthe 1988. *The Literary Absolute: The Theory of Literature in German Romanticism*, P. Bernard & C. Lester (trans.). Albany, NY: SUNY Press.

Nancy, J.-L. 1990. "Sharing Voices", in *Transforming the Hermeneutic Context: from Nietzsche to Nancy*, G. Ormiston & A. Schrift (eds), 211–59. Albany, NY: SUNY Press.

Nancy, J.-L. & P. Lacoue-Labarthe 1990. "The Nazi Myth", B. Holmes (trans.), *Critical Inquiry* 16(2), 291–312.

Nancy, J.-L. 1991. "Of Being in Common". In *Community at Loose Ends*, J. Creech (trans.), The Miami Theory Collective (eds), 1–12. Minneapolis, MN: University of Minnesota Press.

Nancy, J.-L. 1991. *The Inoperative Community*, P. Connor (ed.). Minneapolis, MN: University of Minnesota Press.

Nancy, J.-L. 1992. "*La Comparution*/The Compearance", Tracy B. Strong (trans.), *Political Theory* 20(3) (August), 371–98.

Nancy, J.-L. & P. Lacoue-Labarthe 1992. *The Title of the Letter: A Reading of Lacan*, F. Raffoul & D. Pettigrew (trans.). Albany, NY: State University of New York Press.

Nancy, J.-L. 1993. *The Birth to Presence*, B. Holmes *et al.* (trans.). Stanford, CA: Stanford University Press.

Nancy, J.-L. 1993. *The Experience of Freedom*, B. McDonald (trans.). Stanford, CA: Stanford University Press.

Nancy, J.-L. 1996. *The Muses*, P. Kamuf (trans.). Stanford, CA: Stanford University Press.

Nancy, J.-L. 1997. *The Gravity of Thought*, F. Raffoul & G. Recco (trans.). New Jersey: Humanities Press.

Nancy, J.-L. 1997. *The Sense of the World*, J. S. Librett (trans.). Minneapolis, MN: University of Minnesota Press.

Nancy, J.-L. & P. Lacoue-Labarthe 1997. *Retreating the Political*, S. Sparks (ed.). London: Routledge.

Nancy, J.-L. 1998. "La Déconstruction du christianisme", *Études philosophiques* 4, 503–19.

Nancy, J.-L. 1999. "Responding for Existence", in *Studies in Practical Philosophy* 1(1) (Spring), 1–11.

Nancy, J.-L. 2000. *Being Singular Plural*, R. D. Richardson & A. E. O'Bryne (trans.). Stanford, CA: Stanford University Press.

Nancy, J.-L. 2000. "The Self-Deconstruction of Christianity: A Discussion with Jean-Luc Nancy", the European Graduate School website: www.egs.edu/nancy/nancy-self-deconstruction-of-christianity-2000 (accessed July 2004).

Nancy, J.-L. 2001. *The Speculative Remark (One of Hegel's Bon Mots)*, C. Surprenant (trans.). Stanford, CA: Stanford University Press.

Nancy, J.-L. 2002. *La création du monde ou la mondialisation*. Paris, Galilée.

Nancy, J.-L. 2002. *Hegel: The Restlessness of the Negative*, J. Smith & S. Miller (trans.). Minneapolis, MN: University of Minnesota Press.

Nancy, J.-L. 2002. *"L'Intrus"*, in "At the Heart: Jean-Luc Nancy", a special issue of *The New Centennial Review* **11**(3) (Fall), 1–14.

Nancy, J.-L. 2002. "Is Everything Political? (A Brief Remark)", in "At the Heart: Jean-Luc Nancy", a special issue of *The New Centennial Review* **11**(3) (Fall), 15–22.

Nancy, J.-L. 2003. *A Finite Thinking*, S. Sparks (ed.). Stanford, CA: Stanford University Press.

Other works

Beistegui, M. de 1997. "Sacrifice Revisited". See Sheppard *et al.* (eds) (1997), 157–73.

Bell, D. A. 1993. *Communitarianism and its Critics*. Oxford: Clarendon Press.

Bellah, R. *et al.* 1985. *Habits of the Heart*. Berkeley, CA: University of California Press.

Bernasconi, R. 1993. "On Deconstructing Nostalgia for Community within the West: The Debate Between Nancy and Blanchot", *Research in Phenomenology* **23** (1993), 3–21.

Bernstein, J. M. 2001. *Adorno: Disenchantment and Ethics*. Cambridge: Cambridge University Press.

Blond, P. 1997. *Post-Secular Philosophy: Between Philosophy and Theology*. London: Routledge.

Bowie, M. 1991. *Lacan*. Cambridge, MA: Harvard University Press.

Bruns, G. L. 1997. *Maurice Blanchot: The Refusal of Philosophy*. Baltimore, MD: Johns Hopkins University Press.

Caygill, H. 1997. "The Shared World: Philosophy, Violence, Freedom". See Sheppard *et al.* (eds) (1997), 19–31.

Critchley, S. 1999. *The Ethics of Deconstruction: Derrida and Levinas*, 2nd edn. West Lafayette, IN: Purdue University Press. (First published 1992.)

Critchley, S. 1999. "With Being-With?: Notes on Jean-Luc Nancy's Rewriting of *Being and Time*", in *Ethics–Politics–Subjectivity: Essays on Derrida, Levinas, and Contemporary French Thought*. London: Verso. [Also published in *Studies in Practical Philosophy* **1**(1) (Spring 1999), 53–68.]

Dallmayr, F. 1997. "An 'Inoperative' Global Community? Reflections on Nancy". See Sheppard *et al.* (eds) (1997), 174–96.

Derrida, J. 2000. *Le Toucher: Jean-Luc Nancy*. Paris, Galilée.

Devisch, I. 2000. "A Trembling Voice in the Desert: Jean-Luc Nancy's Rethinking of the Space of the Political", *Cultural Values* **4**(2), 239–55.

Dow, K. 1993. "Ex-posing Identity: Derrida and Nancy on the (Im)possibility", *Philosophy and Social Criticism* **19**(3–4), 261–71.

Egginton, W. 2002. "The Sacred Heart of Dissent", in "At the Heart: Jean-Luc Nancy", a special issue of *The New Centennial Review* **11**(3) (Fall), 109–38.

Etzioni, A. 1997. *The New Golden Rule: Community and Morality in a Democratic Society*. New York: Basic Books.

Fenves, P. 1993. "Foreword: From Empiricism to the Experience of Freedom". In J.-L. Nancy, *The Experience of Freedom*, B. McDonald (trans.). Stanford, CA: Stanford University Press.

Ferry, L. & A. Renaut 1990. *French Philosophy of the Sixties: An Essay on Antihumanism*, M. H. S. Cattani (trans.). Amherst: MA: University of Massachusetts Press.

Fischer, F. 1997. "Jean-Luc Nancy: The Place of a Thinking". See Sheppard *et al.* (eds) (1997), 32–7.

Flahault, F. 2003. *Malice*, L. Heron (trans.). London: Verso.

Fynsk, C. 1991. "Community and the Limits of Theory". In *Community at Loose Ends*, Miami Theory Collective (eds), 19–29. Minneapolis, MN: University of Minnesota Press.

Fynsk, C. 1991. "Foreword: Experiences of Finitude". In *The Inoperative Community*, J.-L. Nancy, P. Connor (ed.), vii–xxxv. Minneapolis, MN: University of Minnesota Press.

Gaillot, M. (ed.) 1998. "An Interview with Jean-Luc Nancy". In *Multiple Meaning Techno: An Artistic and Political Laboratory of the Present*, W. Niesluchowski (trans.). Paris: Dis Voir.

Gilbert-Walsh, J. 2000. "Broken Imperatives: The Ethical Dimension of Nancy's Thought", *Philosophy and Social Criticism* 26(2), 29–50.

Hardt, M. & A. Negri 2000. *Empire*. Cambridge, MA: Harvard University Press.

Hewitt, A. 1996. "The Bad Seed: 'Auschwitz' and the Physiology of Evil". In *Radical Evil*, J. Copjec (ed.), 74–104. London: Verso.

Hohendahl, P. U. 1995. *Prismatic Thought: Theodor W. Adorno*. Lincoln, NE: University of Nebraska Press.

Hudson, W. 1982. *The Marxist Philosophy of Ernst Bloch*. New York: St Martin's Press.

Hutchens, B. C. 2004. *Levinas: A Guide for the Perplexed*. London: Continuum.

Ingram, D. 1988. "The Retreat of the Political in the Modern Age: Jean-Luc Nancy on Totalitarianism and Community", *Research in Phenomenology* 18, 93–124.

Kamuf, P. 1991. "On the Limit". In *Community at Loose Ends*, Miami Theory Collective (eds), 13–18. Minneapolis, MN: University of Minnesota Press.

Kamuf, P. (ed.) 1993. *On the Work of Jean-Luc Nancy*, 16(2).

Kant, I. 1960. *Religion within the Limits of Reason Alone*, T. M. Greene & H. H. Hudson (trans.). LaSalle, IL: Open Court and Harper Brothers.

Kant, I. 1963. *Lectures on Ethics*, L. Infield (trans.). New York: Harper & Row.

Kant, I. 1997. *Critique of Practical Reason*, M. Gregor (trans. and ed.). Cambridge: Cambridge University Press.

Kant, I. 1997. *Groundwork of the Metaphysics of Morals*, M. Gregor (trans. and ed.). Cambridge: Cambridge University Press.

Kundera, M. 1984. *The Unbearable Lightness of Being*, M. H. Heim (trans.). New York: Harper & Row.

Laus, T. 2001. "La Fin du christianisme: Désenchantement, déconstruction, et démocratie", *Revue de Théologie et de Philosophie* 133(4), 475–85.

Lysaker, J. T. 1999. "On What is to be Done with What is Always Already Arriving", *Studies in Practical Philosophy* 1(1) (Spring), 68–85.

MacIntyre, A. 1995. "The Spectre of Communitarianism", *Radical Philosophy* 70, 34–5.

MacIntyre, A. 1998. "Politics, Philosophy and the Common Good". In *The MacIntyre Reader*, K. Knight (ed.), 235–52. Notre Dame, IN: University of Notre Dame Press.

May, T. 1997. *Reconsidering Difference: Nancy, Derrida, Levinas and Deleuze*. University Park, PA: Pennsylvania State University Press.

Miami Theory Collective (eds) 1991. *Community at Loose Ends*. Minneapolis, MN: University of Minnesota Press.

Mulhall, S. & A. Swift 1996. *Liberals and Communitarians*, 2nd edn. Oxford: Blackwell.

Naas, M. 1999. "Practically Not to Be", *Studies in Practical Philosophy* 1(1) (Spring), 68–85.

Norris, A. 2000. "Jean-Luc Nancy and the Myth of the Commons", *Constellations* 7(2), 272–95.

O'Byrne, A. 2002. "The Politics of Intrusion", in "At the Heart: Jean-Luc Nancy", a special issue of *The New Centennial Review* 11(3) (Fall), 169–88.

Raffoul, F. 1997. "Translator's Preface". In J.-L. Nancy, *The Gravity of Thought*, F. Raffoul & G. Recco (trans.), vii–xxxii. New Jersey: Humanities Press.

Raffoul, F. 1999. "The Logic of the With: On Nancy's *Être Singulier Pluriel*", *Studies in Practical Philosophy* 1(1) (Spring), 36–52.

Saramago, J. 1991. *The Year of the Death of Ricardo Reis*, G. Pontiero (trans.). New York: Harcourt Brace.

Schlegel, F. 1991. *Philosophical Fragments*. P. Firchow (trans.). Minneapolis, MN: University of Minneapolis Press.

Shapiro, G. 1994. "Jean-Luc Nancy and the Corpus of Philosophy". In *Thinking Bodies*, J. F. MacCannell & L. Zakarin (eds), 52–62. Stanford, CA: Stanford University Press.

Sheppard, D. *et al.* (eds) 1997. *On Jean Luc-Nancy: The Sense of Philosophy*. London: Routledge.

Smith, J. 2002. Foreword: 'Nancy's Hegel, the state, and us'. In J.-L. Nancy, *Hegel: The Restlessness of the Negative*, J. Smith & S. Miller (trans.), ix–xxix. Minneapolis, MN: University of Minnesota Press.

Surya, M. 2002. *Georges Bataille: An Intellectual Biography*, K. Fijalkowski & M. Richardson (trans.). London: Verso.

Tönnies, F. 1955. *Community and Association*. London: Routledge & Kegan Paul.

van den Abeele, Georges. "Communism, the Proper Name". In *Community at Loose Ends*, Miami Theory Collective (eds), 30–41. Minneapolis, MN: University of Minnesota Press.

Ward, G. 2000. *Theology and Contemporary Critical Theory*, 2nd edn. London: Macmillan. (First published 1996.)

Wurzer, W. S. 1997. "Nancy and the Political Imaginary after Nature". See Sheppard *et al.* (eds) (1997), 92–101.

Ziarek, K. 2002. "Is all Technological? Global Power and Aesthetic Forces", in "At the Heart: Jean-Luc Nancy", a special issue of *The New Centennial Review* 11(3) (Fall), 139–68.

Žižek, S. 1996. "Selfhood as Such in Spirit: F. W. J. Schelling on the Origins of Evil". In *Radical Evil*, J. Copjec (ed.), 1–29. London: Verso.

Žižek, S. 2001. *On Belief*. London: Routledge.

Index